Music
and
the Emotions

International Library of Philosophy

Editor: Ted Honderich
Grote Professor of the Philosophy of Mind and Logic
University College London

Recent books in the series include:

* *Content and Consciousness* Daniel C Dennett
  State Punishment Nicola Lacey
  Modern Anti-Realism and Manufactured Truth Gerald Vision
* *Philosophy of Economics: On the Scope of Reason in Economic Inquiry* Subroto Roy
  Scientism: Philosophy and the Infatuation with Science Tom Sorell
  The Immaterial Self: A Defence of the Cartesian Dualist Conception of the Mind John Foster
* *Wittgenstein's Philosophy of Psychology* Malcolm Budd

*Also available in paperback

Music
and
the Emotions

The Philosophical Theories

Malcolm Budd

London and New York

First published in 1985
by Routledge & Kegan Paul

Paperback edition first published in 1992
by Routledge
11 New Fetter Lane, London EC4P 4EE

Simultaneously published in the USA and Canada
by Routledge, Inc.
29 West 35th Street, New York, NY 10001

Printed in Great Britain by
Biddles Ltd, Guildford and Kings Lynn

British Library Cataloguing in Publication Data
A catalogue record for this book is available from the British
Library.

Library of Congress Cataloging in Publication Data

Budd, Malcolm

Music and the emotions.
Bibliography: p.
Includes index.
1. Music–Philosophy and aesthetics. 2. Music–
Psychology. I. Title
ML3845.B77   1985   781'.15   85–1975

ISBN 0–415–08779–1

For Michael

CONTENTS

PREFACE

Rameau opened his *Treatise on Harmony* by defining music as the science of sounds. But when music is regarded as one of the fine arts it is more accurate to define it not as the science, but as the art of sounds. And if this definition is understood in the sense in which it is intended, it draws into its net just the subject it is meant to capture. For music is essentially the art of uninterpreted sounds. It is not the art of sounds understood as signs with non-auditory meanings and composed in accordance with syntactic rules: it is not the art of speech. And it is not the art of sounds arranged in such a way that something not composed of sounds is to be heard in them: it is not the auditory analogue of the art of pictorial representation. It is the art of sounds that are not given a non-auditory interpretation.

Music is based upon the human capacity to hear sequences of bare sounds in various ways: to hear a rhythm in a series of sounds; to hear two simultaneous rhythms in a series of sounds; to hear a series of sounds as a melody; to hear one melody as a variation of another; to hear sets of sounds as chords; to hear a later chord as resolving an earlier chord; and so on. And these modes of hearing sounds do not possess thought-contents: to hear a rhythm, a melody, a chord, a cadence is in each case to be aware of a form of sounds or a form in sound, and each form can be perceived without anything else being present to or grasped or thought of by the mind than sounds that are experienced in that form. Accordingly, the fundamental appeal of a musical work is as a structure of sounds that is its own *raison d'être*: the experience in which the work is appreciated – the experience that realises its value as music – is both non-propositional and non-representational, and if the work is valued as music, what is valued cannot be separated from the composition of sounds itself. The experience of music is *au fond* purely auditory: it consists of interconnected modes of hearing mere sounds. And the value of music is inherent in the forms of sound that compose the music: it cannot be abstracted from the sounds in which it is located and considered without reference to them. It is for these reasons that it is fruitless to attempt to produce a sense of the value of a musical work in anyone who is unmusical. The significance of any musical work can be revealed only to initiates.

But although musical value is specifically musical, in the sense that the value of a musical work can be appreciated only by those capable of experiencing it with understanding; and although music is characteristically, and in essence, an abstract art, in that music as an art-form is not based upon music's capacity to represent or to refer to items in the physical world; it would be mistaken to conclude that the experience and value of music must be essentially unrelated to the non-musical world. For some musical phenomena exist not only in music, and our familiarity with their non-musical instances can play an important role both in shaping and colouring our experience of music — as when our response is affected by a correspondence between a musical rhythm and the rhythm of a bodily process, or when music succeeds in suggesting a non-musical phenomenon by imitating its rhythm. And it is possible for phenomena specific to music to be related in a musically significant manner to non-musical phenomena — as when a melody is expressive of a state of mind, an attitude, a feeling or an emotion, and the melody is imbued with the significance of that state of mind. At least, this is how the character of music presents itself to a superficial consideration: the truth or falsity of this appearance can be decided only by a more penetrating examination of the subject.

And this introduces the theme of my book. For in the book I investigate the relationship between music and the emotions. However, many kinds of connection between music and the emotions are irrelevant to my concern. For my interest is the nature and significance of music as an art-form and my concern, accordingly, is to isolate those connections, if any, between music and the emotions that are involved in the understanding and appreciation of music and in the proper estimate of musical value and the value of music relative to other values — the values of the other art-forms and the various kinds of non-artistic value. This book is intended as a preliminary step towards the attainment of that end.

The book consists of a set of studies in the philosophy of music: it expounds and assesses certain theories about the relationship between the art of music and the emotions. But it has not been my aim to supply a comprehensive history of the subject. For my interest is philosophical, not historical. I am concerned to understand the artistically significant connections between music and the emotions, not merely to catalogue and relate to one another the numerous different conceptions of these connections that others have put forward. My treatment of the topic is therefore highly selective: the theories I have chosen to examine are still influential; they include what I consider to be the most substantial contributions to the subject; they cover much of the ground that must be worked over; and in general there is something that can be learnt from them about musical experience and value. And my examination is distinctly philosophical: what is at issue is the adequacy of the theories to their subject-matter and the quality of the arguments by which they are supported, and it is from this point of view that they have been evaluated. But although the book is a work of philosophy I have been concerned to write it in such a way that it is as accessible as is possible to the reader who does not have a grounding in philosophy. What *is* presupposed is an acquaintance with music, against which the abstract nature of the argument can be tested; and also a concern to clarify the nature of one's attachment to music — for without this the time and effort required to read the book will be wasted.

The structure of the book is simple. First, I investigate the topic of the emotions and I propose a model of the essence of an emotion. It is clear that this model would need considerable refinement in a complete treatment of the subject; and it makes use of the problematic idea of pleasure and pain as experiential aspects of modes of thought. Furthermore, the topic of the emotions is not exhausted by an account of the essence of an emotion: much the greater part of the subject remains to be explored. But I believe that the model is suitable for its purpose: it helps to correct certain misconceptions about the nature of an emotion, and it serves, I hope, to focus attention upon what an emotion is. However, I have not wanted my examination of the question whether there is an artistically significant relation between music and the emotions to stand or fall with the model's adequacy and, accordingly, I have attempted, so far as is possible, to keep the argument of each of the succeeding chapters free from reliance upon the model.

In these succeeding chapters, which I have tried to make largely independent of one another, I examine a number of theories about the relation between music and the emotions. Now philosophies of music can be divided into two camps. On the one side, there are those theories that maintain that the value of music as an art-form and the different musical values of different musical works must be explained by reference to music's relationship with something outside music and in which we have an independent interest. And by far the most common extramusical phenomenon with which the value of music has been thought to be bound up is emotion. For emotion is something of great extramusical concern to us; it is undeniable that music has the power to move us to emotion; and in the case of certain musical works – those we experience as being expressive of emotion – we hear an emotional quality in the music itself. Hence, emotion is a natural candidate for the role pre-supposed by theories in this camp: the role of that which exists outside music and which determines the value of music according to the relation in which music stands to it. In the opposite camp are those theories that claim that the essential value of music as an art-form is purely musical: the importance of music as an art-form does not lie in any function it performs that involves a reference to anything non-musical; the musical value of each musical work is independent of any connection between the work and anything external to music; and, consequently, it is always unnecessary to experience a musical work as related to any-thing extramusical in order to understand the work and to appreciate its value as music. And, accordingly, the value of music is essentially unrelated to the emotions.

I begin the examination of my chosen theories of music by considering a set of theories drawn from the second camp: each theory attempts, in one way or in all ways, to dissociate music as an art-form from the emotions, and their arguments complement each other. The evaluation of these theories occupies the second, third and fourth chapters. I then turn to a number of theories from the first camp: each of these theories maintains that there is an essential connection between the art of music – or, at least, certain significant musical works – and the emotions. The evaluation of these theories occupies the fifth, sixth and seventh chapters. Finally, I consider a theory that has a foot in each camp with-out, perhaps, being a member of either. And the result of the examination is that each of the theories – the representatives of the first camp as well as those of the second camp, and also the go-between – is found wanting: no theory does justice to the phenomenon of music.

Nevertheless, some of the theories are more insightful than others, and throughout the book I am concerned to specify and to establish certain requirements that any viable theory of music must satisfy. This does not add up to a comprehensive theory of music or to a complete account of the artistically significant relations between music and the emotions. And I do not have such a theory or such an account. My book is therefore not offered as a solution to all the problems with which it deals. But the markers it lays down, and the clearing of the ground it attempts, will, I hope, encourage efforts to make further progress.

I am grateful to Jerrold Levinson, Colin McGinn and, especially, David Landells for their helpful comments on previous versions of some of the chapters, and to Jonathan Sinclair-Wilson for his encouragement. I must thank the Oxford University Press for permission to use as the main content of the second and third chapters material from two articles published in Volumes 20 and 23 of the *British Journal of Aesthetics*. And I am grateful to Katherine Backhouse and Wendy Robins for producing the final typescript.

I

THE EMOTIONS

1   The emotions can be considered either episodically or dispositionally. As an episode, an emotion is an occurrence: it is something felt,
experienced or undergone at a certain time – as when someone blushes
with embarrassment, is petrified with fear, finds a situation amusing or
feels pity for another's misfortune. Understood dispositionally, an
emotion involves a tendency to undergo the emotion when certain
thoughts are present to the mind: under these conditions episodes of the
emotion are likely to occur – as when someone is envious of another's
talent and experiences envy when he thinks of that person's success, or
is afraid of somebody and feels fear when he finds himself in that
person's company. It is true that an emotion in the dispositional sense
involves more than this tendency to undergo the emotion; but the
tendency is essential to it. Hence, the idea of emotion as an episode –
the experience or undergoing of emotion – is basic and it is this conception of emotion we need to understand.

2   There are at least three questions that can be asked about the nature
of the emotions:
(i) What is emotion? (What is necessary, and what is sufficient, for an
occurrence to be an instance of emotion? What separates the experience
of emotion from the experience of other kinds of mental event?)
(ii) How are the different emotions distinguished from each other? (How
are they individuated?)
(iii) How are the different emotions to be defined? (How are they constituted?)
    Let us consider the following list of emotions: embarrassment, envy,

fear, grief, pride, remorse, shame. Perhaps the best procedure would be to try to answer for these emotions the third question first. If we can see what each of these emotions is, we can see what differentiates them – and so answer for these emotions the second question – and also what, if anything, they have in common which is not shared with any-thing that is not an emotion – and so answer the first question, if what is distinctive of these emotions is distinctive of all emotions and all states of mind in which emotion is experienced. If, on the other hand, we find reason to believe that the emotions are not susceptible of definition, this reason is likely to put us in a better position to answer one or both of the other questions. But there are three considerations it is important to bear in mind if this procedure is adopted. Firstly, the adoption of this procedure does not rest on the assumption that each emotion has a name. The fact is that some emotions do have names and no questions are begged by starting from those that do. Secondly, the procedure does not assume that each emotion term, or each of those on the list, stands for a single emotion. Whether an emotion term stands for one or for more than one emotion depends in part upon the answer to the second question – the principle for individuating the emotions – and we are not yet in a position to say what this is or what might be a suitable criterion for the individuation of the emotions. Thirdly, the procedure does not assume that everything that is true of each of the emotions on the list is true of every emotion and contains the essence of emotion. What we regard as the emotions might not form a tightly unified class: some emotions on the list might not be characteristic, and some emotions not on the list might be anomalous.

3   Perhaps it will be helpful at this point to lay out the various positions that might be adopted towards the nature of the experience of each specific kind of emotion. At least four positions can be distinguished: three of the positions agree that the emotions cannot be defined, but differ in the reasons they advance for this conclusion; one position maintains that the emotions are susceptible of definition.

(i) The first position claims that the experience of each emotion is a simple experience in the same sense as that in which the experience of a particular hue is a simple experience: it has no distinguishable compon-ents or aspects, and is for that reason not susceptible of analysis. It is not composed of ingredients or facets whose combination or fusion constitutes it. The different emotions can no more be defined in simpler terms than the different colours can be. Accordingly, the emotions are

2

differentiated from each other in the kind of way that colours are differentiated from each other, and the relation of particular emotion to emotion itself is similar to the relation of particular colour to colour itself.

(ii) The second position maintains that the experience of each emotion is a compound experience, but it is not fully resoluble into its components. Each variety of emotion has a distinctive feature which cannot be analysed into the features of its constituent elements. An emotion is a composite, a blend, but its character is not the sum of the characters of its elements: it has a feature which is not possessed by any of its ingredients — as any minor second has a character which is not possessed by either of the notes that compose it and yet which is not merely the union of their unmerged characters. An emotion is not a combination of its constituents but a fusion of them: when an emotion is experienced the experience is not merely the combined experience of what is experienced when each component or aspect of that emotion is independently experienced. An emotion cannot be resolved without remainder into relations between its components: it is not a set of phenomena combined in some independently specifiable way. Hence, a person cannot know what an emotion is — what it is to experience that emotion — merely by being familiar with each separable element or ingredient of that emotion and knowing that these are combined in the emotion in such-and-such a manner. And hence, the emotions are distinguished by the special quality of the product of the fusion of their constituents and also by their different constituents (if, as this position is likely to hold, emotions with exactly the same constituents cannot be of different kinds).

(iii) The third position claims that the experience of each emotion is composite and it is resoluble without remainder into its components and the way in which they are combined. Accordingly, each emotion is susceptible of definition, and a person can know what the experience of any emotion is like if he understands the definition of the emotion: if he is familiar with the emotion's constituents and understands how they compose the emotion. Furthermore, the emotions are distinguished by their different constituents (if two emotions cannot combine the same constituents in different ways).

(iv) The fourth position rejects an assumption implicit in the other three positions. For it maintains for each emotion that the experience of that emotion does not possess an essence: there is no property common and specific to experiences of the same emotion (except, trivially, the

3

property of being instances of that emotion). Hence, instances of an emotion are united in some other way than by their possession of a distinctive property. And experiences of two different emotions are distinguished by their different relations with other experiences of the two kinds of emotion.

4 Now these rival positions, which have been expressed in an abstract form, can be brought into sharper focus if we adopt the procedure suggested earlier and attempt to define the emotions on the list. Perhaps the most plausible definitions of the emotions are those that follow the lines laid down in Aristotle's *Rhetoric.*[1] Let us consider the following definitions, each of which is put forward as an account of at least one of the kinds of episode to which the term applies:

(i) Embarrassment is discomfort at the thought that some action or condition might make others think less well of one.

(ii) Envy is pain at the thought of an advantage enjoyed by another.

(iii) Fear is distress at the thought of danger to oneself or someone or something one cares about.

(iv) Grief is acute distress at the thought of the death of someone who is dear to one.

(v) Pride is satisfaction at the thought of an achievement, or the possession of a desirable quality, by oneself or someone or something one identifies with.

(vi) Remorse is distress at the thought that one has acted wrongly.

(vii) Shame is discomfort at the thought of the possession of a defect, or the falling short of an ideal, by oneself or someone one identifies with.

One feature of these definitions is that each emotion is defined in such a way as to involve a particular kind of thought: it has this thought as a constituent. Now it is certainly true of each of these emotions that it has a thought as a constituent and, consequently, the first position — the thesis that the experience of each emotion is a simple experience — is mistaken. A concept of a particular thought is part of the concept of each of these emotions: someone experiences one of these emotions only if he is of a certain opinion, or views things in a certain way, or thinks that a certain proposition is true, or a certain thought occurs to him.

Another feature of the definitions is that for each emotion the thought it involves is different from the thought involved in any other emotion. These emotions are differentiated from each other by the thoughts included in them: each emotion involves a thought specific to it: the specification of the thought is sufficient to distinguish the emotion from all others. But although this is true of the emotions on the list it is not universally true of the emotions. Different emotions can involve exactly the same thought – as both pity and *Schadenfreude* involve the thought of someone's misfortune or discomfiture.

A third feature of the definitions is that each emotion is defined in such a way as to involve not only a particular kind of thought but a positive or negative reaction to the content of the thought: a form of satisfaction or dissatisfaction, pleasure or pain, agreeableness or dis-agreeableness, delight or distress. It is because pity and *Schadenfreude* involve different reactions to the same thought – the one reaction is distress, the other is pleasure – that they are different emotions.

These definitions construe each emotion as a form of pain or pleasure which is experienced on account of a certain kind of thought. Hence, a general account of the emotions based on this pattern defines the emotions as the various forms in which kinds of thought can be experienced with kinds of pleasure or pain. Accordingly, two episodes of emotion can differ with respect to the kinds of thought they involve, or in the nature of the pleasurable or painful reaction to the thought, or in both respects. Two episodes will be instances of the same kind of emotion only if they involve the same thought and the same form of pleasure or pain. But the limits of a particular kind of emotion will be drawn more or less narrowly according as the thought the emotion involves is required to be more or less specific. Hence, an emotion term will be said to stand for only one kind of emotion if a liberal criterion for individuating kinds of emotion by reference to kinds of thought is adopted; if a stricter criterion is preferred the term will be said to stand for more than one kind of emotion. And so an emotion term can be said to apply to a number of different kinds of emotion or to a single kind of which these are species: if 'fear' is standardly applied not only to episodes that involve the thought of possible harm but to episodes that do not, there is one kind of emotion that is defined by reference to the thought that unites these different kinds of episode and a more specific kind that is defined by reference to the thought of possible harm.

But is the style of definition illustrated by these accounts – which renders an emotion as a thought experienced with pain or pleasure – acceptable in the particular cases considered and also in general? I shall consider two grounds on which it might be rejected: the conditions laid down by definitions in this style for an episode to be an instance of a certain kind of emotion might be thought to be insufficient or they might be thought to be unnecessary. And if they are thought to be unnecessary, exception might be taken either to the alleged necessity of a specific form of pleasure or pain or to the alleged necessity of a constituent thought. I shall begin with the objection to the supposed necessity of the conditions but I shall put on one side for the moment the objection that some kinds of emotion do not involve particular kinds of thought.

5   The objection to the introduction of an aspect of pleasure or pain into the idea of each emotion can take two forms. The first maintains that the pleasant or unpleasant tone of each kind of emotion is variable: whether a certain emotion is experienced with pleasure or with pain is not dependent solely upon the nature of the emotion but upon the character and situation of the subject of the emotion. But the plausibility of this form of the objection is based upon a conflation of the pleasurable or unpleasurable aspect of an emotion either with a person's attitude towards his experience of the emotion or with the effect of the emotion on the person. The fact that someone experiences a certain thought with pleasure can distress him and, conversely, the fact that he experiences a certain thought with pain can please him: someone can be displeased that he experiences pride or he can derive pleasure from being sad. But this does not imply that his experience of pride can lack a pleasant aspect or his sadness be wholly pleasurable. And although emotions which are in themselves unpleasurable can have pleasurable effects (as Freud insisted),[2] they do not thereby lose their painful aspect.

The second form of the objection to the introduction of an aspect of pleasure or pain into each emotion maintains that for some emotions the thoughts integral to them do not need to be experienced with some particular form of pleasure or pain if they are to be instances of those emotions. Now the significance of this form of the objection is not solely a matter of whether it is justified. For if there are only a few emotions for which an aspect of pleasure or pain does not enter their definitions, the importance of the fact that there are such emotions depends on the extent to which these emotions possess features in common with the other emotions. But the style of definition we are considering credits emotions with just two essential aspects, an aspect of thought and an aspect of pleasure or pain. Hence, unless the emotions defined in this way are only partially defined, there is nothing that one of these emotions and an emotion which does not essentially possess a pleasure–pain aspect could share as part of their nature except the property of having a thought as a constituent. And if this should be so the emotions would fall apart into two kinds of state: thoughts experienced with pleasure or pain, and thoughts not so experienced but which possess some other distinctive property (perhaps a disjunctive property). And the style of definition we are considering would be applicable to much the larger of the two sub-classes. If, however, this style of definition is always or generally incomplete − if it only succeeds in defining the emotions partially − then it is possible that the emotions − both those that do and those that do not essentially involve an aspect of pleasure or pain − might be bound together by further properties. If the definitions in this style are completed, the elements that complete them might unite the emotions they define with those emotions that are not forms of pleasure or pain. The force of this second form of the objection can be assessed, therefore, only after a consideration of the view that the conditions laid down by definitions in this style for an episode to be an instance of a certain kind of emotion are insufficient.

6   If an emotion is not merely a thought experienced with pleasure or pain, it must have a further aspect. And either this further aspect of an emotion will be independently specifiable − specifiable without using the concept of the emotion at issue − or it will resist independent specification. If it is not independently specifiable then some form of the second position I distinguished about the nature of the experience of an emotion − the position that claims that although the experience of an emotion is composite it is not fully resoluble into its separate components − will be correct. If, on the other hand, the further aspect is independently specifiable, and if the addition of this aspect completes the proposed definitions, then the emotions will be definable and both the second and the fourth position will be mistaken. What might this further aspect, if it is independently specifiable, be thought to be? There are two obvious candidates: the first is a desire and the second is a set of bodily feelings. I shall consider firstly the relation between the emotions and desire and then the relation between the emotions and bodily feelings.

7   Desire is related to pleasure and pain in various ways. A person's reason for wanting to do something, or the respect in which he finds it desirable, is often that he finds it pleasurable to do that thing or believes he would find it pleasurable: pleasurable in itself, or pleasurable under the description of the reason or respect, not necessarily pleasurable all-in-all. And his reason for wanting not to do something, or the respect in

which he finds it undesirable, is often that he finds it unpleasurable to do that thing or believes he would find it unpleasurable. A closely connected point is that delight at the thought of performing a certain kind of action is liable to generate the desire to perform the action, distress at the thought of doing something is liable to generate the desire not to do it and distress at the thought that something is the case is liable to generate the desire or wish to ameliorate the situation or, at least, that the situation should be improved. In addition, someone does not desire something if he does not view its prospect with pleasure or the likelihood of its not coming to pass with displeasure. Furthermore, in the case of immediate, rather than long-term, wants – where what is wanted is wanted for now, rather than where the desire looks forward to a future date – the existence of the want, or the consciousness that it is unsatisfied, essentially involves frustration or dissatisfaction: not to have what one wants now to have is unpleasant, the more so the more one wants to have it.[3] Moreover, one way in which pleasure can be realised is precisely through the satisfaction of a desire: just as one form of unpleasantness is the dissatisfaction experienced in the frustration of a desire, so one form of pleasure is the satisfaction of getting what one wants. Finally, an unpleasant experience is something one has no reason in itself to want to have: the fact that an experience is unpleasant does not by itself provide a reason to undergo it. Therefore, unless there are reasons to the contrary, if one is having an unpleasant experience one will want not to be having the experience; and, conversely, if one is having a pleasant experience, in the absence of further reasons one will not want not to be having the experience.

The experience of pleasure or pain is therefore often combined with the presence of a related desire or wish. Consequently, it would be unsurprising to find that for some emotions the definition of the emotion involves a reference to something the subject of the emotion wants – as shame may involve a tendency to conceal from others the object of one's shame, envy a desire to be as well situated as the person envied (either through possessing his advantage oneself or through his not possessing it), anger an impulse to break down opposition or to hurt the person frustrating one and pity an inclination to help the person or creature whose misfortune moves one. And sometimes the thought integral to a certain emotion will be experienced with pain or pleasure precisely because the thought takes the form of a belief whose content is just the content of a pre-existent desire: one discovers or one merely believes that the world is how one has wanted it to be and one experiences

8

pleasure, or the world is or seems to be how one has wanted it not to be and one suffers accordingly.

Nevertheless, an aspect of pleasure or pain is primary in the concepts of the emotions (considered as episodes). For in the absence of an experience of pain or pleasure a combination of a thought and a related desire is never sufficient for someone to be moved by the thought to experience emotion; whereas it is sufficient for someone to react with emotion to a thought that he should experience it with pleasure or pain, even if his experience qualifies as the experience of a certain emotion only if it is accompanied by, or is a result of the real or apparent satisfaction of, a particular desire. And when an emotion has both a thought and a desire or wish as a component and the thought and the desire or wish have the same content or have opposite contents, the emotion is experienced only when the satisfaction or frustration of the desire or wish issues in an affect: the thought is experienced with pleasure or displeasure, delight or distress. Moreover, the introduction of an aspect of desire into the emotions would not always be justified. For some emotions lack desires as constituents.

8   When someone experiences an emotion it will often be the case that processes occur in his body which he experiences as bodily feelings: he may feel his hair erect, his heart pound or his skin prickle, for example. Moreover, the more powerfully someone experiences an emotion the more likely he is to feel changes in his body that are brought about by his being in an emotional condition. But bodily feelings of particular kinds are neither specific nor essential to particular kinds of emotion. It is not a necessary truth that the bodily feelings experienced when a certain emotion is undergone are experienced only when that emotion, and not any other emotion, is undergone. And it is not part of the nature of any emotion that someone experiences that emotion only if he experiences a particular set of bodily feelings. In fact, those changes in the body we may feel when we experience an emotion are not dictated by the concept of that emotion. How an emotion characteristically feels in one's body is dependent upon the kind of creature one is. The bodily feelings that are characteristic of a certain emotion are determined by the constitution of the body of the creature for whom they are characteristic accompaniments of the emotion. It is not a conceptual truth that two creatures, each of whom experiences the same emotion and feels changes in his body, must feel the same processes take place in their bodies. Although certain bodily feelings are frequent elements in

the experience of various emotions, there is no requirement that if someone is to experience a particular emotion he must experience a particular set of bodily feelings. Indeed, it is not clear that there are any emotions which are such that their experience essentially includes the experience of bodily feelings: for most, if not all, emotions it is not an *a priori* truth that the experience of some bodily change or other is part of the experience of the emotion. But even if this should be so, the weaker thesis is secure. Consequently, no matter how close the links between emotions and bodily feelings may be in our lives, it is unnecessary to introduce a reference to particular sets of bodily feelings into the definitions of the emotions, but, at most, in the case of some emotions, a reference to the occurrence of unspecified bodily feelings.

9 I have said that there are two obvious candidates — desires and bodily feelings — for the role of the alleged missing element of the emotions. But there is another possibility which is concealed, as it were, in the definitions themselves and which emerges if we turn back to consider the objection — the objection I referred to but did not discuss — to the thesis that each kind of emotion involves a particular kind of thought. The objection maintains that there are kinds of emotion which do not have a thought as a constituent. And the counter-example to the thesis that the objection cites is the state of excitement, where this is understood not in the more general sense in which someone who is not calm is excited, but in the more specific sense in which excitement is a particular kind of pleasure. One can be excited painfully or pleasurably, and pleasurable excitement is a specific kind of emotion. And, so the objection continues, in the sense in which excitement is a specific form of pleasure, although it is true that one can be excited by a thought or in thinking of something in a certain way a thought is not partly constitutive of excitement. For, in the first place, there is no particular kind of thought someone needs to have present to his mind in order for him to experience excitement. And, secondly, it is possible for someone to be excited by something and for his excitement not to be founded upon a thought at all. Now the fact that there is no thought common to all cases of excitement is not, perhaps, fatal to the thesis that each kind of emotion involves a charge of pleasure or pain on a particular kind of thought. For different kinds of emotion can be distinguished under the general head of 'excitement' by reference to the different kinds of thought that bear a charge of excited pleasure. But the fact that someone can experience excitement when there is no thought which carries the charge of pleasure establishes, so the objection maintains, that there are kinds of emotion that are not partly constituted by a thought.

It is undoubtedly true that states involving pleasure or pain can be grouped into kinds according to different principles. One criterion requires instances of the same kind to be composed in just the same way: if each involves a thought it must involve the same kind of thought and it must be experienced with the same form of pleasure or pain. It is this criterion that governs most of the common terms for the emotions. But a different classification of states involving emotion can be effected by means of a less stringent requirement: two instances of emotion are of the same kind if each involves the same form of pleasure or pain. Now the force of the objection we are considering is not that there is a counter-example to the thesis that each kind of emotion involves a particular kind of thought. For the existence of a counter-example can always be accommodated by the acknowledgement of the disparate nature of the emotions: the centrality of thought in an account of the emotions is not threatened. The force of the objection is that there are differences in kinds of pleasure which are not a matter of differences in the kinds of thought the pleasures involve; and it is not only thoughts that can be experienced with one or another of these kinds of pleasure but also perceptual experiences and activities which do not embody a thought. Accordingly, a particular kind of pleasure can be a charge on a thought or on something that does not involve a thought or on something that does involve a thought but not in virtue of the thought it contains. Hence, an emotion which has a thought as a component can be an instance of some general kind which does not require its instances to be partly constituted by a particular thought but which, rather, subsumes its instances solely by virtue of their involving a particular kind of pleasure. And it is a matter of little significance whether this general kind of state is thought of as a distinct kind of emotion or the title is withheld from it because it lacks a thought as a constituent.

Now the hidden candidate for the role of the missing element of the emotions that emerges from the consideration of this objection to the thesis that each kind of emotion includes a thought as a component is precisely such differences in kinds of pleasure and pain — differences that do not consist in different constituent thoughts or even in different objects of pleasure and pain. The suggestion, therefore, is that the proposed definitions require further specifications of the kinds of pleasure or pain with which the constituent thoughts are experienced; and these more specific kinds of pleasure or pain are not differentiated by what is found pleasing or painful. Fear is not merely distress at the thought of possible harm, but a particular kind of distress at the thought of possible harm; and a similar conclusion holds for each of the other emotions we have attempted to define. Each kind of emotion involves not only a particular thought but a particular form of pleasure or pain.

This suggestion can take two forms. The first allows that the particular kinds of pleasure and pain that the emotions are alleged to involve can be specified independently: the particular kind of discomfort involved in embarrassment can be fully characterised without making use of the concept of embarrassment; and in general the specific kind of pleasure or pain that each emotion includes can be fully characterised without making use of the concept of that emotion. If this should be so, the proposed definitions of the emotions could be completed by the speci-fication of the kinds of pleasure or pain each emotion involves. The second form of the suggestion maintains that the kinds of pleasure or pain involved in each of the emotions are specific to the different emotions and cannot be independently characterised. If this should be so, the emotions would not be fully definable.

Is the suggestion, in either of its forms, acceptable? Are there different kinds of pleasure and pain in the required sense? And if there are, are they integral to the emotions? And if so, are they in the case of each emotion independently specifiable?

The suggestion is founded upon the supposition that there are dif-ferences of a certain sort in kinds of pleasure. Now thoughts, feelings, activities and perceptual experiences can all be experienced with pleasure. Accordingly, two instances of pleasure can differ in the nature of that from which the pleasure is derived: each involves a thought but the thoughts are different; the one pleasure is a pleasurable activity whereas the other is a pleasurable feeling; and so on. But the suggestion we are considering maintains that there is a further way in which instances of pleasure can differ. For pleasures derived from the same source − the same thought, the same feeling, the same activity, the same perceptual experience − can, it is claimed, be of different kinds without their differences consisting in differences in what the pleasures are focused upon. And we are supposed already to have to hand one example of such a specific form of pleasure in the case of excitement. But is excite-ment really a specific form of pleasure in the required sense?

The answer to this question becomes clear if we examine the relation between the more and the less general uses of the term 'excitement'. In the more general sense of the term − in the sense in which someone can experience excitement without thereby experiencing pleasure – rage, indignation, terror and joy are forms of excitement: each involves an inclination to heightened activity of the mind or body. There are two ways in which pleasure can insert itself into an excited state: it can be directed towards the object of excitement or it can have the excited state itself as its object. Accordingly, someone can be excited (in the more general sense) by something and also derive pleasure from that thing, or he can derive pleasure from being excited (in the more general sense). When the term 'excitement' carries the implication that the state referred to is pleasurable, it normally indicates that the situation is one in which the excited person derives pleasure from something that excites him, although it might indicate that the person derives pleasure from his excitement. Excitement is therefore not a particular mode of pleasure but at most an accompaniment or the object of pleasure. Hence, the example of excitement fails to establish that there are differences in kinds of pleasure other than differences in those things in which pleasure is taken. The supposition upon which the suggestion rests therefore lacks its only foundation.

But whilst we must reject the suggestion we can salvage something from it. For, in the first place, the suggestion is right to maintain that an emotion may involve a heightening or lowering of bodily or mental activity – as joy involves an increase in energy and sadness involves diminished vitality. And, secondly, although the suggestion is based on an ill-founded objection to the thesis that each kind of emotion involves a thought, the objection's insistence that pleasure can be a charge on a thought or on something that does not involve a thought or on something that does involve a thought but not in virtue of the thought it involves is beneficial in two different ways. It indicates the need to make good a lack of concreteness in the account of an emotion as a thought experienced with pleasure or pain. For on most occasions when we experience an emotion, the thought we react to with pleasure or pain will not exist in an abstract form but will be conveyed or embodied in an experience – a perceptual experience, an experiential form of memory or an exercise of the imagination – and the progress of the emotion will be governed by the manner in which the experience develops. And the objection exposes the weakness of the assumption that the various kinds of emotion – each of which has a thought as a constituent – form a class that includes all the states of mind in which emotion can be said to be experienced. If the essence of each emotion consists in a thought experienced with pleasure or pain, then there are indefinitely many more states of mind

13

that differ from any of the emotions in only one respect: the pleasure or pain they involve is not a quality of a thought. And this fact is insufficient to disqualify them as instances of emotion.[4]

10 It is now clear, I believe, that it is unrewarding to pursue further the question whether it is possible to sustain an account of the emotions that defines them as the various forms in which kinds of thought can be experienced with kinds of pleasure or pain, or whether this account should be replaced by a more accurate account. The emotions undoubtedly form a heterogeneous class, and one, moreover, of which the membership is uncertain. In this situation it is better to forgo the attempt to capture the essence of an emotion in a definition of the form 'Each emotion is . . .', and, instead, to provide a model to which many emotions conform but from which other emotions or other states of mind diverge in various ways and to different degrees. The idea of an emotion as a thought experienced with pleasure or pain is just such a model: many emotions conform to it, even if the model needs supplementation in some cases. Furthermore, the ease with which the model can be used to explain many of the most significant features of, or facts about, the emotions demonstrates the model's power:

(i) The pleasure or pain with which a thought is experienced can be more or less intense, and, accordingly, other things being equal, the effects on a person's mental state and his bodily state and behaviour more or less pronounced. Hence, the emotions have intensive magnitude.

(ii) A thought experienced with pleasure or pain is not composed of parts homogeneous with it which compose it by being adjoined to each other at their common boundaries. Hence, the emotions lack extensive magnitude.[5]

(iii) The pleasure or pain someone experiences when he reacts with emotion to a thought is not normally regarded as being located in a part of the person's body. Accordingly, an emotion is not itself assigned a location in the body, but only any bodily change that is felt when the emotion is experienced.

(iv) Pleasure and pain are opposites, and it is sometimes possible for a particular thought to be experienced either with pleasure or with pain. Hence, emotions can have opposites.

(v) Thoughts can be composite or multiple, and each element can possess an aspect of pleasure or pain. Hence, a person's emotions can be mixed.

(vi) The pleasure or pain someone experiences need not reveal itself in his outward appearance. Hence, an emotion need not be manifested.

(vii) If a thought experienced with pleasure or pain issues in action, as it need not do, there is no single action, corresponding to the nature of the thought and the pleasurable or painful reaction, in which it must issue. For the connection between a thought experienced with pleasure or pain and action is mediated by the subject's character, situation, desires and beliefs. Accordingly, there are indefinitely many ways in which a kind of emotion can be manifested in behaviour: the way in which an emotion is manifested on any particular occasion is dependent not only upon the nature of the emotion someone experiences, but on a variety of factors that change in an unlimited number of ways from case to case.

(viii) A thought and a pleasurable or painful reaction to a thought are open to assessment in various ways: the thought can be mistaken, or lack an adequate justification, or be based on self-deception, for example, and the reaction to the thought can be unwarranted or inappropriate, or too strong or too weak. Hence, a person's emotions can be misdirected, unfounded, unreasonable, amenable to reason, excessive or of insufficient strength.

(ix) One way in which a certain kind of pleasurable or painful reaction to a particular kind of thought can be judged unfavourably is by its being considered a defect in character to react in that way to that kind of thought. Accordingly, certain kinds of emotion can be thought of as being inherently undesirable and as revealing faults in those who suffer them.

(x) Other things being equal, the more pleasurable or the less painful someone's life is, the happier he will be. Hence, a person's happiness is a function of the kinds of emotion that fill his life.

II

THE REPUDIATION OF EMOTION

1 Music can be considered from many points of view. These points of view include those of the composer, the executant or executants and the listener. But the points of view of the composer, executant and listener are not entirely distinct. For they may overlap – as when music is improvised – and they are interconnected: a composer normally intends his composition to be performed; it may be the intention both of the composer and the executant that the performance of a musical composition should be listened to; an executant's performance is normally guided by his understanding of the composer's intention as to how the music should sound; and not only is a listener aware that what he is hearing is a performance of a musical composition, but the manner in which he attends to what he hears is informed with this awareness – he listens to what he hears with expectations he would not otherwise have.

By the point of view of the listener I mean the point of view of someone who listens to music for its intrinsic rewards. Accordingly, there are two aspects to the listener's attitude to music. Firstly, the listener listens to music. He does not merely hear the music while he is engaged in some other activity that occupies all or part of his attention and which the music is an adjunct or stimulus to or a distraction from or an enhancement of – as when music is danced or marched to or accompanies rhythmical labour or provides a background to a social gathering or is used to induce a mood appropriate to a ceremony. The listener's attention is focused on the music. Secondly, the listener listens to music in the knowledge or hope that he will find the experience of the music intrinsically rewarding and not solely with some other end in mind.

The repudiation of emotion

Now I intend to consider music from the point of view of the listener. But in doing so I am not claiming priority for this point of view. It may well be true that the majority of composers have not thought of their music primarily as something to be listened to, and it may even be true that in many, perhaps most, cultures the listener's attitude has never been cultivated. Undoubtedly, much music has been composed for performance at an occasion when the attention of those present will not be centred on the quality of the music as such, and the music may not have been intended to have any status other than one subordinate to that of the occasion of which it is designed to be a part. And some music has been composed principally or exclusively for those who are capable of taking an active part in its performance. Moreover, the incidental function of music, or the activity involved in its performance, may be just as valuable as, or even more valuable than, the function it performs when it is the object of the listener's attention. But it does not follow from these facts that the point of view of the listener is only of minor importance. For, in the first place, the listener's point of view can be taken up for any music, even music which was not composed with the intention that it should be considered from this point of view. Secondly, the point of view of the listener has a special significance: if music is not rewarding to listen to, then, although there are many kinds of value it may have, there is one important kind of value it lacks. Finally, the adoption of the listener's point of view makes available experiences which are valued in themselves to the highest degree. And, as in the case of any other experiences of the greatest intrinsic value, so in the case of the favoured experiences of the listener, it is natural to want an explanation of the fact that the experiences are inherently rewarding in such an extreme way. Theories that propose an asethetically significant relation between music and the emotions hope to provide at least part of this explanation.

2   A piece of music can be related either to an instance of a certain general kind of emotion or to the kind itself. It can be connected with a particular person's emotion − a particular incident in the history of the world − or with the kind of emotion of which this is one instance. There are three significant instances of emotion with which a piece of music − a musical work or a performance of the work − might in some way be connected: the emotion the composer experienced when he composed the work, or which he experienced on some other specific occasion in his life, the emotion a performer experienced when he

17

performed the work, and the emotion a listener experienced when he heard a performance of the work. But instances of emotion of the first two kinds are irrelevant in themselves from the point of view of music as something to be listened to for its intrinsic rewards. When someone listens to music in this manner there is never any reason for him to be concerned whether the composer felt a certain emotion at a certain time or the performer feels or felt a certain emotion when performing the work. The fact that the composer or performer of a musical work experienced a particular emotion on a certain occasion might be relevant instrumentally to the character of the work or the performance. But the character the work or the performance possesses and the listener must grasp if he is to appreciate what he hears is an audible character the work or the performance has in itself and which the listener can take in through his attention to the performance. And the emotion the composer or performer once felt – that particular episode of emotion – is not a feature of what the listener hears and that he can perceive in the music. The listener may be inclined to infer from the character of the music that the composition or the performance arose from the experience of a particular emotion. But this would be an inference from the music's audible character, not an aspect of that character.

3 In each of the following cases a piece of music is related to a kind of emotion in the way indicated: the third movement of Beethoven's first *Rasoumovsky* string quartet is an expression of sadness of extraordinary depth and sincerity: Elgar's *Sospiri* expresses profound sorrow and a feeling of irrecoverable loss; the opening of Mendelssohn's *Italian* Symphony is imbued with *joie de vivre*; the adagio introduction to the finale of Mozart's string quintet in G minor expresses ultimate despair; the Prelude to Wagner's *Tristan und Isolde* is suffused with yearning. Each piece of music can be said to possess a particular emotional quality or to be expressive of the emotional condition it reveals. Now the intrinsic irrelevance to the aesthetic or artistic appeal of a musical work of the fact that the work's composer on a specific occasion felt an emotion, E, is susceptible of a more specific demonstration when what is in question is the work's appeal as being expressive of E, even if this instance of E plays an important role in the composition of the work and in the formation of the composer's intention that the music should be expressive of E, and even if the composer sees himself as expressing *his* E in the music he composes. For if the composer wishes to express his E by composing music that is an expression of his E he will intend to create

18

music that possesses the quality of emotion E. But the fact that the composer now feels E, or that he felt E on any other specific occasion, and that he intends his music to express his E implies nothing about the audible character of the music he composes. This character may or may not 'match' his E. For it to match his E the music must have a non-relational character – a character it does not possess only because it stands in a certain relation to an individual thing or event – in virtue of which it matches his E. And a piece of music can have this character whether or not its composer felt E on some specific occasion and intended his music to express that instance of E. Of course, the possession of this character is nothing other than the possession of the quality of emotion E. It is this character that the composer intends to give to his music when he wishes to express his E in the music. It is unsurprising, therefore, that a composer does not need to feel an emotion he intends the music he is composing to be expressive of. And the listener can hear a musical work as being expressive of E without being concerned whether the music stands in a certain relation to a particular instance of E that was felt by the composer.

A similar argument can be used to show the intrinsic irrelevance of a performer's emotion to the appeal of a musical work, as he performs it, as being expressive of a certain emotion. For if someone wishes to express an emotion he feels by performing music, and he wishes his emotion to be expressed in the music he plays, then normally he will play music which he considers to possess the quality of emotion he feels, and he will intend the music as he performs it to possess this quality of emotion – perhaps he will intend his performance to make fully manifest the quality of emotion that other performances often fail to reveal. And whether the music as he performs it possesses this quality of emotion is not a matter of whether the performance is generated by an instance of the emotion which the performer feels. If, on the other hand, someone chooses to play a piece of music he considers not to possess the quality of emotion he feels, then his emotion can be expressed in the music he plays only by his playing the music in such a manner that it then has the character it lacks if it is performed in a manner that does justice to the music. And, again, whether the music as he performs it possesses this character is a matter that is determined independently of any fact about the performer's emotion.

4   From the listener's point of view, therefore, neither an instance of emotion experienced by the composer nor an instance of emotion

experienced by a performer is of interest. But we have not yet considered one important instance of emotion – the emotion a listener may experience when he listens to music – and we have not considered the nature or the significance of the musical expression of emotion. Can the value of music from the point of view of the listener ever be explained by reference to the emotion aroused in the listener by the music he listens to? And can it ever be explained by reference to the expressive character of the music? Or is there some other relation in which music can stand to the emotions and which is relevant to the explanation of the value of music to the listener? The best-known attempt to establish that a negative answer should be given to each of these questions is Eduard Hanslick's book *The Beautiful in Music*,[1] and I shall now present and examine the arguments he puts forward against the view that the value of music as an art-form is located in some connection between music and emotion.

5   Hanslick tries to establish three negative conclusions about the relationship between music and the emotions. He argues, firstly, that it is impossible for any definite emotion to be represented by a piece of music, and, hence, that the musical value, the 'beauty', of a piece of music can never be due to the fact that it represents a definite emotion or to the manner in which it represents the emotion. Furthermore, so the argument continues, the value of the forms of sound constructed in music would not depend upon their being accurate representations of definite emotions, even if the musical representation of definite emotions were possible. He argues, secondly, that emotion terms cannot be used to characterise music in a manner that is both properly musical and ineliminable. Accordingly, to experience a melody as sad, for example, is not to experience it in a way that essentially relates it to the emotion of sadness. And he argues, finally, that the aim of music that aspires to musical value is not to evoke or excite emotion in the listener: the musical value of a musical work is never dependent upon its capacity to arouse definite emotions or to establish a mood. His conclusion is that music is an end in itself, not merely a means for the achievement of something to do with the emotions; it pleases in its own right, like an arabesque, or a flower; its value as music, its beauty, is specifically musical.[2]

I begin by considering the issue of the musical representation of the emotions.

6   Hanslick's main concern is to deny that feelings or emotions are the subject-matter which music is intended to illustrate or represent.[3] But this formulation is not precise enough to engage with directly. Hanslick refers to Roland's exploits as the subject of a poem and to a flower-girl as the subject of a painting, and he assumes that the idea of the subject of a work of art is thereby made clear. But the relation in which the subject stands to the work of art is different in the two cases: in one the subject is what is described in the work, in the other the subject is what is seen, and is intended to be seen, in the work. Hence, although Hanslick wishes to deny that the emotions stand in a certain relation to musical works, the nature of this relation is not something that he makes specially clear at the outset. But in the course of his argument the nature of the relation he has in mind emerges, and it turns out to be a relation neither identical with nor included in either of the ones mentioned above, although perhaps reflecting a false conception of the nature of visual representation.

The conclusion of Hanslick's argument is that it is not possible to represent definite feelings or emotions by purely musical means. His argument may perhaps be rendered in this way: (i) Music cannot represent thoughts. (ii) Definite feelings and emotions, hope, sadness and love, for example, involve or contain thoughts. Therefore, (iii) music cannot represent definite feelings or emotions.[4]

Whatever our understanding of the concept of representation may be, the formal validity of this argument depends upon the validity of the principle that if one thing involves another thing then in order for something to represent the first thing it must represent the second thing. But the validity of this principle does depend upon the way in which the concept of representation is to be understood. It also depends upon the idea of one phenomenon involving or containing another. Now when Hanslick asserts that the feeling of hope is inseparable from the conception of a happier state that is to come, his view appears to be that the concept of hope includes the concept of the thought that what is wanted may possibly come about; and in general that a definite emotion or feeling involves or contains a thought in the sense that the concept of that thought is part of the concept of the emotion or feeling. Accordingly, a person is correctly characterised as experiencing a definite feeling or emotion only if a thought occurs to him or engages his mind. And each distinct kind of definite feeling or emotion requires this thought to be of a certain kind.

If we consider a particular definite feeling or emotion that someone has, that is to say, a specific instance of a definite feeling or emotion of a certain kind, and subtract from it the thought it contains, what is left? Hanslick does not give a clear answer to this question, but he refers to the strength of the feeling, and the manner of its development. He also mentions 'a general feeling of satisfaction or discomfort'.[5] In fact, he asserts that a feeling always involves satisfaction or discomfort.[6] Perhaps he would have accepted the view we have already discussed in the case of emotions that definite feelings or emotions involve desires or aversions, or pleasure or pain, as joy involves pleasure at the attainment of something one desires, shame distress at something one regards as a defect, and envy wanting something that another possesses; so that if we subtract the idea of what is desired, or what is found distressing, or that in which pleasure is taken, all that remains is 'a general feeling of satisfaction or discomfort'. And since the thought, or the thinking of it, does not have degrees of intensity, Hanslick must regard the strength of a person's feeling or emotion as the degree of his satisfaction or discomfort. Whether this is so or not, Hanslick's general point of view is clear. Everything by which one kind of definite feeling or emotion is distinguished from every other kind involves a thought, that music cannot represent, so that every other feature of a feeling or emotion can be shared with different feelings or emotions. If different kinds of feeling or emotion were to differ not only in the nature of the contained thoughts, but in some other respect that distinguished them from all other feelings or emotions, then the possibility of representing at least something that is distinctive of a certain kind of feeling or emotion might remain. It is Hanslick's contention that there is nothing else by which the different kinds of definite feeling or emotion can be distinguished.

Hanslick concedes that music can represent the 'dynamic properties' of feelings: their strength and the manner in which they develop; their 'speed, slowness, strength, weakness, increasing and decreasing intensity'.[7] But particular instances of these dynamic characteristics of feelings are not proprietary to particular kinds of feeling. Rather, they may be possessed by different feelings. A feeling of joy may have the same strength as a feeling of sadness, and it may well up and diminish in the same fashion.

The reason why Hanslick allows that music can represent the dynamic properties of feelings or emotions, but no other properties of them, is that he is concerned with those features of feelings or emotions that music can 'reproduce' or 'incorporate', or that music and feelings or emotions can 'have in common';[8] and the dynamic qualities of feelings or emotions are the only aspects of them that music can, as far as Hanslick can see, reproduce. When Hanslick thinks about music's capacity to represent a phenomenon all he considers is music's ability to match or resemble the phenomenon, and so the possibility that the phenomenon should be imitated in, or copied or simulated by, music.

This allows an amplification or modification of his argument against the musical representation of definite feelings or emotions. Reformulated, the initial premise would be that music can neither imitate a thought nor otherwise present it. Music cannot express thoughts as do words; and since music can represent a phenomenon only to the extent that it can imitate it, music cannot represent a thought. By collapsing the notion of representation, where this is understood after the manner of visual representation, into the notion of imitation, Hanslick reaches the conclusion that music cannot present a thought either in the way in which literature can present something or in the way in which painting can present something. And since these seem to him to exhaust the possibilities, he believes that music can never present the thought that forms the core of a definite feeling or emotion, and, consequently, music can never represent a definite feeling or emotion.

Now it is in fact clear that music lacks the essential features of language, and that it cannot present the content of a thought by resembling the thought. If the only way of being a non-verbal representation of something were by being a replica of that thing, music could not represent the all-important thought located, according to Hanslick, at the heart of a definite feeling or emotion, and would thereby, and in this sense, be prevented from representing definite feelings and emotions. It is also clear that there can be no true parallel, in the case of the musical representation of emotion, to visual representation in its straightforward form; that is to say, to visual representation which is such that R is a representation of O only if O can be seen in R. For music would have to be of such a nature that an emotion can be heard in it. And the reason the exact parallel cannot be maintained is that it is only the signs or expressions of emotion that can be heard, not the emotion itself; and since something can, in the required sense, be seen in something else only if it can itself be seen, so, likewise, something can, in the required sense, be heard in something else only if it can itself be heard. Just as there could not be a picture of an emotion, but only of a person emotionally affected, for an emotion can no more be seen than it can be heard, so there could not be a musical representation – a musical counterpart of a straightforward visual representation – of an emotion, but only of an emotion's expression in a person's voice.

Hanslick claims that the only features of emotions that can be copied in music are their dynamic properties, which can be common to different kinds of emotion. But if this is so we can go further. These dynamic features music can reproduce are not peculiar to the emotions. Other processes in the natural world, as in a musical work, may end more or less suddenly; may increase or decrease in strength; may involve growth to a culmination or climax. So the features of emotions that music can reproduce, their dynamic properties, have nothing specially to do with the emotions, but are features of many other processes as well. Therefore, the conclusion should be that there is nothing music can represent, in the sense of copy, which particularly concerns the emotions, unless the ways in which emotions progress are distinctive of them.[9] Music can represent the dynamic properties possessed by episodes of emotion, but it cannot represent them *as* properties of, specifically, episodes of emotion. It is, therefore, unsurprising that Hanslick maintains that there is *nothing* extraneous to the musical notes that can properly be called the subject that a 'pure' musical work represents.[10]

7   But was Hanslick right to locate a thought at the heart of each definite feeling or emotion? Now there is a difficulty in answering this question. For Hanslick does not explain the concept of a definite feeling. He merely gives instances of what he considers to be definite feelings. The feelings he mentions as being resistant to representation in music include sadness, hope, cheerfulness, hatred, piety, religious fervour, love, joy, grief and longing. Most of these are emotions; and Hanslick himself writes indiscriminately of feelings and emotions. And we have already assessed the plausibility of the thesis that each emotion has a thought as a constituent. I believe the best procedure is not in fact to question whether Hanslick was right to place a thought at the heart of each 'definite' feeling, but instead to introduce the idea of a definite feeling as a feeling which is partly constituted by a thought. The class of definite feelings will then include at least most of the phenomena we would think of as emotions, and at least most of the feelings Hanslick claims to be resistant to representation in music. If there are feelings or emotions that do not include a thought, they will be untouched by Hanslick's argument against the possibility of the representation in music of definite feelings, since the argument turns essentially upon the consideration that music cannot represent a thought. Hanslick presents cheerfulness as a definite feeling that cannot be represented in music. But cheerfulness seems rather to be either a quality of character or a

mood, which in either case consists in being in good spirit, and which does not include a specific thought. Hence, Hanslick's argument cannot be used to establish the impossibility of its musical representation. And this holds good for any similar quality of mood or character.

8 Hanslick drops without further mention the 'general feeling of satisfaction or discomfort'. Now this glancing reference is not to something he makes particularly clear. But suppose it were true — we have already explored the supposition that it is true — that it is part of our experience, whenever we feel an emotion, or a definite feeling of a certain kind, to experience it with some measure of satisfaction, dissatisfaction, pleasure, distress or discomfort; and, further, that in the continuation of an emotion the degree of pleasure or pain can vary, and in the transition from one emotion to an emotion of another kind there can be changes from pleasure to pain or vice versa. Then if music could represent the experience of satisfaction and dissatisfaction, in the sense that it could in some way reproduce or copy them, there would after all be a connection, of the kind Hanslick denies, between music and at least something integral and peculiar to emotions and other allied phenomena. Or if, at least, there are musical analogues of pleasure and pain and the different ways in which they arise and develop, then a musical work might stand in a significant symbolic relation to an important element of the emotions. Accordingly, although music cannot articulate the thought an emotion involves, it is not thereby prevented from delineating that element of the experience of an emotion without which the experience would not be emotional. And if this essential element of emotional experience can in some way be made manifest by music, its appearance in a musical work might be sufficient to endow the work with musical value or to make the music intrinsically rewarding from the listener's point of view. Moreover, it is not difficult to imagine what might be thought to provide the foundation of music's capacity to present an appearance of this element of emotional experience: the nature of tonality and the phenomena of consonance and dissonance. For dissonance and consonance, understood in the sense of those musical sounds that do, and those that do not, stand in need of resolution, give to tonal music the movement from tension to resolution that is integral to it. And there is a natural correspondence between musical tension and resolution, on the one hand, and the experience of dissatisfaction and satisfaction, on the other hand. I shall later examine at length a theory of the nature and value of music as an art-form that construes a

musical work as a counterpart of a process which involves satisfaction and dissatisfaction.[11]

9   We have seen that Hanslick has argued that it is not possible to represent definite feelings or emotions by musical means. He attempts to buttress his position by the additional argument that musical value would not depend upon the (accurate) representation of feelings even if such a representation were possible.[12] We may give his arguments more general application by considering them not only in relation to, but also in abstraction from, his particular idea of representation, and of the limits of representation in music.

The first claim is that some valuable pieces of music do not represent a definite feeling. This is certainly true. But, clearly, it counts against only the stronger view that each valuable work represents definite emotions and its musical value is in some way dependent upon this function. It leaves untouched the view that the value of some music is a matter of the music's representing, or is dependent upon the manner in which it represents, definite emotions; and this weaker view is inconsistent with Hanslick's idea that musical value, the beauty of music, is purely musical.

Hanslick's second consideration is that vocal music, as it represents feelings more perfectly, becomes musically less beautiful. But this presents difficulties for Hanslick. He would be able to secure the conclusion he wants if he could show that as music most accurately represents a definite feeling so it becomes less beautiful. But since Hanslick believes that music cannot represent definite feelings, clearly he cannot establish this. What he tries to show is that as vocal music most accurately represents a definite feeling, so the music itself becomes less beautiful. But, according to Hanslick, it is the words, rather than the music, which represent the feeling. Hence, what he attempts to establish is that, as a definite feeling is more accurately represented by the words, supported by all that the music can represent, namely, the dynamic qualities of the feeling, so the music becomes less beautiful. And because he considers the recitative to be the form of music which is most concerned to represent definite feelings accurately, he finds it easy to reach his conclusion. But in recitative, although a singer's voice sometimes imitates the natural inflections of the voice under the varying conditions of emotional excitement, which is Hanslick's reason for taking it as the prime example of vocal music concerned to represent definite emotions, the words do not imitate the emotions themselves. Hanslick calls the recitative a copy of rapidly changing states of mind. What it copies, however, if it copies anything at all, are various speech-inflections and speech-rhythms and certain features of the natural expression of emotional states in the human voice.

The third consideration Hanslick brings forward in support of the claim that musical value would not depend upon the accurate representation of definite feelings, even if such a representation were possible, is the assertion that in any song slight alterations can be made to the music which do not affect the accuracy of the representation of feeling at all, but which destroy the beauty of the theme. This consideration would indeed show that the beauty of vocal music was never dependent upon the accurate representation of feeling; but the sense in which it is true that the beauty of a theme can always be destroyed by slight alterations which do not affect the accuracy of representation – at least, this is all that Hanslick intends – is merely that the reference made by the words of the song to the particular feelings will always remain. The related point Hanslick mentions, that many songs may adequately express the drift of a poem whilst having no musical merit, would show only that the musical merit of vocal music is not solely dependent upon its accurately representing feelings.

Hence, Hanslick fails to show that even if music could represent definite feelings, it would never be the case that the beauty of a piece of music was dependent upon its fulfilling this function. Therefore, this part of his argument for the thesis that the beauty of music is specifically musical must rest squarely upon the alleged impossibility that music should represent a definite feeling.

10 Hanslick emphasises that his principal negative concern is to show that music cannot represent definite feelings or emotions, and so have them as its subject matter. And we have seen that his central consideration is that music cannot imitate or reproduce that feature of emotions which helps to make them definite, or the particular kinds of emotion that they are. But the demonstration that a musical work cannot represent an emotion is not sufficient to establish that the value of music is unrelated to the emotions. For there are more ways than this in which an emotion might be thought to stand in an aesthetically important relation to a piece of music. Hanslick recognises two other ways in which an emotion might be thought to be related to a musical work in a relevant manner: his criticisms of these two possibilities complete his attempt to show that musical value is unrelated to the emotions.

11   One way in which an emotion might be thought to stand in an aesthetically important relation to a piece of music is by the emotion's being excited in a listener by the work. Now Hanslick not only acknowledges, but stresses the fact that music can arouse emotion. However, as he insists, this is not the question at issue. The question is whether the arousal of (a definite) emotion is ever an aesthetically relevant, perhaps the appropriate, response to a piece of music; or whether it is ever required in an adequate or full understanding of the work; or whether the experience of an emotion can form a valuable part of an aesthetic response to music. But Hanslick's treatment of this issue, although in places penetrating, is inconclusive.[13] He rightly rejects as unaesthetic the arousal of emotion by music in any way which fails to involve an understanding of the music; for example, in a manner analogous to that in which the taking of opium may be related to the dreams it induces. And it is true, as he emphasises, that people often use music merely as a stimulus to their private emotional flights, rather than attend to, and allow their response to be governed by, the detailed development of the music, which is the musical listener's method of listening to it; so that the musical excitation of feelings is often not of aesthetic significance. But this is not enough to show that an emotion in a person's response is never aesthetically relevant, or never required, or of no importance. He also insists that there is no causal nexus between a musical composition and the feelings it may excite, and that music can be equally admired at different times even though its emotional qualities are thought of as, or the emotions it arouses are, different. But this establishes neither that an emotion in a person's response to music is never necessary if the music is fully to be understood, nor that an emotion cannot be a possible element in an aesthetic response and an integral feature of the value of the experience.

Hanslick's anxiety to repudiate the role commonly assigned to the emotions in the experience of music leads him to construe the experience as essentially one consisting in the passionless contemplation of the various 'purely musical' features of the music, which contemplation may yield pleasure, although this is not essential to the recognition of the beauty of the music. Now if someone were to insist against this that the experience of music may properly, and directly, be an emotional one, he would not be denying that the experience may be pleasurable. Rather, he would be giving an alternative characterisation of the nature of the pleasure that may be experienced. That is to say, he would be insisting that what may be pleasurable is an experience that is not purely contemplative and free from the experience of emotion but rather one that involves the experience of emotion. He would be claiming that the experience of the listener to music might in one respect sometimes be similar to that of, let us say, a person who likes to watch horror films, who takes pleasure *in being* (imaginatively) *frightened*. The response that a horror film invites, and is designed to draw out from the audience, involves feeling a definite emotion, fear or horror, and someone who does not experience this emotion in watching the film thereby fails to have the experience the film can provide, and to this extent, or in this respect, will attach no value to his experience. Someone may of course not value the experience if he does experience fear, either because he does not delight in the imaginative experience of fear, or because, although he does enjoy the experience, on other grounds he attaches no importance to it. And just as in this case, so for theories of music that stress the musical arousal of emotion, there are questions as to the enjoyment of a particular emotion experienced in response to the work of art. There is, firstly, the question how this enjoyment is possible, especially when the emotion experienced is normally distressing; and, secondly, the question what value the experience of the emotion has: the emotion can, after all, be aroused by non-musical stimuli in ordinary life. These are in fact the final considerations Hanslick presses in his treatment of the musical arousal of emotion; but he fails to establish that there are no acceptable answers to these questions.

Now pure music is a non-representational form of art and in that respect differs from the film. Therefore, if a definite emotion can be involved in an aesthetic response to a musical work it will be necessary to provide a different explanation of how this is possible from that which would be invoked in the case of the film. Recourse cannot be had to the mechanisms of identification, empathy and sympathy, for example, at least in a fashion analogous to that in which they are brought into play by films, and also by works of fiction and by other 'representative' works of art. It will also be necessary to meet the objection that a theory of music that construes musical value as the capacity to arouse emotions renders music theoretically superfluous.[14] If the value of music is located in the emotions it arouses then there will be the possibility that something other than the music can arouse the same emotions. But this would make the music in principle dispensable, and would thus credit the music only with instrumental and not with intrinsic value. If music is valued only as a means to an independently specifiable end, in this case the arousal of extra-musical emotions, then it must be possible that there should be other, and perhaps even better, means of achieving what music aims at; so that music could be dispensed with, and replaced by whatever else can achieve the same effect. If different musical works can arouse the same emotions, and if music is valued only as a means of emotional arousal, then any music we admire would be replaceable as an object of our affection by any other musical work that excites the same emotions. Further, if there should be some non-musical way of arousing the same emotions that a piece of music arouses, and if the music is valued only for the emotions it excites, then that non-musical phenomenon will have the same value as the music. And yet it is clear that music could not be displaced in this kind of way from the position it in fact occupies in our life.[15]

If this objection to theories of music that explain the value of music in terms of its capacity to engender emotions in the listener is to be met successfully, what is needed is an account of emotion which explains how there can be an emotion whose essence is given by these two characteristics: it is an instance of some generic kind of extra-musical emotion, and it involves the experience of hearing a specific piece of music. The emotion must fall under the head of some general kind of extra-musical emotion, and it must be individuated from other forms of that emotion by involving the experience of hearing the music. This emotion will then in one sense be an extra-musical emotion without thereby being separable from a certain piece of music. The emotion will be, say, grief, but the kind of grief that it is will involve the experience of a particular piece of music; so that the emotion can be experienced only if the music is. The experience of hearing the music will not be a mere cause of the emotion but will instead be integral to the experience of the emotion. Only in this way can the objection be overcome.

The difficulty of explaining how an extra-musical emotion can be experienced in an aesthetic response to music, so that the music is not rendered in principle dispensable, is easily circumscribed in the case of some emotions. For the emotion can take as its object the music itself, and the music, since it is the object of the emotion and not merely its cause, is not made vulnerable to replacement by something that could produce the same effect. If the music is intended to arouse the emotion it will also be intended to arouse the emotion through being its object. An example of an emotion whose aesthetic arousal by music presents no problem is amusement. But grief, for instance, if aroused by music, would not have the music as its object, in the sense that the music would not be what it is that is being grieved over. It is when an emotion does

30

not have the music as its object that it is hard to see how, if the music is valued because it arouses the emotion, it is being valued aesthetically; for the music would seem to be merely its cause, and its value only that of an instrument for the production of the emotion.[16]

12   With hindsight it is possible to see that in considering the musical arousal of emotion a distinction can be drawn that Hanslick fails to recognise. Either the emotion that is felt in response to music might be a definite extra-musical emotion, that is, such an emotion as sadness, which can be elicited by non-musical stimuli as well as by music itself, or it might not be a definite extra-musical emotion. There are two ways in which this last possibility could be realised: the emotion might not be extra-musical, or it might not be definite. By this I refer, in the former instance, to the idea of an emotion that is *sui generis*, or specifically musical, associated in particular with the theory of Edmund Gurney,[17] and, in the latter instance, to the idea that the emotions have a common core of emotion *per se*, which idea is the central element of Leonard Meyer's theory of the affective response to music.[18] It is in fact unnecessary to deny, as Hanslick does, that a definite extra-musical emotion can be experienced in an aesthetic response to music in order to maintain the doctrine of the specifically musical nature of the beauty of music; for the emotion might be one that has the music as its object. The position with respect to an emotion for which the music is not its object is perhaps as yet unclear. But it is certainly unnecessary to disallow either a *sui generis* emotion, or emotion *per se*. If music can move us without arousing a definite extra-musical emotion, its abstract purity will not be compromised by the possibility of an aesthetic response of an emotional kind. I shall later consider whether a viable theory of music can be built either upon the idea of an emotion which is specific to music or upon the idea of emotion *per se*.[19]

13   The second way in which it might be thought that music can be related to an emotion in an aesthetically significant manner is by music's being expressive of an emotion or by music's possessing an emotional quality.[20] Hanslick argues against this that it is allowable to characterise a piece of music by means of terms used to name or to describe emotions, e.g. 'proud', 'gloomy', 'tender', 'ardent', 'longing', as long as these terms are used *figuratively* to express certain analogies between the musical work and the emotional states they designate.[21] Accordingly, such terms serve to indicate merely the musical character of the piece, so

that terms taken from a different order of phenomena, e.g., 'sweet', 'fresh', 'cloudy', 'cold', might equally well, or with just as much justification, have been used. Clearly, if one order of terms would do as well as another, characterising a musical theme by means of terminology drawn from descriptions of the emotions does not imply a relation specifically to the emotions. Only a use of emotional terminology not so replaceable would carry that implication, and Hanslick does not countenance an undeletable or ineliminable use.

But it is unclear how this figurative use of words which signify emotional states is supposed to work. For the only analogy Hanslick allows between an emotion and a piece of music is their dynamic features. Accordingly, the use of such words as 'proud', 'gloomy' and 'longing' must be to indicate certain dynamic features of the musical work, which can be as well indicated by such terms as 'sweet', 'fresh', 'cloudy', 'cold'; and yet neither set of terms ordinarily signifies dynamic features of processes. It is, perhaps, only by using a set of such terms, drawn from a particular realm, and exploiting the relationships between the terms to characterise different pieces of music, that an indication of dynamic features of a musical work becomes possible.

It is true that a word is often used metaphorically, its use transferred from one kind of phenomenon to another, in order to designate a property for which there is no name in the language. That is to say, rather than coin a new term, we economise in vocabulary by making use of an old term to do a new job. A specially important instance is when we trade upon similarities between the two kinds of phenomenon. A clear example of such a use, within the field of music, is that of the words 'higher' and 'lower' to stand for relations between the pitch of notes.[22] Tones differ not only in duration, timbre and loudness, but also in another respect, which exhibits a one-dimensional ordering that can be marked, for example, by the use of the terms 'higher' and 'lower'. Hanslick licenses the application of names or descriptions of feelings or emotions to music if they are used in this way; that is to say, if they are used solely to designate certain features of musical works, as, to vary the example, the terms 'smooth' or 'round' can be used to stand for features of the sound of notes. These musical features must be identifiable without reference to the emotions whose names are used to signify them.

It is clear that not all transferred uses of terms can be understood on this model. There are two other possibilities. The first is that a figurative use of a word may attribute a property whose identification involves an essential reference to the phenomenon the term literally designates. An instance of this kind of use would arise in the sphere of music if to characterise a melody as sad were to say, or express, the fact that it arouses sadness in one; or that it makes one think of, or imagine, sadness; or that the melody seems to match or correspond with sadness; or that the music can be experienced as if it were the vocal expression of sadness; and so on. The second possibility is that a transferred use is resorted to, not through poverty of the language, to designate an otherwise nameless property, and not because the specification of the property involves a reference to the phenomenon the word is normally used to designate, but for some quite different reason. A term used metaphorically may in fact not attribute a property at all, but rather, for instance,[23] as I.A. Richards and others have pointed out,[24] be used to express an attitude to the term's new referent similar to that experienced towards its original referent.

Hanslick's claim is that the characterisation of music by emotion terms is either improper or deletable: improper if their use is to involve an essential reference to the emotions; deletable if they can be replaced by sets of terms drawn from different realms which would serve exactly the same purpose; which sets in their turn are deletable in favour of purely musical characterisations, that is, in terms of words, which are not used figuratively, but literally when they are applied to music.

Now in general there is no requirement that whenever a certain term is used figuratively as the name of a property it must be used as the name of the same property. It is not clear from Hanslick's account whether the permissible figurative use of an emotion term to describe music is supposed to be uniform, either in the uses of different people or even in the different uses of the same person. If an individual's use of an emotion term to describe music is intended to be uniform, so that he always uses the term to refer to the same musical character, then the position Hanslick advocates is congruent with the thesis that emotion terms are used as terms of 'purely sensible description' when they are applied to music.[25] According to this thesis, there are various 'purely audible features' that music can possess – features which stand in the same relation to auditory experience as colour stands to visual experience – and, because we lack terms which stand directly for any of these features, we commandeer the language of the emotions and use words that describe our emotions as names of these purely audible features. It follows from this thesis that if the word 'sad' is used to stand for a purely audible feature of music – in lieu of a word the specific function of which is to name this feature – it must be possible in principle to identify this feature without making use of the concept of sadness: it is part of the force of the phrase 'purely sensible description' that it is not integral to the identification or recognition of this feature that it should be brought under the concept of sadness. Hence, it is an assumption of the thesis – and so an assumption of this version of the position Hanslick advocates – that there is a feature common to all sad music (or to all music that is sad for a particular person), and this feature is not possessed by any music which is not sad, and the feature can be specified independently of the concept of sadness in purely audible terms.[26]

Hanslick's view appears to be that there is no special reason why 'sad' should be used to stand for this property; the term is no more appropriate than many other words. But there is sometimes thought to be a special suitability in using the term 'sad' as a name of this purely audible property.[27] For, so it is claimed, music that possesses this purely audible property also possesses some of the characteristics of people who are sad. Characteristically, sad music is slow, quiet and low in pitch, and sad people move relatively slowly and speak both softly and low in pitch. Now this alleged correspondence might be intended to provide the outline of a causal explanation of the fact that the term 'sad' is used to stand for a certain purely audible feature, or it might be intended to provide a justification for this use. But if it is intended to provide a justification for using the word 'sad' to stand for a certain purely audible feature, the justification it provides is exceedingly weak. For even if there is a purely audible feature F which music possesses only if it is sad, and if music possesses F only if it is relatively slow, soft and low in pitch, and even if sad people characteristically move more slowly and speak more softly and at a lower pitch than they would do if they were not sad, much music that is not sad – and does not possess F – resembles sad people in these respects just as much as sad music does. This correspondence therefore provides no more reason for calling music which possesses F sad than for calling music which is slow, soft and low in pitch but which does not possess F sad. Furthermore, there are many things other than sad people that move slowly and make soft, low sounds. Hence this correspondence fails to show that 'sad' is a more appropriate word to stand for F than any other available word.

The thesis that emotion terms are used as terms of purely sensible description when they are applied to music – the purely sensible description thesis – asserts that an emotion term is used to attribute to music a purely audible feature. Hence, if a piece of music possesses an emotional quality it is not thereby related to an emotion in a manner that might be integral to the value of the music – for it is not thereby related to an emotion. Now the purely sensible description thesis does not attempt to characterise the purely audible feature that, according to the thesis, an emotion term is used to attribute to music. Of course, an adherent of the thesis would deny that this is a weakness in the view. For it is precisely his contention that the reason emotion terms are used to attribute purely audible features to music is that the purely audible features they stand for lack names. But in the absence of a characterisation of these alleged features, and given that we have not been provided with good reason for using emotion terms to stand for them, the purely sensible description thesis does not inspire conviction: it merely asserts that there is a purely audible feature that 'sad' is used to stand for, and a different purely audible feature for each emotion term that is properly used to describe music. A theory that construes emotion terms as designating purely audible features of music would be more plausible if it offered some account of these purely audible features which would enable us to understand the strength and prevalence of the inclination to regard emotion terms as pre-eminently suitable words to stand for these features.

Now if the purely sensible description thesis is offered as an account of the way in which emotion terms are actually applied to music I believe it is an inaccurate account. It must be conceded to the thesis that it is sometimes true that when emotion terms are applied to music they may properly be treated less than seriously. For when someone says that a certain melody is anguished, for example, he might mean only that the melody contains extreme melodic leaps to dissonant intervals. In fact, people often intend something less definite or specific than their words might imply. But whilst a person's use of words transferred from one kind of phenomenon to another can sometimes be taken unseriously, in that although he mentions, he intends no undeletable reference to, the first kind of phenomenon, this is often not so.[28] Someone who describes a piece of music with a term which designates an emotional reaction will not always allow that his meaning can be captured by some description of purely audible features: his meaning involves an essential reference to the emotional reaction. When this is so, the purely sensible description thesis misrepresents the function of an emotion term. Moreover, an ineliminable use of an emotion term appears often to be justified: the word 'sad', for instance, seems sometimes to

35

be the *mot juste*, rather than a makeshift, intimating, perhaps by analogy, something that has nothing specifically to do with sadness. And it is easy to give an indisputable example of a justified undeletable use of an emotion term: the characterisation of Mozart's Masonic Funeral Music (KV 477) as mournful – no description of the music in purely audible terms can be substituted for the emotional characterisation without losing the point of the emotional characterisation. It is clear that there is a sense in which a musical work can justifiably be characterised as having a certain emotional quality, where the reference to the emotional quality is ineliminable.

But this is insufficient to show that Hanslick's attitude to the application of emotion terms to music is misplaced. For it does not follow from the fact that there is an ineliminable use of emotion terms to describe music that the existence of this ineliminable use is ever of importance in an aesthetic response to music or in an explanation of its value to the listener. And if it is never relevant to the musical value of a work that it possesses, ineliminably, an emotional quality Hanslick's position would not be threatened – from the point of view of the musical value of a work, there would be no proper use of an emotion term to characterise music in a manner that would relate the music specifically to an emotion. Furthermore – to put the point slightly differently than before – a theory that maintains that emotion terms are applied to music in a properly musical way only if they designate purely audible features of music would become attractive if it could be shown that the purely audible features in question were such that it was understandable why there should be such a strong and widespread inclination, on the part of composers and listeners alike, to characterise music by using words drawn from the language of the emotions. For if this were true, there would be less reason to accept at face value our natural estimate of the significance of the emotional qualities of music – that the value of the Masonic Funeral Music, for instance, is a function of the emotional quality it possesses ineliminably.

In the following chapter I examine the best-known, but least understood, attempt to provide an account of the purely audible features emotion terms are supposed to designate when they are applied to music in a properly musical manner, which would explain the exceptional suitability of these words as names of these features.

III
MOTION AND EMOTION
IN MUSIC

1   In *The Meaning of Music* Carroll C. Pratt posed in the following way the problem of the apparent ascription of emotional qualities to music.[1] Let us say that what a person experiences as outside his body is for that person objective and that what he experiences as belonging to or inside his body is for him subjective. By this criterion moods and emotions are subjective for the person who feels them: what someone feels when he feels worry, anxiety, uneasiness, fear and joy belongs to or lies within his body. An emotion is subjective in the sense that what is felt is located within, rather than outside, the subject's body. When a person experiences an emotion he feels the contraction of his brow, the tension of his muscles, the pounding of his blood, or some other happenings in or to his body. But moods and emotions are sometimes spoken of as though it were thought that they could be properties of phenomena that are for each person objective – in particular, as though they could be properties of music. Yet it cannot be literally true that music embodies emotion, for it is not a living body which feels its own bodily processes. How, then, are we to understand the characterisation of music as agitated, calm, wistful, seductive, restless, pompous, passionate, sombre, triumphant or yearning?

The main theory that Pratt was concerned to present an alternative to was the theory that these are merely moods or feelings which the listener has erroneously transferred from himself to the music because he has become a victim of the pathetic fallacy. Ruskin believed that our emotions can induce a falsity in our experience of the external world.[2] Physical objects can assume false appearances under the influence of violent emotion, so that we impute characteristics to such objects that really they lack. We attribute to inanimate objects characteristics that are specific to living things and we credit to other kinds of living things qualities that only human beings possess. Although we know that non-human creatures lack specifically human characteristics and that inanimate objects are not forms of life, the emotions have the power to make it appear to us otherwise: these objects can then seem to be qualified by properties that they are incapable of possessing. The excited state of our feelings makes us for the time irrational. With our reason temporarily unhinged, we imagine the objects we perceive to have characteristics which we know they cannot have. Ruskin gave the name 'the pathetic fallacy' to this falseness in our impressions of external things induced by strong emotion.

If someone who listens to music is so powerfully affected by the music that he comes to think of it as animate and to perceive it as something which is in an emotional state then this falseness in his consciousness is an instance of the pathetic fallacy: the strength of the feelings has led him to project the emotion that he feels into the music. However, if the fact is that music arouses emotions in the listener it is hard to see how he could be genuinely under the impression that the subject of the emotions he feels is the music and not himself. An illusion which involves the mislocation of an emotion's subject in an inanimate thing is not something that recommends itself on independent grounds. Furthermore, if the description of music in emotive terms is the commission of the pathetic fallacy then such description is always unwarranted: a character has been wrongly transferred from the listener to the music. But the description of music as joyful, sad or triumphant is not always inappropriate.

Perhaps, then, the emotive description of music is merely a fanciful manner of speaking in which the emotion apparently attributed to the music should be understood as felt by the listener, so that what the listener means by what he says may be true even though he expresses himself in a misleading manner. But this suggestion is little better than the previous one: for although it does not require the listener to experience violent emotion which unhinges his reason, it does require him to feel the emotion that seemingly he attributes to the music. And yet it is unnecessary for someone to feel triumph, sadness or joy if he is properly to characterise music by the names for these emotions.

How, then, is the ostensible attribution of moods and emotions to music to be understood?

2   Pratt's solution to this problem is in outline as follows. There are movements both of and in the body: our body can move about and it is itself a locus of movements. Some of these movements we feel by kin-aesthesis and organic sensation. The fact that we can feel bodily move-ment kinaesthetically and organically is what is chiefly responsible for the many words which, when used to describe how we feel, signify the dynamic character of movement. The words 'forceful', 'weak', 'languid', 'agitated', 'restless', 'calm', 'excited', 'quiet', 'indecisive', 'graceful', 'awkward', 'clumsy', 'tripping', 'rhythmic' and 'fluent', for example, can appropriately be used to characterise how we feel.[3] But these words apply equally to qualities of the bodily movements we experience. Therefore, if there is another species of movement that possesses these same characteristics of felt bodily movement these words can be applied equally accurately to this other species of movement. In consequence there will be no pathetic fallacy involved in such a use of the words. And in fact musical movement possesses characteristics of the required kind. Hence, such a sentence as 'The music is anguished' is, when true, literally true.

3   However, the notion of musical movement is problematic. For although we use the language of movement in talking about music it is shorn of an essential implication. If I throw a ball into the air, as it gets higher it moves from one position to another. But if a note is succeeded by a higher note there is nothing that in fact moves from one position through an intervening gap to a higher position.[4] Furthermore, nothing even seems to move from one position to another: my perception of a higher note following a lower note is not *as of* movement in the sense that the perception of a wave moving across the sea is the perception as of something moving across the sea, or in the sense in which the experi-ence of the motion picture is the experience as of motion.

4   Before proceeding further with the topic of movement in music there is a prior matter that needs attention. For movement requires not only something that moves but also positions between which movement takes place. Does the temporal art of music have a spatial or quasi-spatial aspect of the required kind? The obvious candidate for the role of position in 'musical space' is pitch level. There must be a good reason why the standard way of referring to differences in the pitch of tones is by means of words which refer to relative position in space; and if this reason is made explicit it may allow us properly to regard pitch levels on the model of spatial positions.

A common view is that when the terms 'high' and 'low' are applied to tones they are used metaphorically and spatial metaphors are used to describe differences of pitch because by certain associations differences of pitch remind people of differences of height. Pratt, on the contrary, maintains that prior to any association each tone has 'an intrinsic spatial characteristic'. Of course, his claim is not that it is literally true of two sounds of different pitch that one is higher than the other in the sense that it comes from a higher position in space. His view is more nearly that it is literally true that one of the tones seems to come — it is heard as if it were coming — from a higher position in space: it is *phenomenologically* higher in space. But it is clearly not unrestrictedly true that 'high tones are phenomenologically higher in space than low ones'. For a low note can be heard as coming from above us while at the same time a high note is heard as coming from below us. When a higher note does in fact come from a lower position in space than a lower note it can seem to be coming from below the lower note. The view licensed by the experiments Pratt bases his claim upon is that if two sounds in fact come from the same position the sound that is heard as higher in pitch is heard to come from a higher position in space. A high tone seems to come from a higher position than a low tone when the tones are emitted from the same point in space. Pratt's claim is that it is this fact that explains (and perhaps is signalled by) our calling one tone higher than another when it has the greater frequency.

Now whilst it is true that a musical instrument usually emits both high and low notes from the same place, so that in listening to a musical instrument the condition under which (according to Pratt) high notes are heard as coming from a higher position is characteristically satisfied, it is not in fact integral to the experience of different notes that they should be heard as if they were coming from different heights. It is not necessary to suffer the *illusion* that low notes are coming from a lower position than high notes in order to hear notes as higher or lower. The perception of forms in music also does not require that different notes should seem as if they were coming from different heights. For example, if the lower notes that compose a melody are both actually and manifestly produced at a higher position than higher notes — the phenomenological position in space of lower notes is their real position and this position is higher than that of higher notes — nevertheless we can hear the notes as composing that melody.

Pratt's thesis that high notes sound as if they come from a higher spatial position than low notes is not important in describing the experience of music. Furthermore, it fails to explain how difference of pitch is itself experienced. Pratt claims that *in addition* to hearing a difference in pitch between different notes we hear high notes as if they were coming from a higher position in space than lower notes and, in virtue of this fact, we describe difference in pitch with spatial terms.[5] This leaves uncharacterised the experience of hearing difference in pitch itself. But the nature of this experience is something that can and should be described. For an understanding of the physical basis of difference in pitch no more provides an account of the experience of pitch than an understanding of the physical basis of difference of timbre provides an account of the experience of timbre. Just as timbre is not heard as a multiplicity of tones – although difference in timbre is a function of the number and relative intensities of overtones – so pitch is not heard as rate of vibration or frequency of pendular motion.

A better view, which involves a characterisation of the experience of pitch itself, was put forward by Edmund Gurney:

> among the simple impressions of sense, differences of pitch present the absolutely unique peculiarity, that they are neither differences of *kind*, as between red and blue colours, or between bitter and sweet tastes, or between a violin-note and a clarionet-note; nor differences of *strength* or *degree of intensity*, as between bright and moderate light, or between very sweet and slightly sweet tastes, or between a loud note and a soft note; but they are differences of *distance and direction*, clearly and indisputably felt as such . . .[6]

Gurney attempts to bring out this peculiarity of pitch by contrasting our experience of the scale of pitch with our experience of the colour spectrum:

> When a spectrum is thrown on a screen, the distances from each other of the various colours give no feeling of cogency or necessity. Presented as they are, the space-distance of any tint from any other could of course be mechanically measured for any particular adjustment of the screen and the prism: but such measurements would have no general or essential validity; by imagining the spectrum indefinitely lengthened or contracted at any point we can vary indefinitely the relative distances of the colours, so that distance in space is clearly quite irrelevant to their differences. The *order* of the spectrum, moreover, is, as far as our sensations go, perfectly accidental and arbitrary; we can construct or imagine other orders, presenting

41

just as much, or rather just as little cogency, and whose gradation would look just as natural; for instance, we might make blue shade into red *via* purple. Again, if a bright spot of yellow (the middle colour of the spectrum) be thrown on a screen, and, by the gradual intervention of coloured glasses between it and the source of light, the colour be gradually changed to *red*, and a similar process be repeated so as to change the spot from yellow to *green*, we have absolutely no sense of having passed in *opposite directions* in the two cases; nor have we any sense of *going further* in looking from the leaves to the flower of a scarlet geranium than in looking from the leaves to the flower of a buttercup: whereas if we hear first a middle note on a piano followed by a bass note, and then a middle note followed by a treble note, the impression of opposite directions is irresistible; as is the impression of going further in the passage from a bass note to a treble note, as compared with the passage from a bass note to a middle note.[7]

It is clear, as Gurney here demonstrates, that difference in pitch is not experienced as difference merely in kind or quality, as between different hues.[8] But neither is it experienced as difference in strength or degree of intensity. For when a phenomenon exhibits degrees of intensity of a quality in the manner of sweetness, the difference between the instances of the phenomenon is experienced as more or less of that quality. An ordering of instances along a 'dimension' is effected by the degree of the quality that the instances are experienced to possess. The ordering just is the relative values of the degree of the quality. But sounds of different pitch are not heard as having different degrees of some quality, in accordance with which they can be ordered along a scale. As far as is true of our experience, there is no less and no more of the phenomenon in a note of low pitch than there is in a note of higher pitch. This is clear also from the fact that when there is an intensive 'continuum' in the manner of sweetness there is the possibility that the degree of intensity of the quality should be zero. Tastes can be more or less sweet or they can be lacking in sweetness altogether. But as we proceed in either direction along the scale of pitch, although we come to positions where we cannot proceed further − we cannot hear notes of higher and higher pitch or notes of lower and lower pitch − the limits of our hearing of pitch are not points at which the degree of intensity of a phenomenon (pitch) is experienced as having become zero. Neither as we ascend nor as we descend the scale does the phenomenon of pitch approach a point at which there is no longer any amount of it left.

The sense in which differences of pitch are differences of 'distance and direction' is therefore that sounds of different pitch are experienced as ordered along a scale and the ordering is not determined by a quality's being experienced to different degrees: the sounds are experienced as ordered without the order being produced by the varying strength of some feature heard in the sounds. And it is in this sense that pitch levels can be said to provide 'positions' in musical 'space': they are the musical analogues for musical 'space' of points in real space. But it must be remembered that this is nothing more than an analogy, the limited basis of which I have attempted to make clear.[9]

5   We can now return to Pratt's treatment of the idea of movement in music. We have seen that differences in pitch are experienced as differences of 'distance and direction'; and the two directions that the scale of pitch presents are usually characterised as 'up' and 'down'.[10] But when one note is followed by another note do we always experience the succession merely as a tone at one position of the scale followed by a tone at a higher or lower position? Isn't it sometimes the case that we hear movement within the 'dimension' that pitch provides, so that a later note is heard as the end of an upward or downward movement? Pratt, like many others, took seriously the fact that terminology denoting movement is used to describe music. Moreover, his account of the correct understanding of the description of music by means of terms that stand for emotions and moods requires a notion of musical movement that does not diverge radically from the notion of movement in space. Yet the idea of movement that can be heard in music is problematic, as we have seen, because not only is there nothing that moves from the position of one note to the position of a succeeding note but there is not even the appearance or illusion of something that moves between the positions.

Pratt hoped to resolve the problem by indicating a parallel between, on the one hand, some of the processes we hear in music and, on the other hand, our perception of movement by sight and kinaesthesis. Physical movement is change of spatial location. If we consider a simple case of translational movement then we perceive movement by sight by virtue of the fact that our visual field successively contains similar visual qualities at different positions. When a musical instrument follows one note with a note of a different pitch we hear, one after the other, similar sounds at different pitch levels. Now if we accept Pratt's thesis about the experience of pitch then our hearing of pitch involves, phenomenologically, the experience of a spatial dimension.[11] Therefore, when a musical instrument plays successively notes of different pitch our auditory field contains successively similar auditory qualities at different positions. This parallel between the experience of a series of notes of different pitch and the perception of movement by sight is sufficient, Pratt claims, to ground the attribution to music of characteristics of movement. Music can contain processes which possess properties that are similar to those that other kinds of movement, or movement properly so-called, can possess. In particular, musical 'movement' is capable of embodying counterparts of the forms and patterns of bodily movement. Musical movement − which is objective − possesses properties very similar to those of bodily movement − which is subjective (for the person whose body it is). The close likeness between the features of the two kinds of movement licenses the univocal application to them of words that stand for these characteristics.

But it is clear that Pratt's attempted resolution of the problem of movement heard in music fails. In the first place, it is wrong to represent the experience of forms of movement in music as a perceptual illusion;[12] and yet this is all that the likening of the experience of musical sounds to the visual and kinaesthetic perception of movement could result in. In any case, the experience of a series of notes of different pitch does not involve the experience of a siren-like continuous alteration in the pitch of a sound, whereas when an object moves across our field of view our experience involves a continuous change in the position of the appearance of the object.[13] Secondly, it is not always true that we hear a succession of notes of different pitch (but of similar timbre) as an upwards and downward movement. But Pratt's explanation of the phenomenon of musical movement implies that we should hear each such succession as a movement. Thirdly, Pratt's explanation cannot account for the possibility of counterpoint: we can hear two melodies proceeding together even when the melodies are produced by instruments with the same or similar timbre. But the manifest discontinuity of the change in pitch of successive notes disallows the modelling of the experience of counterpoint on the visual perception of two concurrent movements.

Perhaps the comparison between the experience of music and the perception of movement was not intended to imply that the experience of music involves the illusion of movement but only that it resembles perception of movement in the respect that it involves the change of the position of sensory quality. Even so, the last two objections would apply with equal force: the experience of movement in music would not be accounted for. A resemblance between the experience of a series of notes of different pitch and the perception of movement is too general a phenomenon to explain the particular ways in which ideas of movement occur in the description of music.

It is clear that when the concept of movement is applied to music music is not brought under the concept in the same manner in which an object that is thought of as moving is subsumed under the concept. The experience of movement in music is not a form of perceptual illusion (nor some close relative of illusion which likewise involves the thought that what is perceived is moving). How, then, should the description of music by means of words that signify movement be understood? There are two obvious possibilities. The first declines to take the talk of movement seriously and maintains that when we speak of an ascending phrase all we mean is that later notes of the phrase increase in pitch. The second construes as metaphorical the description of music in terms that stand for forms of movement. Clearly, it is only the second interpretation that assigns to the concept of movement a significant role in the experience and description of music. But the role it assigns is obscure. For the function of metaphor is manifold and unless the underlying point of a metaphor is understood its characterisation as a metaphor is unrevealing. Furthermore, to characterise as metaphorical the description of music in terms that stand for movement is not to describe the experience of hearing movement in music. For the experience of hearing movement in music is the experience that is expressed by the description of music in terms which signify movement; and since the characterisation of the description as metaphorical fails to illuminate the description it likewise fails to illuminate the experience.

6   The close parallel Pratt purported to find between so-called 'movement' in music and real movement does not exist. But it is unclear how damaging this is to his suggestion as to how the apparent attribution to music of subjective characteristics should be understood. For although the suggestion seeks to exploit the supposed parallel it is uncertain that it requires that music is, or is experienced as, a form of movement: it may require no more than that music can possess various features of forms of movement. It is therefore necessary to consider in more detail the account Pratt presents of the use of emotion terms to describe music.

Motion and emotion in music

The account is based upon the proposition that emotions and moods are subjective experiences: when we experience an emotion or are subject to a mood what we feel (organically or kinaesthetically) are processes which involve movements of or within our body. Now if a movement, or an inclination to movement, is involved in a certain psychological state there will be a character, C, of the movement which we feel when we are in that state. And it might be that we are said to feel C when we are in that psychological state precisely because this is just what we feel when we are in that state. But this character might be shared by a piece of music − in which case the music could properly be characterised as C. And the characterisation of the music as C would not be figurative but literal. It would not depend for its force upon the primary application of the term 'C' to a psychological state. Rather, the psychological state would derive its name from a quality of movement which is common to bodily and musical movement. We would both be and feel C; the music would not feel C, but merely be C. It is precisely this kind of possibility that Pratt proposes as the correct understanding of the use of emotion terms to describe music.

Pratt presents a number of psychological states which are supposed to be illustrative of his account. One is the state of agitation. When someone is in an agitated state he is liable to behave agitatedly; and if he does behave agitatedly he feels the agitated movements that his body makes. But the agitated character of these movements can be shared by many other kinds of phenomena, and in particular by music. And if a piece of music has this agitated character then its description as agitated is literally true. Another state is restlessness. If someone feels restless he does not feel at rest. He feels such things as an inability to keep still and an increased rate of breathing and heartbeat. Much the same kinds or aspects of movement can be found in music:

> Staccato passages, trills, strong accents, quavers, rapid accelerandos and crescendos, shakes, wide jumps in pitch − all such devices conduce to the creation of an auditory structure which is appropriately described as restless.[14]

A third illustration is provided by the state of vacillation. Pratt maintains that the reason musical phrases can contain movements which possess the character of indecision and vacillation is that they can have the same character as a bodily movement which is part of a subjective state that is appropriately described as indecisive and vacillating.[15] Finally, Pratt claims that most of the words 'playful', 'whimsical', 'triumphant', 'powerful', 'martial', 'majestic', 'calm', 'peaceful', 'hurry-ing', 'struggling', 'bewildering', 'tumultuous', 'uncertain' and 'suspense' can be used for emotions and moods; and when they are so used they

> stand for psychological experiences which include among their com-
> ponents various forms of movement. In so far as similar forms of
> movement may be presented tonally, the same words apply equally
> well to musical effects.[16]

In short: music can be agitated, restless, triumphant or calm since it can possess the character of the bodily movements which are involved in the moods and emotions that are given these names precisely because it is this character of the bodily movements which is felt when the mood or emotion is experienced.

7   Emotion, therefore, is not really experienced as embodied in music. Its apparent embodiment is explained by two facts: that musical move-ments have properties very similar to characteristics of felt bodily move-ments, and that emotions are described by terms for these characteristics because they include movements with these characteristics and it is these movements which are felt when the emotions are experienced. There are characteristics of musical movement that bear a close resemblance to certain features of bodily movement. These characteristics are frequently described by words which also stand for moods and emotions. But these characteristics 'merely *sound* the way moods *feel*'.[17] Words that signify moods and emotions can be used to describe the auditory structures of music because the form of experiences of one sense modality can duplicate the form of experiences of another sense modality. Objective phenomenal structures can exhibit a striking re-semblance to the forms of subjective bodily reverberations and in consequence be thought of, erroneously, as the embodiments of emotions and moods. But they do not embody emotions and moods. Rather, 'they merely sound and look the way emotions feel.'[18] Music embodies not psychological conditions but the characters of the bodily move-ments (the feelings of) which are included in or compose psychological conditions.

8   It is important to realise that Pratt's account is an account only of the correct interpretation of a particular form of speech: the description of what is objective (music) in terms of what is subjective (mood and emotion). The account does not specify a relation between the objective

and the subjective that is supposed to be important from the point of view of music as art. The fact that a piece of music possesses a feature in common with an emotional state is not assigned an importance different from the fact that the music possesses this feature. The common possession of the property is significant only in grounding one type of description of music. The suggestion is not that it is integral to the musical value of some works of music – that it is of importance from the point of view of the value of music as music – that music should be experienced as having properties in common with the bodily processes which are felt when moods or emotions are experienced. It is necessary to appreciate the auditory structure of a musical work but not to appreciate its resemblance to a pattern of bodily movement.[19]

9   It is clear that whether or not this account ever correctly represents how the description of music in emotion terms should be understood it could work only for a psychological condition which is such that
(i) there is a way that a person feels when he is in the condition,
(ii) this way is so characterised because there are bodily movements (the feelings of which are) 'included' in the psychological condition, the subject feels these bodily movements when he experiences the condition and they have a property which gives its name to the condition,
(iii) music can share with these bodily movements the property that gives its name to the psychological condition.
For the account is essentially that there are features of movement that can be perceived in two different ways: by organic and kinaesthetic feeling in the perception of bodily movement and by hearing in the perception of musical movement.

Now there are psychological conditions that more or less, or with some show of plausibility, fit the schema, and it is unsurprising that Pratt's account appears to be based upon these. Restlessness and agitation are perhaps the two examples that provide the greatest support for his account. Something is in a restless state if it is ceaselessly moving about. Someone who is restless finds it difficult to be still and he will move restlessly. He can perceive the ceaseless movement of his body by bodily feeling, in which case he feels, or he is aware of feeling, restless. And music can be in a state of ceaseless change. Again, something is in an agitated state if it is moving to and fro or shaking. Someone who is agitated will behave in an agitated fashion unless he represses his inclination; and he can feel the agitated movements that his body makes. And music can be in a state similar to agitation. But there do not appear

48

to be many psychological conditions that satisfy the schema. Further-more, many of the subjective states that music is said to express or whose names are used to describe music do not satisfy the schema.

The movement of an object can be characterised with respect to the number of movements that it is making, the parts of the object that are in motion, the manner, extent, speed and force of each movement and the resistance with which each movement is met. It is only psychological conditions that can be defined by a set of such features that can fit the schema. But there is no set of such features that defines the emotion of sadness, for example, in the sense that it specifies what a person feels when he feels sad and it is in virtue of this that his feeling is characterised as sadness. For sadness is a form of unhappiness, and when someone feels unhappy there is no set of features of bodily movement which gives its name to that feeling. Moreover, sadness is a specific kind of unhappiness: it is unhappiness at loss, suffering or disappointment. And the bodily movements that are indicative of unhappiness are not in themselves sufficient to determine what kind of thing the unhappiness they are signs of is about: there are no bodily movements that are specific to sadness amongst the various forms of unhappiness. Therefore, the characterisation of music as sad cannot be understood in accordance with the model that Pratt suggests.

It would not be an adequate reply to this argument to claim that a certain kind of bodily movement is a part, but only a part, of what someone feels when he feels sad. For even if this were true it would not be sufficient to license the attribution of sadness to music in the style Pratt advocates. If a person feels more than this kind of movement when he feels sad then − in accordance with Pratt's model − we should attribute less than the full emotional condition to music that embodies this movement. Pratt maintains that certain words, when used for emotions and moods 'stand for psychological experiences which include among their components various forms of movement.' But the conclusion he draws from this does not follow: 'In so far as similar forms of move-ment may be presented tonally, the same words apply equally well to musical effects.' If we feel F in experiencing E, and C is a component of E (or is a part of what we feel when we experience E), but C is not identical with F and C does not imply F, then if we are to comply with Pratt's account we cannot properly apply 'F' to music that instantiates C. If my chest puffs out with pride this is not a sufficient basis for me to attribute pride to music that has an expansive quality. A form of bodily movement must be *all* that a person feels when he experiences a certain emotion — it must also give its name to the emotion — in order for music that instantiates the same form to be correctly characterised by the name of the emotion (according to Pratt's account).

Pratt's suggestion therefore could not provide a general solution to the problem of the apparent attribution to music of what is subjective. There are many moods and emotions that music is said to be qualified by which are such that the characterisation of music by the use of words that signify these moods or emotions cannot be understood on the model that Pratt recommends. Furthermore, Pratt exaggerates not only generally but specifically the proper scope of his model. For example, he characterises the Prelude to *Tristan und Isolde* as 'ardent, erotic, full of suspense, longing, unfulfillment', with the implication that this characterisation can be accommodated by his theory.[20] But not all these features are qualities of, or derive from characteristics of, bodily movement. When we experience a passionate erotic desire that is uncertain of fulfilment our condition does not derive its name from the kinds of bodily movement that we may feel when in that condition.

10   We are now in a position to pick up the discussion of the purely sensible description thesis at the point at which it was broken off at the end of the previous chapter. I said in effect that the purely sensible description thesis can be understood in two different ways. It can be understood either as an account of the function that emotion terms are in fact intended to serve when they are applied to music, or as an account of the function that emotion terms must be intended to serve if they are to be applied to music in a musically relevant manner. And I said that if the thesis is interpreted in the first way it is clear that it is incorrect. But it is the second interpretation that it is important to evaluate. And I said that although the thesis interpreted in this fashion appeared to be false — for the musical value of some works appears to be a function of the emotional qualities they possess ineliminably — it would appear in a better light if the nature of the purely audible features that the thesis allows emotion terms to ascribe to music were to be made clear and their nature should be such that there is a specially good reason why emotion terms should be thought of as pre-eminently suitable words for them. Now if it were true, as Pratt's theory maintains, that emotion terms designate forms of movement which can be realised both in the body and in music (as well as in objects of other sense modalities), then two conclusions would follow. Firstly, there would be a special suitability in the use of emotion terms to describe music, as long as emotion terms were used to stand for forms of movement in music. But, secondly, if emotion terms were applied to music in the manner for which Pratt's account renders them specially suitable, their application to music would not relate music specifically to the emotions. And this would provide some support for the second interpretation of the purely sensible description thesis. However, we have seen that the account offered by Pratt's theory of the link between the features emotion terms are supposed to ascribe to music and the natures of the experiences of the emotions they name is a failure. Hence, the second interpretation of the purely sensible description thesis receives no support from Pratt's theory.

Now there may be other ways in which it might be thought that the alleged special suitability of emotion terms to stand for various purely audible features of music could be explained. But I believe there is little point in pursuing any further suggestions. For no explanation of the exceptional appropriateness of emotion terms to name purely audible features of music would be sufficient to establish the purely sensible description thesis – the most it could do would be to place the thesis in a more favourable light. To establish the purely sensible description thesis it would be necessary to prove that any use of emotion terms other than the one favoured by the thesis is irrelevant to considerations of musical value. But from the point of view of the listener musical value consists in the degree to which and the manner in which the listener finds the experience of music intrinsically rewarding. Hence, a proof of the purely sensible description thesis would need to show that when a listener experiences music as having an emotional quality and he also finds the music intrinsically rewarding, the fact that the music is related specifically to a certain emotion can never form part of the listener's reason for valuing the music as music. And, conversely, it would need to show that when a listener experiences music as having an emotional quality and he finds the music repulsive, his reason for disliking the music can never include the fact that the music possesses the emotional quality (ineliminably). I believe it is clear that there can be no such proof. But this implies nothing about the scope and the importance of the emotional qualities of music.

IV
SEXUAL EMOTION IN
IDEAL MOTION

1   It is clear that in general a musical work is not related to the audible
appearance of the world as a representational painting or a work of one of
the other representational arts is related to the visual appearance of the
world; neither does it express propositions as the arts based upon the use
of language do. But although music is characteristically not designed to
give rise to thoughts about something other than its medium and which
are essential to its appreciation in the manner either of the representational or of the literary arts, many people have thought that music can be a
humanistic art. Adherents of a humanist theory of music believe that
works which consist solely of music can resemble the typical products of
the arts of literature and representation in engaging and providing
sustenance for some of the most important human values and sympathies.
Although 'absolute' music is essentially a form of abstract, and not
representational, art and it lacks the resources of a true language, the
humanist maintains that its non-representational and non-propositional
nature does not prevent many of its products from having a significance
that can be explained only by their relation to what we are familiar with
outside music. In these works there are embodied, reflected, expressed,
symbolised or in some other way presented phenomena that are integral
to human life: we recognise moods, feelings, emotions, attitudes and
various other states and activities of our inner life manifested in such a
way that, if we are sensitive to their presence and responsive to the
manner in which music makes them present to us, we value these musical
works because of their essential human reference.

The most impressive representative of the opposed formalist theory
that the abstract art of music is devoid of any human meaning and is

merely the source of a distinctive kind of deep and harmless pleasure was Edmund Gurney; and the severest challenge to a humanist theory of music is presented by his massive and remarkable work *The Power of Sound.*[1] In this work Gurney attempted to show that we need bring to music no special qualities of character or intellect, and no extra-musical interests or values, but only an isolated sense of abstract proportion; for music presents forms that have no important connection with anything outside music, and the rewards of music are entirely self-contained. Our love of music is essentially unrelated to anything else that we value: music speaks of nothing that independently matters to us.

Gurney's book contains a wealth of insights and is certainly the most thorough and wide-ranging work of distinction written on the philosophy of music. In this chapter I attempt to extract and examine the principal theses which Gurney put forward about the nature and value of music and which, if true, would establish the formalist position.

2   For Gurney the cardinal units of music were melodic forms: short series of musical sounds of different pitch that are heard as unities. And it is from a consideration of melodic forms that an investigation of music should begin. For our response to music on a larger scale is founded upon our response to these relatively compact melodic forms, and melodic forms themselves present the central fact and problem of music.

Someone who has the ability to perceive melodic forms will characteristically find it rewarding to listen to some, but not all melodic forms; and of those that he finds rewarding he will regard some as finer pieces of music than others. Gurney believed that there is a pleasurable emotion of a distinctive kind which is experienced when and only when a melodic form is found musically impressive or rewarding to listen to as music: when and only when a melodic form is experienced as 'beautiful'. The central fact to which Gurney believed the aesthetics of music should address itself was precisely that for any individual only some melodic forms will impress him favourably, will be experienced as beautiful, will yield the distinctive pleasurable emotion. And the principal problem that music presents concerns the explanation of melodic beauty: Why is it that for any individual, at any given stage of his life, it is only in listening to certain melodic forms that he feels the characteristic pleasurable emotion that is correlative with the experience of finding a melodic form beautiful? What is it about the melodic forms that yield him this pleasure that differentiates them from those that do not?

A complete answer to this problem would consist of two parts. It would for each individual specify a criterion that would distinguish the melodic forms that he finds impressive from those that he does not; and it would offer an explanation of the fact that he experiences the distinctive pleasurable emotion in response to any melodic form that satisfies the criterion but not in response to any melodic form which does not.

Gurney's claim is that no satisfactory criterion for separating the melodic forms that impress a person from those that do not can be produced. For:

(i) In no individual's case are there purely musical criteria (for example, principles concerning the structure of the notes that constitute melodic forms) that determine whether for him a melodic form is or is not beautiful.

(ii) In no individual's case is there an extra-musical phenomenon and a relationship between it and particular melodic forms such that the relation in which a melodic form stands to this phenomenon determines whether it is for that individual beautiful.

There are no rules or laws of a purely musical nature – not even inductive generalisations that capture all and only pleasure-giving melodic forms – in accordance with which all beautiful and no non-beautiful melodic forms are constructed (and so, *a fortiori*, no real explanation of why it is *these* melodic forms that impress this individual). And no person finds a melodic form beautiful if and only if, for example, it closely resembles (and so suggests) (a) physical movements of certain kinds, (b) the cadences of emotional speech: two melodic forms can resemble equally any bodily movement, or other kind of physical movement, or the pattern of the voice under the stress of emotion, and yet differ completely in that one is highly pleasurable and the other is not pleasurable at all. Furthermore, any attempt to combine the criteria mentioned in (i) and (ii), so as to specify a criterion which requires both a certain kind of musical structure and a specific relation to a particular extra-musical phenomenon, or which requires either the one or the other, will founder on the fact that two melodic forms can equally satisfy the suggested criterion and yet differ in the crucial respect: the one is experienced as beautiful and the other is not.

For any person melodic beauty is therefore both specifically musical and anomalous.

3   This thesis does not fully capture Gurney's radical theory of musical impressiveness. We must add to it a contrast between vision and hearing

and the arts correlative to these senses. Unlike the visual arts, where a body of visual habit and instinct engendered by our visual experience of the world informs our response even to abstract visual patterns, our response to melodic forms is unconstrained by our auditory experience of the world. In contrast to the phenomena that engage the eye, those that meet the ear are in general formless and bear no relation to the definite proportions of melodic forms: melodic forms are artificial exceptions to the various unshaped successions of sounds which our ears naturally receive. Our reaction even to the most abstract visual forms is everywhere influenced by their likeness to the forms of phenomena in the natural world: we do not respond to them *in complete abstraction* from reference to the natural world. But our reaction to melodic form is undetermined by any resemblance to similar forms in the natural world: we respond to them in complete abstraction from reference to the natural world. In consequence, whereas we cannot speak of an *independent* faculty by which the beauty of visual forms is judged, the musical faculty – the ability to perceive and to derive pleasure from melodic forms – is independent, and it is unique. Its independence resides in the fact that the characteristic melodic pleasure is experienced independently of any relation in which particular melodic forms stand to anything outside the musical faculty; its objects are isolated from the facts and interests of life; and its possession is compatible with the presence or the absence of any particular qualities of character or intellect. Its uniqueness lies primarily not in the fact that the ear is the sole means by which melodic forms can be perceived but in the distinctive nature of a melodic form, or the process which constitutes the perception of a melodic form, the process by which a melodic form is realised in its evolution moment by moment: the process to which Gurney gave the name 'Ideal Motion'. The musical faculty is an independent and unique sense of abstract proportion which judges each melodic form on its own merits and does not proceed in accordance with any laws.

4   It is clear that Gurney does not produce a demonstrative proof that for each person melodic beauty is unlawgoverned. He advances no considerations that show *a priori* that, in any individual's case, there cannot be laws to the effect that the individual is impressed by a melodic form if and only if the melodic form is of a particular kind. And to establish the thesis otherwise it would be necessary both to examine a sufficient number of individuals to ground the generalisation, and to provide

convincing reasons for concluding from the failure in each person's case to find a law that there are no such laws to be found. It is true that a law that governs an individual's sense of melodic beauty would need to apply not merely to the finite number of melodic forms with which he is familiar but also to the indefinitely many melodic forms that he would find impressive, or that he would not find impressive, if at any point in his life he were to hear them. But this is no reason to doubt the existence of any such laws.

5   Gurney believed that an impressive melodic form, or impressive music in general, is impressive in virtue of its being 'productive of a sort of emotion which . . . is unknown outside the region of musical phenomena':[2]

> The prime characteristic of Music, the *alpha* and *omega* of its essential effect [is] its perpetual production in us of an emotional excitement of a very intense kind, which yet cannot be defined under any known head of emotion.[3]

Therefore, not only is melodic beauty for each person both specifically musical and anomalous; the emotion experienced in the appreciation of melodic beauty is itself specific to music. This supposed 'fused and indescribable' emotion Gurney explained by reference to a theory of Darwin's that connects music and sexual excitement.[4]

6   In *The Descent of Man*[5] Darwin advanced the view that the vocal organs of animals were primarily used and developed in relation to the propagation of the species: to call, charm, allure and excite the opposite sex. Moreover, the sounds that some species produce during the mating season are 'musical': they have a definite pitch and compose short melodic phrases or songs. Furthermore, those species which make musical sounds in a certain order and rhythm clearly derive pleasure from these sounds, for they charm and excite.

If we now turn to the musical experience of human beings we find, so Darwin thought, a set of facts that requires explanation. In the first place, the ability to produce vocally and to enjoy musical sounds is of no use in the daily habits of life; the ability is present to some degree of development in all races of mankind; and although it is uncertain whether the half-human progenitors of man possessed the ability, it was certainly possessed by man at a very remote period. Secondly, the emotions that music arouses are the gentler feelings of tenderness and love, and the sense of triumph and ardour for war, but not the more terrible ones of horror, fear and rage; and these powerful and sometimes mingled feelings can give rise to the sense of sublimity. Thirdly, there is an instinctive recourse to musical cadences and rhythm when strong emotions are expressed in impassioned speech. Finally, the feelings excited in us by music or the cadences of impassioned speech appear, Darwin writes, 'from their vagueness, yet depth, like mental reversions to the emotions and thoughts of a long-past age'.

Darwin proposed to explain these facts on the assumption that the power of making musical sounds was used in the pre-human stage of development for sexual purposes:

> Musical tones and rhythm were used by our half-human ancestors, during the season of courtship, when animals of all kinds are excited not only by love, but by the strong passions of jealousy, rivalry and triumph. From the deeply-laid principle of inherited associations, musical tones in this case would be likely to call up vaguely and indefinitely the strong emotions of a long-past age. As we have every reason to suppose that articulate speech is one of the latest, as it certainly is the highest, of the arts acquired by man, and as the instinctive power of producing musical notes and rhythms is developed low down in the animal series, it would be altogether opposed to the principle of evolution, if we were to admit that man's musical capacity has been developed from the tones used in impassioned speech. We must suppose that the rhythms and cadences of oratory are derived from previously developed musical powers. We can thus understand how it is that music, dancing, song, and poetry are such very ancient arts. . . . The impassioned orator, bard, or musician, when with his varied tones and cadences he excites the strongest emotions in his hearers, little suspects that he uses the same means by which his half-human ancestors long ago aroused each other's ardent passions, during their courtship and rivalry.[6]

7 Gurney wished to make use of Darwin's theory to explain the characteristic pleasurable emotion, the distinctive but indefinable emotional excitement, of impressive music. The experience of music is suffused with highly exciting emotional elements because of music's resemblance to the inarticulate use of the voice in sexual excitement by our distant ancestors. The emotion specific to music is a distillate from, it is the sublimated quintessence of, primitive sexual passions, and it has

descended to us by inherited associations through the ages. The root of the impressiveness of music lies in the fusion and the sublimation of the strongest elementary emotions which, according to Darwin, were associated with the primeval activity of following musical sounds and rhythms with pleasure. The 'peculiar delight which is at once perfectly distinct and perfectly indescribable'[7] has been derived by principles of hereditary association from what were the deepest emotions experienced by our progenitors. The singular character of musical emotion – the fact that 'Music is perpetually felt as strongly emotional while defying all attempts to analyse the experience or to define it even in the most general way in terms of definite emotions'[8] – can be explained by tracing it to its origin in the gradual fusion and transfiguration of primitive sexual feelings.

A number of points about Gurney's proposed application of Darwin's theory must be noticed:

(i) It is intended specifically to explain the peculiar impressiveness of *melodic forms* and not various other characteristics or effects of music – effects that are due, for example, to massiveness of sound or complexity of structure.

(ii) It cannot explain, and it is not intended to explain, why any individual finds those particular melodic forms impressive that in fact he does. It offers no explanation of why contact with the emotional spring suggested by Darwin is made in the case of certain melodic forms but is broken in the case of all others. What it attempts to explain is the power and depth of the emotion with which a melodic form can be experienced when it is found impressive.

(iii) The explanation Gurney proposes is therefore not that some melodic forms more closely resemble certain primeval series of sounds than do others. It is not the possession of common melodic forms that unites us with our semi-human progenitors. The common element is the sense or process – Ideal Motion – by which melodic forms are realised. Although this sense is no longer in an embryonic state, and it can now grasp melodic forms of a complexity previously denied to it, nevertheless, its highly developed state is a later state of the same sense and thereby links us with our primitive ancestors. And it is when this sense of proportion is exercised in a manner that *satisfies* the listener that contact is made with the emotional source from which the embryonic sense was flooded when the embryonic sense was itself exercised *satisfactorily*. In consequence, our emotional response to music is charged with the strength of the passions with which musical sounds were originally experienced.

This explanation seemed to Gurney to be uniquely adequate to account for the power of the emotions that developed music excites. At the same time he recognised a difficulty; and this difficulty eventually came to appear to him sufficiently grave not only to diminish the attraction of Darwin's theory but to preclude its use. The difficulty is that Gurney's position is a conjunction of two propositions that do not fit happily together: (i) each melodic form satisfies, or fails to satisfy, the musical faculty independently of any association, or lack of association, with Darwin's emotional source — which is to say that the satisfaction a melodic form provides is yielded independently of any emotion that accrues in virtue of the opening up of the channel to that source, and yet (ii) this satisfaction is not felt in independence of the emotional flow from the associational source to which it opens a passage, and to which the satisfactoriness or impressiveness as we experience it should be mainly due.[9] The increment that the exercise of the musical faculty, when satisfactory, is supposed to receive from association is postulated in order to explain the strength of the emotion created by an impressive melodic form. However, the exercise is supposed to receive this increment *whenever* it is satisfactory. But there is no access to the strength of the emotion that supposedly would have been felt without the increment. No one can separate out, either in his own or in another's experience, the amount of satisfaction that a melodic form is suited to give on its own account and, subtracting this from all that he feels, form a conception of the residue which must in some fashion be accounted for: a conception of the amount which accrues to the experience (in accordance with Darwin's suggestion) by association with the sexual excitement with which melodic forms were once realised. There is therefore no reason to suppose that the strength of the emotion that an impressive melodic form does in fact arouse exceeds what would have been felt in some counter-factual situation, and that the discrepancy can be made good only by assuming an increment from some external source. If we agree that whether a melodic form is found satisfying is independent of its relation to the alleged origin of musical pleasure, then *this* satisfaction will not be explained by reference to this supposed source; and it is unclear that there is a problem about some further satisfaction for which Darwin's suggestion might provide a solution.

8   Gurney considered the pleasurable emotion that impressive music yields to be of an extremely valuable kind: it has the 'power of relieving the mind and steeping it as it were in a totally new atmosphere . . .

indescribable suggestions of infinity, and . . . freedom from any kind of deleterious after-effects'.[10] But music must be judged solely by reference to the amount of pleasure (the specifically musical emotional pleasure) that it affords and not by its consequences. The emotional pleasure may be of a valuable kind but the value of music as music is entirely self-contained. Music is never valuable as music because of a possible connection with anything else we might value. Music can lend itself to many sorts of ulterior purposes and it can be experienced in a variety of ways different from that of listening to it in a connected manner as a developing process: listening to it as music. But for those in whose lives music is an important element its value lies not in its reflecting any of our deeper values or in its expressing desirable qualities of emotion or character, nor in its soothing or exciting us when we desire peace or crave excitement, but in its own special appeal, isolated from the facts and interests of life: the presentation of melodic forms which arouse an indefinable pleasurable emotion.

However, it is not the nature, but only the strength, of the pleasure that a musical work yields that determines its value as a work of art. It is only the pleasurable element of the emotion music arouses that is relevant to an assessment of its merit because the character of the emotion aroused by impressive music is always the same. Hence terms of praise or dispraise must properly be used only with reference to the amount of pleasure to which a musical work gives access:

> the word *bad* may be fairly used (absolutely or relatively) of music
> − (1) which gives no pleasure, (2) which gives extremely slight and
> transitory pleasure, (3) which gives pleasure superior in these respects,
> but shown by experience to be incompatible with more deep and
> lasting pleasure given by other music.[11]

If, therefore, experience does not show that the appreciation of a particular musical work is incompatible with the appreciation of works that give, and give repeatedly, great pleasure all that can be said against the work in question is that the pleasure it gives is small or fleeting. No criticism of a person's taste in music is possible if he is not precluded from appreciating works capable of giving great pleasure; and which works can give the greatest pleasure is a matter of fact which is resistant to explanation. The positive response to music is always unanalysable and it is as little susceptible of criticism as it is capable of justification.[12]

9   Gurney's theory as to the nature of the impressiveness that music

may possess consists of two principal theses. The first maintains that there is a distinct kind of emotion that music which is experienced as impressive always yields and this emotion is experienced only in response to music (which impresses). The second advances the Darwinian derivation of this emotion from primitive sexual excitement. I have explained that Gurney recognised the problematic nature of the second thesis and finally felt compelled to abandon it. But the first thesis is equally vulnerable.

In the first place, if someone experiences emotion in finding a piece of music impressive, this emotion may not be of one specific sort. The emotional response to music as impressive is not of a unitary kind, but it is in fact variable. This point is, as we shall see, impossible to press home within the framework of Gurney's own theory, for unless one is prepared to embrace the existence of a variety of different kinds of specifically musical emotions, that is, of emotions that are not extra-musical, any emotion experienced in response to music either must be of a single kind not experienced outside music, or it must be an extra-musical emotion, in which case, according to Gurney's theory of expression, the emotion experienced is expressed by the music and does not constitute the listener's being impressed by the music. But a more adequate account of expression than the one Gurney offers will not require that any (extra-musical) emotion experienced in an aesthetic response to music is an instance of the musical expression of emotion.

Secondly, it is clear that the emotional response to music as impressive need not be a form of excitement. And yet it is precisely Gurney's claim that the specifically musical emotion is a distinct kind of emotional excitement.

Thirdly, it would be a falsification of the experience of someone who finds a musical work always distinguished to represent it as one in which a distinct kind of emotion is constantly felt, differing from point to point in the music only in degree. On the contrary, emotion comes and goes. Perhaps it would be said that music cannot be experienced as impressive unless it is listened to with pleasure, and that a part of a work from which no pleasure is derived is precisely one that is found unimpressive, or of no musical value. But even if this should be so it would not be enough to establish Gurney's thesis, for, in the wide sense in which the idea of pleasure would here need to be understood, we can derive pleasure from something that does not move us, or that does not emotionally arouse us. *A fortiori*, the existence of a specifically musical emotion would not be secured by the existence of a specifically aesthetic manner of deriving pleasure from a musical work by attending to it in a certain way.

Finally, Gurney's belief that the pleasurable emotion aroused by impressive music cannot be analysed or even in any way described in terms of other familiar emotions — in other words, the supposed indefinability of musical pleasure — appears to have arisen through a misrepresentation of the fact that we may take deep pleasure *in* music. The pleasurable emotion is specifically musical in the sense that music is its object: not in the sense that music arouses an emotion of a kind that for some reason nothing else arouses. If we take pleasure in listening to music we take pleasure in an activity that is different from any other activity. But there are not two independent phenomena, a kind of pleasure and a certain activity, each of which is different from anything else and which are so related that the one attaches to the other and never to anything else.[13] The uniqueness of the pleasure is the uniqueness of the activity in which the pleasure is found.

10   I now turn to the topic of the musical expression of emotion. Gurney wanted to show that the significance commonly attached to the expressive power of music is misplaced. He presents this account of the musical expression of qualities and feelings: for music to express quality Q (i) Q should be in a certain sense separable from the music, and (ii) the music should make us experience feeling F, where either F is identical with Q or F is the feeling identified with the contemplation of Q.[14] I shall put aside the first condition and consider only the second condition. 'A melody may be *simple*', Gurney writes, 'but as it does not make us feel *simple*, and as we have no definite mode of feeling identified with the contemplation of so general a quality, we should not naturally say that it *expressed* simplicity.'[15] Again, the reason why a pedal bass continued for a long period of time cannot properly be said to express *permanence* is that 'the perception of something going on for a considerable time neither makes us feel permanent, as, e.g., triumphant music makes us feel triumphant, nor wakens any feeling which corresponds with it in the way that, e.g. the feeling of amusement corresponds with the perception of caprice or pursuit.'[16] And he writes:

> The feeling in ourselves need not necessarily be the *same* as the quality attributed to the music: the special feeling corresponding to melancholy music is melancholy, but the special feeling corresponding to capricious or humorous music is not capriciousness or humorousness,

62

but surprise or amusement: clearly, however, this mode of feeling is sufficiently identified with the contemplation of the quality.[17]

Gurney's account of the expression by music of qualities and feelings is not intended merely to be stipulative. For it is intended to capture the idea of the attribution to music of emotional and other qualities. Music may be sombre, gay, plaintive, majestic, mournful, confident or mysterious in the sense — this is Gurney's thesis — that it arouses the feeling that corresponds with the quality attributed to the music. Attributing an emotional quality to music, saying that it is melancholy or triumphant, for example, is tantamount to saying that the music causes the emotion: it causes us to feel melancholy or triumphant.

11 Gurney's account of the musical expression of qualities and emotions is multiply ill-defined, and in consequence it is unclear how it is to be understood. It was probably intended to be taken in an intra-subjective fashion. Even so, it could be understood in a fully relativised form, so that the emotion a piece of music is said to express is relative to the emotion aroused in a particular person on a particular occasion; alternatively, the intention might be that a reference to the music's apt-ness to arouse the emotion it is said to express is to be understood. Certainly a piece of music might for adventitious reasons make someone feel melancholy, so that he himself would not regard it as expressing melancholy: as when the music's effect is mediated by a personal association. And when the feeling that music arouses is not the same as the quality that the music is said to express but is instead the feeling 'identified with the contemplation' of that quality, it is not sufficient that music should arouse the feeling. The music must be the object towards which the feeling is directed: humorous music must itself be found amusing and not merely cause someone to feel amusement (about something else). It is clear that no viable theory of expression that locates music's expressive nature in its capacity to arouse (extra-musical) emotions will allow that each case of the arousal of emotion by music is thereby an instance of music's expressing that emotion, or being qualified by that emotional quality.[18]

12 There are many considerations that count against the identification of the musical expression of an (extra-musical) emotion with the arousal of that emotion. I shall mention two considerations which are of special relevance in this context. The first is that Gurney regards as a case of expression the well-known and puzzling phenomenon that the minor triad of C played after the otherwise isolated major triad sounds, or is experienced as, melancholy.[19] But the minor triad, in this context, does not create melancholy in us, and it does not need to do so in order that it should be heard as melancholy. The possession by music of emotional qualities is not the same phenomenon as, and need not involve, the music's arousing the emotions that qualify it. A theory of expression along these lines is really no more plausible than the thesis that the sound of a horn can be heard as golden only if it makes us (feel) golden, or that a theme is feminine only if it makes us (feel) feminine.

This objection might be met with the reply that whilst indeed we do not need to be turned to gold if we are to experience a sound as golden, the phenomenon of visual-auditory synaesthesia,[20] or so-called 'colour hearing' is real; and the experience of a piece of music as being qualified by an emotion is to be assimilated to this phenomenon. But in fact it is not necessary to be subject to 'colour-hearing' in order to hear a sound as golden. The thesis that a sound or key or other musical phenomenon can be said to be of a certain colour only if it causes someone to see that colour thus truly parallels the doctrine that music can be said to be sad only if it causes someone to feel sad. Each account fails to capture its subject.

A further feature of the musical expression of emotion that Gurney himself draws attention to is hard to reconcile with the assumption he makes as to what expression consists in. He notices that 'the most mournful music, if sufficiently beautiful, may make us happy.'[21] But if we are happy in hearing the music it seems that we cannot, at the same time, be feeling mournful; in which case the theory that the expression of an emotion consists in the arousal of the emotion must be incorrect. This conclusion can be resisted only if it is possible to explain how it is that in the experience of music we can derive pleasure from the experience of what is normally a dispiriting emotion. I later consider the explanation of this problematic feature that Gurney appears to advance.

13 Gurney supplements his account of the musical expression of emotion with a theory of the means at music's disposal to express extra-musical emotions. This theory seeks to explain how it is possible for music to express emotions and so to determine the scope and limits of expression in music. He locates music's power to express emotions mainly[22] in the parallels that may exist between, on the one hand, the pace and rhythm of music, or the process by which it is followed, and, on the other hand, movements of the human body that are literally expressive of emotions. 'Musical motions express extra-musical moods and feelings through their resemblance to physical motions':[23] that is to say, to physical movements expressive of these moods and feelings. Confidence and good spirits are expressed in rapid and decisive movements, agitation by spasmodic movements, dejection by drooping and collapse; and it is in virtue of the affinities that may exist between the features of music and movements of the body in which definite emotions are expressed that music can, through association, express, that is to say, arouse, these emotions.

It might be suggested that Gurney should be understood as maintaining that a piece of music expresses emotion E if and only if (i) the music resembles the movements that are expressive of E (and so suggests E) and (ii) the music makes us feel E.[24] But this cannot be correct, for the first condition refers only to the most important feature of the *means* at music's disposal to express emotions. Gurney allows that music can express E where (i) does not hold.

One objection that must be lodged against Gurney's account is that the nature of the psychic mechanism by means of which, supposedly, the experience of abstract musical motion that resembles physical motion expressive of a particular emotion is converted into the experience of that emotion is left quite unexplained. This omission is facilitated by Gurney's habit of freely moving between the idea that music expresses an emotion if it awakens the emotion and the idea that music expresses an emotion if it suggests the emotion; for a resemblance between music and the behavioural expression of an emotion will, if noticed, suggest the emotion, but it is unlikely therefore to awaken it. Physical movements recognised to be expressive of a certain emotion may themselves arouse no emotion at all, and when they do arouse an emotion it is only when the response is empathic, rather than sympathetic, that this emotion will be of the same kind as the emotion expressed. It is hardly surprising, therefore, that an explanation of the manner in which music that resembles behaviour expressive of a particular emotion is supposed to arouse that emotion in those who listen to it should be necessary, and it is a significant defect in Gurney's account that such an explanation is unforthcoming.

14   A theory of musical value that locates a value of music in its capacity to express emotions can be more or less ambitious. The strongest thesis would be that all valuable music derives its value as music solely

from the fact that it expresses emotions. This thesis can be weakened in one or both of two ways: by replacing the claim that the value derives solely from the music's expression of emotions with the claim that it derives in part from this, and by advancing the claim not about all valuable music but about all valuable music of some independently specified, and perhaps especially important, class, or merely about some valuable music, where the class is left unspecified. Thus it might be claimed, as Deryck Cooke did,[25] that (nearly) all valuable Western harmonic music since 1400 is valuable because it is the expression of emotion. Or it might be claimed that if a work of music is the expression of emotion — as is true of some, but not all, valuable works — then this is always (alternatively, it is sometimes) an aesthetically significant feature of the musical work and contributes to the kind of value the work possesses.

Gurney advances five considerations[26] against the view that music is primarily an art of 'definable expression': the view that music's essential power and value derives principally from its expression of extra-musical emotions. The thesis to which Gurney addresses himself is therefore a near-relative of the very strong thesis outlined above. It is important to bear in mind that music's capacity to express extra-musical emotions is understood by Gurney to involve the arousal of the emotions.[27] I shall consider Gurney's arguments in the order in which he presents them.

The first consideration: Much beautiful music expresses no definable emotion. There is therefore no reason to suppose that a piece of music which possesses a definable expression owes its value to its expression, or is enjoyed because it is triumphant or pathetic.

Gurney attempts to show that the greater part of *im*pressive music lacks definable *ex*pressiveness in the following way. Whereas it is pointless to analyse the structure of impressive music in order to explain its impressiveness, the expressive aspect of music cannot be resistant to analysis. An examination of its structure will enable those features of the music which account for the emotional quality of the music to be identified. Gurney therefore proceeds to look for these features. In the first place, he searches for rules which assign to particular elements or features of music a definite emotional quality. In other words: he looks for a constant emotional effect of a particular musical characteristic or for an emotional character which music always possesses when the music has a specific musical feature. But Gurney recognises that one musical feature in one context may be associated with one emotional quality and in the context of different musical features may be associated with a different emotional quality. The emotional quality of a piece of music is a function of the totality of musical features of the piece. It is therefore unsurprising that Gurney finds few, if any, rules that link to a musical feature a constant emotion quality. The search for the features of music to which the expression of emotion can be attributed therefore assumes a different form. It becomes particular rather than general: What are the features of various pieces of music which, in each particular case, are responsible for the (different) emotional qualities that they possess? But the consideration of this question cannot show that *any* impressive music lacks an expressive aspect and it is therefore strictly irrelevant. Gurney's strategy in the attention that he devotes to the issue is that the study of a number of samples of the emotional qualities music can express should induce or further the conviction that our interest in most of the music we care about is barely or not at all engaged by whatever emotional qualities, if any, might be forced upon the music: the effect is rarely the suggestion of a recognisable emotion, and even when it is the suggestion is incidental to the essential effect.

Gurney's demonstration that the greater part of impressive music lacks an expressive aspect is therefore inconclusive. But the view is surely correct, although the conclusion Gurney derives from this is uncertain. If impressive music was always expressive of emotion there would be some reason to suppose that the expressive aspect of music was of aesthetic importance and not merely an accidental or insignificant accompaniment of the music. (This supposition would be strengthened if no unimpressive music was expressive of emotion.) But if much impressive music lacks an expressive aspect the view that music which is both impressive and expressive 'owes its value to' its being expressive of emotion lacks this support. Nevertheless, the fact that an expressive aspect is not necessary for music to be impressive can show nothing about the importance of the expressive aspect of music which is both impressive and expressive. The expressive aspect of a piece of impressive music might be integral to its value and constitute a specific reason for admiration. We can be impressed by different things for different reasons. The impressiveness of one painting might be a function of the manner in which it integrates the pictorial surface − a feature that another impressive painting lacks. Particular pieces of music might be heard as impressive only if heard as expressive; and impressive music might gain when experienced as the expression of emotion: even if much impressive music is not the expression of emotion.

A comparison with the expression of emotion in the human face can

help us to see the musical expression of emotion in the right way. Two faces can express the same emotion, joy, say, and yet one of the faces be more pleasing to look at when each expresses joy. Furthermore, this face may not be very pleasing to look at generally, but only or especially when it is expressive of joy and it is seen to be so. Hence a face can wear an expression of joy and be visually pleasing only in virtue of doing so, and yet the same expression – the expression of the same emotion – be less pleasing on another face. So the thesis that the character of a certain face is attractive to look at only because it is expressive of joy does not imply that any face which expresses joy is equally attractive nor that the face in question is 'independently beautiful'. It will be the realisation of joy *in the particular form which this face assumes* when it expresses joy that makes it so attractive to us, and the special appeal it then has does not need to derive from some further fact about the face. In this respect expressive music is similar: what appeals to us is the instantiation of an emotional quality *by a particular arrangement of notes*. Whereas Gurney believed that the beauty of a melody and the emotional quality, if any, it possesses are always independent features, in fact a melody can be found beautiful as an expression of a certain emotion. (It is clear that Gurney's arousal theory of musical expression prevented him from seeing this possibility.)
The second consideration:

> The very features which may be often indisputably connected with definable expression are perpetually present in cases where, the music not being perceived as impressive or beautiful, they produce no effect on us. The essential conditions of musical beauty . . . must therefore be quite outside these special features of effect. On the other hand, if any music expresses distinct feeling, it expresses it *better*, we say, the more beautiful it is.

Gurney's suggestion has been that music can express definite emotions by embodying counterparts of features of physical movements that are expressive of those emotions. And his position appears to be that it is *only if* music is impressive that the embodied counterparts of physical movements that are expressive of definite emotions will give the music a particular expressive character. If music is slow *and impressive* then slowness becomes solemnity; if it is quick *and impressive* then quickness becomes merriment or agitation; if it is abrupt *and impressive* then abruptness becomes passion.[28] But if music is unimpressive then slowness, quickness and abruptness remain only themselves.

This position is sometimes apparently weakened to the claim that music which is not on its own merits impressive cannot be expressive, except in a perfectly barren sense:[29]

> no music is really expressive in any valuable way which does not also impress us as having the essential characteristic of musical beauty; an unpleasing tune may be lugubrious but not melancholy.[30]

The distinction between lugubriousness and melancholy is a fine one, but it is in any case clear that, in accordance with Gurney's theory of expression, there is no reason why an unpleasing tune should not express (be) melancholy. For to express melancholy it is necessay only that a tune should suggest or awaken melancholy; and an unpleasing tune could produce this effect − by resembling the physical movements expressive of melancholy − but lack beauty. However, if a tune that awakens melancholy is unpleasing then we will not, in itself, wish to listen to it, and the experience will be, literally, a melancholy one. Moreover, this conclusion holds for every emotion that music can express that is not in itself an emotion we wish to experience. Hence, if an emotion is of a dispiriting or distressing kind its musical arousal will be valueless if the music that arouses the emotion is unimpressive. But Gurney's theory of expression gives no support to the view that music can express 'positive' emotions only if it is otherwise impressive. And if an unpleasing tune could by joyful − and Gurney has produced no consideration that shows that it could not − its expressive character would seem to be valuable. However, this value would not be *musical* value, for the music is unimpressive (as music). The reason for listening to it would be of the same kind as the reason for swallowing an unpleasant medicine. Music that expresses an emotion but which is unimpressive is devoid of musical value. No viable theory of musical value that locates a value of music in its capacity to express an emotion can maintain both that the bare fact that music expresses emotion gives the music musical value and that unimpressive music can express emotion. If it is allowed that unimpressive music can express emotion then such a theory will hold that it is the nature of the emotion or the manner in which emotion is expressed by music that gives the music value and that no unimpressive music can express emotion of this nature or in this manner.

The third consideration: Music often wears a definable expression to one person but a different expression, or none at all, to another person, although each person equally enjoys the music.

Gurney's fundamental concern is with the music that is found impressive by a single individual at a certain stage of his life. The fact that two people can find a piece of music equally impressive but variously expressive does not bear on the issue whether, for each individual, music is primarily an art of definable expression. And the fact that someone can find impressive but non-expressive music that another finds both impressive and expressive merely repeats in its first clause the heart of Gurney's first consideration. Furthermore, the fact that another is not alive to the emotion I experience the music to be suffused with is not sufficient to lessen for me the importance of the expressive aspect of the music. Inter-subjective disagreements about the expressive characteristics of musical works are therefore not strictly relevant to Gurney's basic concern.

The existence of differences of opinion – whether of one person with another, or of a person with his former self – about the expressive aspects of musical works is something that any theory that assigns a significant rôle to the emotional qualities music may have will need to accommodate. Such a theory will naturally wish to insist that it is possible to fail to understand the emotional quality of a piece of music and that a failure of this kind may show a lack of appreciation of the work. The idea of a failure to understand or adequately to respond to a musical work that derives from a failure to appreciate its emotional qualities is something that is not available to Gurney. His ill-defined theory of musical expression as arousal – whether of emotion or the thought of emotion – makes no room for such an idea. Gurney offers no account of expression which is such that a person who fails to feel emotion E (or to think of E) in response to the music might fail fully to understand or to appreciate the music, which does indeed express E. But it is clear that an emotional characterisation of a piece of music – as joyful, triumphant, mournful – can be correct and it can be incorrect. Further, an incorrect characterisation can be indicative of a failure of appreciation of the music: in which case experiencing a work, or part of a work, under a particular emotional characterisation can be necessary fully to appreciate the music. Moreover, without the possibility that someone should fail properly to understand the feeling of a musical work, and without the possibility of justifying a particular emotional characterisation of the work, the phenomenon of expression would be merely an individual matter, and the importance to an individual that he experiences a work under a particular emotional characterisation would be something split off from anything in the music that he might expect to share with others. Gurney's third consideration, that a piece of music may be equally enjoyed by people who experience it differently with respect to the emotions, if any, that for them it expresses, does not show that there are no pieces of music which must be experienced as expressing some particular emotion or sequence of emotions if they are fully to be appreciated. What in effect it does is to throw down a challenge, that any successful theory of expression must take up, to show how there can be any such works.

The fourth consideration: If the sole purpose of a piece of music is to arouse a particular definable emotion then I am no richer for knowing other (impressive) pieces of music that express the same emotion. I might, indifferently, listen to any such piece. But in fact each piece of music is 'a new source of otherwise unknown delight': it is an individual possessing a beauty of its own.

Gurney's thesis as to the nature of the impressiveness of music is that it is the emotion that a piece of impressive music yields that gives the music its value as music, and that this emotion is always of the same kind. The impressiveness of a melodic form corresponds to a characteristic, indefinable, pleasurable emotion which is unknown outside the experience of music. There is therefore a sense in which each impressive melodic form affects us in the same way and yields only what any other impressive melodic form yields: the distinctive emotional pleasure. Now Gurney would maintain of each impressive melodic form that, whilst it yields the specifically musical emotion – from which fact its value derives – it is a new source of delight and it has a value distinct from the value of any other melodic form. It can therefore fairly be replied that each melodic form that is expressive of an extra-musical, pleasurable emotion derives its value from this fact and yet is at the same time a new source of delight. The justice of this reply is underscored by the fact that it is solely the imposition of the separability condition[31] that prevents Gurney's theory of musical expression from yielding the conclusion that each impressive piece of music is expressive of (the same) emotion. For each impressive piece of music arouses the specifically musical emotion which, but for the separability condition, it could properly be said to express. And the fact that the emotion specific to music does not satisfy the separability condition, whereas the emotion of joy or triumph does, is not sufficient to differentiate the emotions with respect to the musical value of their arousal by music. If the proposition that each impressive melodic form has a value of its own is compatible with the proposition that different melodic forms arouse the same *specifically musical* pleasurable emotion and derive their value from the emotion that they arouse, it is compatible with the proposition that different melodic forms arouse the same *extra-musical* pleasurable emotion (joy or triumph, for instance) and derive their value from the emotion that they arouse. Gurney's fourth consideration therefore fails to discriminate against the excitation of extra-musical emotions. The truth is that it is if a pleasurable emotion is or involves delight *in* the forms music presents that an impressive piece of music which arouses this pleasurable emotion is not rendered dispensable by the existence of other pieces of impressive music that also arouse this emotion. If a 'definable' (extra-musical) emotion is not merely aroused by, but is directed towards, the music the individuality of the music guarantees its indispensability.

The fifth consideration: Expressive music could not have so powerful an effect – in particular, it could not be so much greater than that of the corresponding physical movements that are expressive of the emotion and by resembling which, in the main, the music expresses (awakens or suggests) the emotion – without some independent means of powerfully affecting us. The mere expression of an emotion by abstract musical motion would be far less adequate to stir us than the expression of that emotion by the gestures of some uninteresting person. There must therefore be some independent source of impressiveness. And it is this independent source that transfigures any emotion music may suggest. 'The extraordinary intensification which known emotions undergo in musical expression, the movingness of the pathetic, the jubilance of the exulting strains' is due to the fact that 'the particular expression is a phase in an independent mode of deep and mighty impression, whose depth and might it thus makes its own.'

This consideration runs together a number of issues which must be disentangled before the force of Gurney's argument can be assessed.

It is a false contrast to compare unfavourably the effect that the mere musical expression of an emotion might have with the effect that the expression of that emotion in a person's bodily movements might have, for the notion of 'expression' is here equivocal and the relation in which the emotion experienced stands to what expresses the emotion is different in the two cases. The musical expression of emotion is understood by Gurney to bring about the emotion, whereas the behavioural expression of emotion is brought about by the emotion.

A comparison between the effect of music which resembles the bodily expression of an emotion and the effect of that bodily expression itself

72

forces upon us a dual realisation. In the first place, there is the problem as to how it is that any such resemblance is capable, as Gurney assumes, of arousing the emotion in us, rather than of merely calling the emotion to mind – the problem that is concealed from Gurney by his use of the term 'suggest' to mean not just the calling up of the idea of an emotion (by association) but the calling up of the emotion itself. Secondly, our response to the bodily expression of emotion E will not in general be E but – when our response is an emotion – a different emotion.

Gurney's question is not how it is possible for music (through resemblance to the bodily expression of the emotion) to arouse an extra-musical emotion, but how it can arouse such an emotion so powerfully. 'The element of expression', he writes, 'may reach the very extreme of intensity and profundity, since the whole mass of musical feeling which is stirred up appears steeped in the colour of any special emotion it may suggest.'[32] This question must be distinguished from one from which Gurney does not sharply separate it: If music arouses an extra-musical emotion why should the emotion it arouses be experienced as highly pleasurable when in general this emotion may not be experienced with pleasure?

Gurney's opposition to the theory that music is primarily an art of 'definable expression' does not preclude the possibility that some music is valued by us partly because it expresses a particular emotion. In fact he appears to advance a theory as to how music can so matter; and his solution to the problem of the power of the extra-musical emotions that music can arouse is also an answer to the problem of the pleasant character of their experience in music. The thesis that Gurney disallows is that the impressiveness of a piece of music derives solely from the fact that it expresses an extra-musical emotion. On the contrary, it always derives from the specifically musical emotion. But when we experience a piece of music both as expressive of an extra-musical emotion and as impressive then, on Gurney's theory, we experience both the emotion expressed and the emotion specific to music (sublimated sexual excitement). And Gurney construes the resultant state of consciousness as an extraordinary *intensification* of the emotion expressed. But the experience of emotion expressed by a piece of music – let the emotion be melancholy – when conjoined with the indefinable musical emotion would not seem to amount to very intense melancholy, and, if it did, the music would be shunned. Perhaps it was Gurney's intention that the experience of the emotion expressed by a piece of impressive music should draw not only its strength but also its pleasurable character from the distinctive musical emotion. If so then Gurney would have added together melancholy (for example) and the powerful, pleasurable emotion specific to music, and found them to make a very powerful pleasurable melancholy. The problem of the intensity of the emotion expressed and the problem of the delight that it affords would be solved with the same stroke. But if it really is possible to take delight in the forms that music presents and at the same time to feel melancholy then the true sum of melancholy and the emotion specific to music would appear to remain disjoint: a feeling of melancholy and, in addition, the feeling of the specifically musical emotion. And if it is not possible to take delight in music and at the same time to feel melancholy then Gurney's theory of the musical expression of emotion as the musical arousal of emotion must be incorrect. If the most mournful music, when sufficiently beautiful, may make us happy our happiness will not lie in an experience of sorrow that the music arouses in us.

15   Any theory which locates a value of music in its capacity to express emotions must explain how this feature can be a virtue of music. It has been characteristic to look for this explanation partly in the supposed fact that a musical work that expresses a definite emotion always expresses a particular emotion or a nuance of emotion not expressed by any other piece of music or in any other way: so that every (impressive) piece of music that expresses melancholy expresses a different melancholy from every other piece. However, without an account of the nature and mechanism of expression from which this follows, the sense of difference between two pieces felt to express melancholy can always be said to concern not the melancholy which they express but their individual musical structure. Gurney draws a parallel with the case of two children of different physiognomy being told a piece of bad news which affects them exactly alike: the same sentiment will be expressed by their totally different and individual faces.[33] The temptation to believe that each musical work that expresses an emotion necessarily expresses a particular emotion not expressed by any other work was also explored by Wittgenstein, whose well-known diagnosis centres on his distinction between a transitive and an intransitive use of the word 'particular'.[34]

But these negative points are not conclusive against a theory that explains the value of the musical expression of emotion at least in part by reference to the claim that musical works can express kinds or nuances of emotion which cannot be expressed in any other way, for example, by other pieces of music. For it remains possible that some feature of the means whereby music can express emotion should be such that any difference in the music will necessitate a difference in the nature of the emotion, if any, expressed, and that the identity of the emotion expressed will be tied to the particular work that expresses it. If the emotion expressed by a melody were a function of the harmonic relations between its constituent notes, the intervals between them, and their relative durations such that different complexes were mapped one-to-one on to different kinds of emotion, then each melody that expresses an emotion would express a different emotion from that expressed by any other melody.[35] Certainly, if music is thought to express emotion only as Gurney in the main supposes, in virtue of possible correspondences between features of the music and features of the expression of emotion in behaviour, then the further argument that he himself produces against the theory that music is superior to the behavioural expression of emotion in the variety and nuances of emotion it can express would be equally decisive against the view that each expressive work expresses a different emotion from any other.[36] For, in the first place, music could not be in a better position to express emotion than the bodily movements upon the resemblance to which its power to express emotion is entirely dependent. Secondly, the non-verbal behavioural expression of emotion is capable of representing only the crudest differences between emotions, and the features of bodily movement to which musical movement can correspond are so entirely general as to allow that very different pieces of music equally resemble the same feature, and so express, and express only, the same emotion. Furthermore, the limits to the musical expression of emotion would be exactly as Gurney draws them.[37]

These conclusions can be avoided only if Gurney's explanation of music's capacity to express emotion is rejected, and it is replaced by an alternative explanation of such a nature as to secure the desired consequence that the musical expression of emotion is inherently particular. If such an explanation is unavailable then the value of the musical expression of emotion cannot be a result of music's capacity to express emotions incapable of expression by any other means.

V

THE WORLD AS EMBODIED MUSIC

---

1   Schopenhauer is the artist's, and more especially the musician's, philosopher. His principal work, *The World as Will and Representation*,[1] which Thomas Mann was fond of describing as a symphony in four movements,[2] is based on a single thought, announced at the outset, which is developed in unforeseen ways that, nevertheless, seem to be inevitable. This apparently simple thought is repeated many times in the work as a recurrent ground-bass to varied melody and harmony and it informs the reader's consciousness in much the same way that a theme is heard in the variations composed on it. A quarter of the work — its third movement — is given over to an account of the nature of art and aesthetic experience and these are represented as being of singular importance in human life. And Schopenhauer's discussion of art culminates in a celebration of music unrivalled in philosophical writing and which assigns to music pride of place amongst the arts. Moreover, the quality of his finest prose is itself musical: it is expressive of emotion controlled in the manner characteristic of music by subtle rhythmic organisation of sentences, paragraphs, even whole pages, through which the line of thought flows with perfect lucidity.

It is natural to be attracted to a theory of art that credits the products of art with a significance commensurate with the value these works have for us. And this attraction is more clearly felt in the case of Schopenhauer's theory of music because of the absence of rival theories of distinction which compete for our allegiance. But just as the appeal of an object seen from a distance can diminish when it is approached and seen for what it is, so a more perfect understanding of a theory can disclose weaknesses in it which dispel the theory's charm. And this is the situation with Schopenhauer's theory of music: the better we understand it the less likely it is to cast a spell over us.

Now Schopenhauer's theory of music cannot be considered in isolation from the rest of his philosophy, for it is impregnated with his metaphysical conception of the nature of the world, his general theory of art and aesthetic experience and his vision of human life. What we need to do is to see his theory against the background from which it emerges. Only then will we be in a position to understand it as it was intended and to filter out whatever is undesirable in its inheritance. I shall attempt to sketch the essential features of this background despite the obscurity of some parts of it.

2   The first thing it is necessary to understand is the leading idea of Schopenhauer's metaphysical conception of the nature of the world. His principal thought is this: the world has two aspects: from the point of view of its outward face it exists only as representation, from the point of view of its inward face it exists only as will. And the world's existence as will is primary; its existence as representation is derivative. I shall now explain what this means.

According to Schopenhauer, each person has a twofold existence. On the one hand, a person is an individual knowing subject. He exists in space and time, and he acquires knowledge through his senses of items that exist in space and time. Now an object of perception, as it presents itself, or in so far as it presents itself, to an individual knowing subject, is called by Schopenhauer a *phenomenon*. But an object is presented to a subject by a *representation*: a mental 'picture' or image of which he is aware and which has been constructed by his brain in response to the input from his senses. Hence, Schopenhauer concludes, an object of perception as a phenomenon is a representation which exists only in the consciousness of a subject. But the most fundamental characteristics of any object of perception, as it presents itself to an individual knowing subject, are not determined by the nature of the object itself. These properties are imposed on each representation of an object by the mental faculties by means of which an individual knowing subject is aware of any object of perception. One essential characteristic of a material object is its spatiality. We see material things in space, they occupy space and we ourselves are located in that space. But this space is not something really independent of us and of which we become aware by using our senses. Rather, it is merely the form in which our perceptual experience must be realised. Just as the colour we see objects to have when we look at them through a sheet of coloured glass does not attach to the objects themselves but is an appearance they are given by the coloured glass through which we see them so, Schopenhauer argues, the spatial characteristics of objects are imposed on them by the only form in which we can be perceptually aware of them. And whereas we can see the true colours of objects by taking away the sheet of coloured glass, the spatial appearance of objects can never be removed because we can never free ourselves from any feature of perception that is integral to perception, and perception must represent objects spatially. The representations of each individual knowing subject are governed by laws imposed on the representations by the subject's own inalienable nature. And space is one of the forms that a person's representations must conform to. In fact, the status of individual knowing subject dictates that the world is represented as being extended both in space and time and that any change in the state of its contents is caused by a preceding state – the phenomenal world is bound by the law of causality. Hence, if we consider the world only as it is presented to us by our senses and not as it may be *in itself* we are concerned with the world as representation, in which each object – indeed, the entire objective world – is a representation of a subject and so is conditioned by the subject's forms of representation. Each of us can say, 'The world is my representation'.

But we cannot say this from the position we occupy as an individual knowing subject. No person can properly think of the world as his representation if he considers himself as an individual. It is only in so far as each of us has a double existence that we can consider the world to be our representation. For each person, according to Schopenhauer, exists not only as an individual knowing subject, but as *the* subject of knowing. 'The world is my representation' is true for each individual knowing subject only in so far as he is *the* subject of knowing. Now this doctrine that each of us has a twofold existence, as an individual knowing subject and as the knowing subject, is difficult to make sense of. Schopenhauer tells us that the subject of knowing does not exist either in space or in time and that in consequence neither unity nor plurality belongs to it. And he also tells us that the subject 'is whole and undivided in every representing being'. But this makes it look as if Schopenhauer is calling the *property* of knowing *the* subject of knowing. However, we do not need to examine too closely Schopenhauer's conception of the knowing subject. All we need to do is to make ourselves familiar with the properties Schopenhauer attributes to the subject of knowing and to pass on.

3 Schopenhauer's thesis is that each object, considered as it presents itself to an individual knowing subject, is a representation. But the aspect an object presents to a subject cannot exhaust the object's nature. Each object must have a nature of its own and not merely the nature credited to it by the representation a subject manufactures in becoming aware of it in perception. But an object's 'inner' nature is not revealed to any individual knowing subject by his representations. For these reveal only the aspect the object presents to the subject. Hence, they can neither directly disclose the further aspect nor provide any adequate ground for rational speculation about what its nature might be. No matter how any individual knowing subject may examine what he perceives, his forms of representation dictate that it appears to him as being in space and time and subject to the law of causality. What it may be in itself — not as represented as being in space and time — is undiscoverable by direct inspection or by scientific investigation of the phenomenal world.

It is at this point that Schopenhauer gives his distinctive twist to a story familiar to readers of Kant's *Critique of Pure Reason*. So far he has told us that if we start our quest for knowledge of the nature of the world from the perceptual representation of the objective world we cannot get further than phenomena, which are only representations. What the inner nature of objects is, what things are in themselves and not merely as we represent them in perception, always remains beyond us and is not accessible by this path. But there is another route to this goal, so Schopenhauer believes. For we are not merely knowing subjects; we are rooted in the world as individual physical things; we ourselves are among the entities whose inner nature we require to know. In consequence:

> a way *from within* stands open to us to that real inner nature of
> things to which we cannot penetrate *from without*. It is, so to speak,
> a subterranean passage, a secret alliance, which, as if by treachery,
> places us all at once in the fortress that could not be taken by attack
> from without.[3]

Each of us can come to know one object otherwise than by perceiving that object. For our body is not merely one of the many objects in our world of representation. If we consider our body and the physical changes that occur in it as they are known to us in perception then their position is no different from that of any other items we perceive. For our body, as object of perception, is only a representation; and the inner nature of physical changes in our body as they are represented to us is no more comprehensible than the inner nature of anything else represented to us. But, according to Schopenhauer, intentional action and the experience of pleasure and pain provide us with immediate knowledge of the inner nature of changes in our body. And this inner nature is there revealed to us as what Schopenhauer calls *will*. Our body is given to us in two quite different ways: the first by perception as representation, the second immediately as will. When it is given to us in the first way it is subject to space, time and causality, the forms of representation. But when it is given to us in the second way — when we are immediately aware of it in self-consciousness — it is subject only to the form of time. For our knowledge of the will in self-consciousness is not a perception of it but an absolutely immediate awareness of it as manifested in time. An intentional action is an act of will; and although an act of will is one and the same thing as a movement of the body, when we are aware of it in self-consciousness we are not aware of it as a movement of the body. Similarly, when we experience pain we are aware of a physical change in our body but we are not aware of it as such a change. Our immediate awareness of the will in self-consciousness reveals something we experience only as a temporal occurrence. What kind of temporal occurrence an act of will or the experience of pleasure or pain is supposed by Schopenhauer to be I shall leave unexplained at this point.

Schopenhauer's view is that we have available a route to the inner nature of various changes in our body — the route of self-consciousness. But this route cannot quite take us to our destination. For what we want to know is the inner nature of these changes absolutely independently of how they present themselves to us. But anything we become aware of in self-consciousness is stamped with the form of time. Hence, Schopenhauer concludes, what is encountered in self-consciousness is only relatively, not absolutely, our true inner nature, our being-in-itself. We are more closely acquainted with the being-in-itself of these changes in our body than with the being-in-itself of anything else. For our knowledge of anything else proceeds by way of perception, which represents objects under the three forms of space, time and causality, whereas our knowledge of these changes proceeds by way of self-consciousness, which renders them under the form of time alone. But the being-in-itself of something is what it is like in itself, not by way of how it appears to anything. Hence, so Schopenhauer's train of thought goes, we are aware in self-consciousness only of the successive manifestations in time of our being-in-itself but this being-in-itself lies outside time. Nevertheless, Schopenhauer recommends that we call our true being-in-itself 'the will' out of consideration for the manifestation in which it appears most unveiled.[4]

4 This double knowledge which each of us has of his own body is used by Schopenhauer as the key to the being-in-itself of every item in the phenomenal world. With the exception of our own body, whatever we are aware of we experience as representation. But in intentional action and in feeling pain or pleasure we are aware of our body in a different way and we experience it as will. Now in the case of our immediate awareness of the activity of the will in intentional action the will's operation is not only accompanied by knowledge or representation, it is guided by it. But, according to Schopenhauer, each of these is an inessential feature of the will's activity: the will need not be guided by knowledge nor accompanied by knowledge. Hence, there is no logical absurdity involved in positing the will as the inner nature of things whose movements are not guided by knowledge — as the action of a young spider in spinning its web is not guided by the thought of the prey the web is designed to catch — or even of things which entirely lack knowledge, such as plants. And this is precisely what Schopenhauer urges that we must do. For he argues that there is no essential difference between our own body and any other object of perception; the special position of our own body is determined solely by the fact that it is the only object into which we have this twofold insight. Accordingly, he reaches the conclusion that the will constitutes the inner nature of every phenomenon. The will is not only the being-in-itself of each intentional movement of our body and of those changes we experience as painful or pleasurable; it is the inner nature of every change in our body, of all animate and inanimate change, of our entire body itself, of all animate and inanimate objects and of every natural force.

5 We have followed the path that leads Schopenhauer to his view of the world's nature. Considered from one point of view, everything in the world is mere representation: it is an object for a knowing subject. But from another, and more revealing, point of view, everything is will. And since the being-in-itself of every object is will, the world as representation can be called *the objectivity of the will*: it is the will experienced as object or representation. Accordingly, the physical changes we experience as pain or pleasure and the bodily movements that are acts of

will are nothing but the will objectified. Now at this point Schopenhauer introduces a new conception. For he distinguishes indefinitely many fixed *grades of the objectification of the will*. These grades of the objectification of the will are the various levels at which the will can be experienced as representation or object and they are higher or lower grades according as the will is revealed more or less distinctly and completely in them. The lowest grades of the will's objectification are the universal natural forces that manifest themselves in accordance with the laws of nature. Above these are the essential forms and properties of organic and inorganic natural bodies. Finally, there are the various species, with the human being occupying the highest grade of the will's objectification. At each grade there is a plurality of phenomena: a multitude of individuals of a certain structure or the various manifestations of a certain force. The individual things at a certain grade exist in space and time and are therefore subject to change. But the grades themselves are not spatio-temporal items and are not subject to change. Schopenhauer identifies these grades of the objectification of the will with the Platonic Ideas: the eternal forms of transient things. And he likens our encounter with different individuals of the same grade to our seeing a flower through a many-faceted glass: the flower gives rise to innumerable images whose essential nature is the same.[5]

6   The introduction of the Platonic Ideas into Schopenhauer's account of the nature of the world gains its significance from the role they play in his theory of aesthetic experience and art. In Schopenhauer's view, when we acquire knowledge of particular objects of perception in our ordinary experience of the world, this perceptual knowledge is always in the service of our will for the accomplishment of its aims. The world as representation has interest for us only in so far as it is seen as connected, directly or indirectly, with our desires or purposes. Now an object of perception is considered by Schopenhauer to be only an indirect objectification of the will, since it is bound by the various conditions under which anything can be an object or a representation to an individual knowing subject: it must be represented as in space and time and it must conform to the law of causality. The will is therefore multiply obscured in an object of perception by the form imposed upon the object by the conditions which must obtain if we are to have knowledge of it. A Platonic Idea is a more adequate objectification of the will. For a Platonic Idea, a grade of the objectification of the will, differs from the inner nature of the world — the will itself — in only

one respect: it is a representation, an object for a subject; it is not, however, an object with a location in space or time. But how is this possible: how can something be an object for a subject and yet be free from the constraints of the subject's forms of representation?

The answer Schopenhauer gives to this question yields his theory of aesthetic experience and then his theory of art. His answer is that *as individual knowing subjects* we cannot be aware of the Ideas. For as individual knowing subjects whatever can be represented to us in perception must conform to the forms of representation of an individual knowing subject. Hence, awareness of the Ideas is possible only if there is a change in the knowing subject. This change consists in the individual knowing subject's losing his individuality: he ceases to be an individual, governed by the individual's forms of representation, for whom the world as representation has no interest other than as the source of the motives that move his will. We have seen that Schopenhauer attributes a twofold existence to each of us — as an individual knowing subject and as the knowing subject. If we are to be aware of the Ideas we must assume our status as the knowing subject — the pure, will-less subject of knowledge — and rest in fixed contemplation of the object represented to us. We must regard the perceived object in a special way: we must not consider the relations in which it stands to anything else, we must disregard its position in time and space and thus its individuality and we must forget any significance it may have for our will. We must let our whole consciousness be taken up in the dispassionate contemplation of the object:

> We (must) *lose* ourselves entirely in this object . . . forget our
> individuality, our will, and continue to exist only as pure subject,
> as clear mirror of the object, so that it is as though the object alone
> existed without anyone to perceive it, and thus we are no longer able
> to separate the perceiver from the perception, but the two have
> become one, since the entire consciousness is filled and occupied
> by a single image of perception.[6]

If this comes about, what is known is no longer the particular object of perception as such but the Idea it manifests. The perceiving individual loses his individuality and becomes the pure, will-less, timeless knowing subject; and the object becomes in his perception, so to speak, the Idea it embodies. The Idea is in a certain sense an object for a subject. But subject and object in this case have equal weight. In fact, they can no longer be distinguished. For the object is nothing but the representation of the subject and the consciousness of the subject is entirely filled by the object represented. Subject and object, Schopenhauer writes, 'reciprocally fill and penetrate each other completely'. The world as will disappears and the world as representation alone remains. The pure, will-less subject which lies outside space and time finds its perfect correlative in a Platonic Idea.

Now this yields Schopenhauer's theory of aesthetic experience and art in a very simple way. For he considers aesthetic experience to consist precisely in the state of pure, will-less contemplation of an object. And he considers aesthetic pleasure to be of a uniform nature, whether it is called forth by the contemplation of nature or the contemplation of a work of art. He maintains that aesthetic pleasure arises from two inseparable aspects of aesthetic experience: the pure, will-less state of contemplation and the correlative awareness of an Idea. Whether the pleasure accrues more from the one aspect than from the other depends on the nature of the object contemplated: the lower the grade of the objectivity of the will realised by the object the more the pleasure of its contemplation is due to the first of the two aspects. And Schopenhauer's theory of art asserts that the various arts, in so far as they are successful, make available for our contemplation different grades of the objectification of the will. Architecture, considered as a fine art, is concerned to bring to clear perception certain of the Ideas that form the lowest grades of the objectification of the will: gravity, rigidity and the nature of light. Hence, in this case, the aesthetic pleasure – the pleasure in looking at a fine building – lies primarily in the state of pure will-less contemplation itself. At the opposite extreme, the aesthetic pleasure of poetry – above all, of tragedy – is due predominantly to poetry's presentation of the highest grade of the will's objectification: the nature of human life.

Schopenhauer believes that we derive pleasure from being in the state of pure, will-less contemplation in which, according to his theory, aesthetic experience consists. But why should the lack of involvement of the will result in a state we are specially pleased to be in? A famous passage in which Schopenhauer expresses his view of the essential nature of human life provides an answer to this question:

> All *willing* springs from lack, from deficiency, and thus from suffering. Fulfilment brings this to an end; yet for one wish that is fulfilled there remain at least ten that are denied. Further, desiring lasts a long time, demands and requests go on to infinity; fulfilment is short

and meted out sparingly. But even the final satisfaction itself is only apparent; the wish fulfilled at once makes way for a new one; the former is a known delusion, the latter a delusion not as yet known. No attained object of willing can give a satisfaction that lasts and no longer declines; but it is always like the alms thrown to a beggar, which reprieves him today so that his misery may be prolonged till tomorrow. Therefore, so long as our consciousness is filled by our will, so long as we are given up to the throng of desires with its constant hopes and fears, so long as we are the subject of willing, we never obtain lasting happiness or peace. Essentially, it is all the same whether we pursue or flee, fear harm or aspire to enjoyment; care for the constantly demanding will, no matter in what form, continually fills and moves consciousness; but without peace and calm, true well-being is absolutely impossible. Thus the subject of willing is constantly lying on the revolving wheel of Ixion, is always drawing water in the sieve of the Danaids, and is the eternally thirsting Tantalus.

When, however, an external cause or inward disposition suddenly raises us out of the endless stream of willing, and snatches knowledge from the thraldom of the will, the attention is now no longer directed to the motives of willing, but comprehends things free from their relation to the will. Thus it considers things without interest, without subjectivity, purely objectively; it is entirely given up to them in so far as they are merely representations, and not motives. Then all at once the peace, always sought but always escaping on that first path of willing, comes to us of its own accord, and all is well with us. It is the painless state, prized by Epicurus as the highest good and as the state of the gods; for that moment we are delivered from the miserable pressure of the will. We celebrate the Sabbath of the penal servitude of willing; the wheel of Ixion stands still.[7]

Now this painless state just is the state of pure will-less contemplation that Schopenhauer has identified with the aesthetic state. And Schopenhauer's perception of the suffering that is involved, essentially, in human life leads him to assign a high value to the painless state of aesthetic contemplation. Human life is so miserable that it has no genuine intrinsic worth. Aesthetic experience delivers us from life, if only for a brief period; it is an occasional consolation for and release from the endless striving and suffering of the will. And if we now introduce Schopenhauer's doctrine of the negative nature of pleasure — pleasure is merely the absence of pain — we can derive the conclusion that the state of aesthetic contemplation can be said not only to be painless but to be intrinsically pleasurable.

7   The art of music has been conspicuous by its absence from my exposition of Schopenhauer's account of art — which runs parallel to his own. But the omission is deliberate. For music has a special and superior position in Schopenhauer's theory of art. In virtue of its exceptional nature it is not only the most powerful of the arts, but the most important. It is set apart from the other arts by its distinctive aim. The aim of each of the other arts is to construct something that facilitates the contemplation of one or more grades of the will's objectification. But music can create something that has a more significant function than this. For whilst there is only an indirect relation between the other arts and the inner nature of the world, music's relation to the world's inner nature is immediate. The other arts do not enable us to become conscious of the will itself; they make available only the Ideas, grades of the will's objectification. But there is a direct relation between music and the will — a relation that is unmediated by the Ideas. Music is a direct representation or copy of the innermost essence of the world, the will.

But this account of the nature is paradoxical. For Schopenhauer's doctrine is that only a representation can be represented. And yet his theory of the metaphysical significance of music asserts that music is the representation of the will — something which, not being a representation, cannot be represented. Schopenhauer concedes that it is impossible to demonstrate his explanation of the nature of music's 'imitative relation to the world', for the reason that

> it assumes and establishes a relation of music as a representation to that which of its essence can never be representation, and claims to regard music as the copy of an original that can itself never be directly represented.[8]

But the difficulty with his explanation is not that it cannot be demonstrated. His explanation is problematic because if the term 'representation' is taken seriously the explanation does not make sense. What cannot be represented cannot be represented — even by music. The solution to the problem is to understand the thesis that music is a representation of the will in a non-literal way. I believe the sense it is possible to give the thesis — the sense Schopenhauer had in mind — can be discovered by a consideration of what Schopenhauer says about the relation between music and the Ideas.

8 Schopenhauer's view is that whereas music is entirely independent of the phenomenal world, and so of the Ideas, and is related to the will immediately, the other arts objectify the will indirectly, by means of the Ideas. Nevertheless, Schopenhauer believes that there must be some kind of parallel or analogy between music and the Ideas. For although music is related to the will directly, and not by virtue of the capacity to render Ideas perceptible, both music and the Ideas make the will manifest. There must therefore be some analogy between the nature of music and the grades of the objectification of the will; and Schopenhauer believes that the exposition of this analogy will make it easier to understand his explanation of the metaphysical significance of music.

But although this is so, in every case except one the parallels Schopenhauer draws between music and the Ideas are merely fanciful: they bear no significant relation to the experience of music. (His comparison of impure discords of no definite interval to monstrous abortions between different species of animal is typical.) The exception is his treatment of melody. Schopenhauer believes that melody is related in an important way to certain features of human life. We can distinguish in his account three kinds of correspondence that are alleged to hold between melody and human life. Each of the first two kinds relates melody *as such* to an aspect of human life: one aspect is distinctive of human life, the other is essential to human life but not distinctive of it. The third kind of correspondence is the child of the other two and concerns the various types of melody, not melody as such.

Schopenhauer begins with a partial characterisation of the notion of a melody, which enables him to assert a highly abstract correspondence between the nature of melody and what he regards as being distinctive of human nature. A melody is a temporal sequence of different tones connected together in a particular way: it is a process with a beginning and an end; its stages are heard in relation to preceding segments of the process and to expected continuations of it; it runs its course and in doing so is grasped as a single entity. There is therefore an analogy between the nature of melody and the connected consciousness that, according to Schopenhauer, distinguishes the life of a human being from the life of any other living thing. A human life possesses a distinctive kind of unity, which it acquires by the exercise of the capacity to look backwards and forwards in time – in memory, deliberation and anticipation.

A human life is one in which the different parts are bound together by relations of consciousness so that it is unified across time: it does not fall apart into a set of psychologically independent stages. A person's conscious life is a temporal sequence united by self-consciousness. Accordingly, a human being has a sense of his life extending backwards into the past and forwards into the future, and he may have a conception of his life as having a beginning and an end. In virtue of this distinctive feature of human life there is a correspondence between the phenomenon of melody and the unique nature of the will's clearest manifestation — as it is realised by the will enlightened by the intellect.

But this correspondence between melody and the connected consciousness of a human being is extremely slight: it is pitched at such a level of abstraction that its implications for music's significance as an art-form appear negligible. It could not show that the significance of music's melodic aspect lies in a relation in which this aspect stands to life that is distinctively human. However, Schopenhauer's further characterisation of the nature of melody reveals a second correspondence between melody and human life. For human life is a specific form of animal life and a parallel can be drawn between the nature of melody and the realisation of the will in the conscious life of an animal. An animal experiences its life as a succession of states involving desire and satisfaction of desire: its life is a continual alternation of partial or complete satisfaction and lesser or greater dissatisfaction: the animal strives for some goal which, perhaps, it attains and is momentarily satisfied, only for a new desire to spring up and to become a new source of dissatisfaction. Corresponding to this, a melody is a process in which there is a progression from one point of relative repose to another such point: the interlocking phrases which compose the melody form shorter processes whose final notes are their goals; but these goals are merely temporary and the melodic process is complete only when the melody returns to the keynote with finality. And Schopenhauer's analysis of the nature of melody explains how this comes about and further articulates the correspondence. For the nature of melody consists in an alternating *discord* and *reconciliation* of two elements: a rhythmical element and a harmonious element. On the harmonic level, there is deviation from the keynote until, after a longer or shorter time, a harmonious note, the dominant, for example, is reached, and this is a point at which there is an *incomplete satisfaction*; and then, by some route or other, the melody returns to the fundamental note, which is a point of *complete satisfaction*. But for there to be a melody this process must take place in such a way that the harmonious stages of the process are reached at points favoured by the rhythm, namely, at accented parts of a bar. For the two elements of accented beat and harmonious interval may be united or disunited, and if in a musical process they are always disunited there will be no melody. Melodies require points of satisfaction or points of rest and these are obtained only when a harmonious note is reached on an accented beat − that is, when there is a reconciliation of rhythm and harmony. It is not until there is a point of union of the two elements that there is satisfaction, rest, and hence a melodic phrase. And Schopenhauer's thesis is that the constant discord and reconciliation of the two elements a melody requires is an analogue of the origination of new desires and their satisfaction.

Now this general correspondence between melody and what is distinctive of animal (or sentient) life makes possible more specific correspondences between kinds of melody and the various forms in which the will is realised in human life. Here are some of Schopenhauer's examples:

> as rapid transition from wish to satisfaction and from this to a new wish are happiness and well-being, so rapid melodies without great deviations are cheerful. Slow melodies that strike painful discords and wind back to the keynote only through many bars, are sad, on the analogy of delayed and hard-won satisfaction. . . . The short, intelligible phrases of rapid dance music seem to speak only of ordinary happiness which is easy of attainment. On the other hand, the *allegro maestoso* in great phrases, long passages, and wide deviations expresses a greater, nobler effort towards a distant goal, and its final attainment. The *adagio* speaks of the suffering of a great and noble endeavour that disdains all trifling happiness.[9]

In this fashion analogies can be drawn between different kinds of melody and different kinds of emotion or other modes of will. It is for this reason that music has often been thought of as the 'language' of the emotions. In fact, Schopenhauer declares, there is a melodic counterpart to each form in which the will is realised in human life. And it is important to understand how wide − and yet, as we shall see, how narrow − melody casts its net:

> For not only willing and deciding in the narrowest sense, but also all striving, wishing, shunning, hoping, fearing, loving, hating, in short all that directly constitutes our own weal and woe, desire and

disinclination, is obviously only affection of the will, is a stirring, a modification, of willing and not-willing . . .[10]

The forms in which we are affected by the will include, Schopenhauer writes, 'everything which the faculty of reason summarizes under the wide and negative concept of feeling, and which cannot be further taken up into the abstractions of reason': everything of this kind can be captured by melody. Hence, the view of Plato and Aristotle that music can imitate states of the soul – in particular, those states in which emotion is experienced – is vindicated.

9   Now it is easy to misunderstand this doctrine of Schopenhauer's. He is at pains to stress that music is not directly related to the analogues he has brought forward, but only indirectly related. And this is the reason he gives:

> (music) never expresses the phenomenon, but only the inner nature, the in-itself, of every phenomenon, the will itself. Therefore music does not express this or that particular and definite pleasure, this or that affliction, pain, sorrow, horror, gaiety, merriment, or peace of mind, but joy, pain, sorrow, horror, gaiety, merriment, peace of mind *themselves*, to a certain extent in the abstract, their essential nature, without any accessories, and so also without the motives for them.[11]

What does Schopenhauer mean by his claim that music does not express or represent any particular and definite emotion but that emotion itself, its essential nature but not its motive? Consider sorrow: sorrow is unhappiness at the thought of the loss of someone or something dear to one. A particular instance of sorrow would be a certain man's sorrow at the death of his wife. But the distinction Schopenhauer is drawing between the essential nature of sorrow and some particular and definite sorrow is not the distinction I have just drawn. It is not the distinction between a kind of emotion and an instance of that kind. Schopenhauer's doctrine is not that music can express unhappiness at the loss of someone or something dear to one, but neither unhappiness at any particular loss nor some particular person's unhappiness at a loss. For not only can music not represent a particular person's thought of the death of his wife, it cannot represent even so much as the unattached thought of some loss or other. All music can represent is that element of an emotion that has to do with the will: ease or unease, tension or relaxation, satisfaction or desire – the mere fact of desire, not the object of desire

– pleasure or pain. It is the element of the will contained in each emotion – this and nothing else – that Schopenhauer considers to be the essential nature of the emotion.

There are many reasons for interpreting Schopenhauer's account of the metaphysical significance of the melodic aspect of music in this way. In the first place, a thought is one kind of representation – it is an abstract representation, not a representation of perception – whereas pleasure and pain are not representations. But Schopenhauer's theory is precisely that music is a representation of that which can never be represented – that is, can never be a representation. Hence, music cannot represent the thought a certain kind of emotion may involve but only that aspect of the emotion which is not representation but is a function of the will: pleasure and pain, desire and satisfaction. Secondly, most of Schopenhauer's examples of emotions can readily be understood as being merely what he would regard as affections of the will. Joy is great pleasure, merriment is animated enjoyment; and in Schopenhauer's view pain, pleasure and peace of mind are mere indexes of desire and satisfaction of desire. More importantly, Schopenhauer explicitly defines and consistently construes joy as satisfaction of the will, sorrow as the will impeded, suffering as hindrance of the will from attaining its temporary goal, and satisfaction, happiness and well-being as the attainment of the will's temporary goal.[12] Thirdly, Schopenhauer's articulation of analogies between certain kinds of melody and varieties of feeling indicates parallels between, on the one hand, the ways in which tension is created and resolved as the progress of the melodic curve generates expectations that are satisfied either at once or only after a more or less drawn out postponement, and, on the other hand, the will-aspect of feelings. He does not attempt to explain how a melody could reflect any other component of an emotion. Fourthly, if we put together Schopenhauer's general definition of emotion and his account of the idea of a motive we can derive the interpretation I have argued for. Schopenhauer defines an emotion as 'a stirring of the will' by a motive and he regards something as affecting the will only if it is felt pleasantly or painfully.[13] But a motive just is a representation: it is either a sensuous representation of one of the senses, as is always so in the case of nonhuman animals, or an abstract representation, a concept, as is nearly always so in the case of human beings. Hence, Schopenhauer's claim that music expresses only the essential nature of an emotion, not its motive, implies that music can express only the element of pleasure or pain an emotion contains, and not any perception or concept sometimes, usually or necessarily involved in the experience of the emotion. Music can express an emotion only in so far as the emotion is an affection of the will: it can represent only that component of an emotion that derives from the provenance of the will. Finally, the identification of the essential nature of an emotion with the element of the will it contains is confirmed by Schopenhauer's characterisation of 'all movements of the human heart, i.e., of the will': he declares their 'essential nature' to be 'always satisfaction and dissatisfaction'.[14]

Hence, although each emotion can be caught in melody's net, its chaff of representation escapes through the mesh and an emotion surrenders to music only its grain of will. Music in its melodic aspect conveys impressions not exactly of the emotions but of their non-representational component. The melodic analogues of the various kinds of emotion articulate the dynamic structures the will assumes when the emotions are experienced, but they do not articulate the conceptual contents of the emotions. When Schopenhauer declares that 'all the human passions and emotions' are exhibited in a symphony by Beethoven, 'yet all, as it were, only in the abstract and without any particularization', it is solely in this restricted sense that his assertion should be understood. The melodies we hear in music are analogues only of the 'extracted quintessence' of the emotions; and the most important part of any emotion is the affection of the will that lies at its heart. The melodic aspect of music corresponds to the will-aspect of emotion.

10   But when we listen to a musical work in what way is the relation in which it stands to the emotions relevant to our experience? Do we in any sense experience or appreciate the extracted quintessence of the emotions represented in the music? And if we do not, how can the representation of the core of emotion explain the value of musical experience? The answer Schopenhauer gives to these questions is in part clear and in part obscure. The parallelism Schopenhauer articulates between musical works and the Ideas, and in particular his correlation of melody with the experience of the intellectually enlightened will, is intended to explain his cryptic doctrine that music is a representation of that which cannot be represented. But it serves a further function. For in Schopenhauer's view not only does this parallelism exist but when we listen to the musical analogues of the activities of the will all that happens is that we undergo an experience which has elements that are analogous to the manifestations of the will in feeling (and in the other forms it assumes in the world as representation). Schopenhauer does not maintain that music excites the listener's will: it does not make us feel the will-aspects of the emotions. According to Schopenhauer, it would be undesirable if it did arouse our emotions, for our experience of music would then not be free from pain, and a pain-free existence is the only condition that is truly desirable. Indeed, it is one of the virtues of music that it can deliver us momentarily from our normal mode of existence, which is governed by the nature of the will embodied in us and whose essence is endless striving — which we experience as suffering.

This feature of Schopenhauer's view is made especially clear in his consideration of the connection of music's metaphysical aspect with its physical aspect. His account is founded on a certain theory of the physical basis of harmony which he expounds in this way: when the vibrations of two tones have a rational relation to each other, expressible in a small number, the tones can be taken together in our apprehension because of the regular coincidence of their vibrations — they blend and form a consonance; but when this is not so the tones resist being taken together and form a dissonance. And he expresses his view of the relation between the metaphysical significance he has ascribed to music and the physical medium of music in this passage:

The connexion of the metaphysical significance of music with this its physical and arithmetical basis rests on the fact that what resists our *apprehension*, namely the irrational relation of dissonance, becomes the natural image of what resists our *will*; and, conversely, the consonance or the rational relation, by easily adapting itself to our *apprehension*, becomes the image of the satisfaction of the *will*. Now as that rational and irrational element in the numerical relations of the vibrations admits of innumerable degrees, nuances, sequences, and variations, music by means of it becomes the material in which all movements of the human heart, i.e., of the will, movements whose essential nature is always satisfaction and dissatisfaction, although in innumerable degrees, can be faithfully portrayed and reproduced in all their finest shades and modifications; and this takes place by means of the invention of the melody. Thus we here see the movements of the will linked with the province of the mere *representation* that is the exclusive scene of all the fine arts. For these positively demand that the *will itself* be left out of account, and that we behave in every way as purely *knowing* beings. Therefore the affections of the will itself, and hence actual pain and actual pleasure, must not be excited, but only their substitutes, that which is in conformity with the *intellect* as a *picture or image* of the will's satisfaction, and that which more or less opposes it as a *picture or image* of greater or lesser pain. Only in this way does music never cause us actual suffering, but still remains pleasant even in its most painful chords; and we like to hear in its language the secret history of our will and of all its stirrings and strivings with their many different delays, postponements, hindrances, and afflictions, even in the most sorrowful melodies. On the other hand, where in real life and its terrors our *will itself* is that which is roused and tormented, we are then not concerned with tones and their numerical relations; on the contrary, we ourselves are now the vibrating string that is stretched and plucked.[15]

Accordingly, Schopenhauer does not put forward the thesis that we experience satisfaction in hearing each consonance and striving and dissatisfaction in hearing each dissonance. In fact, he maintains that the affections of the will must not be excited when we listen to music. His view is that the consonance is an analogue – 'a picture or image' – of satisfaction and the dissonance of dissatisfaction, and that in consequence music in its melodic aspect is experienced as an analogue of the passage from satisfaction to greater or less dissatisfaction to partial or complete satisfaction – the passage we are familiar with in our own conscious life as the experience of the will.

Now the solution to the problem created by Schopenhauer's paradoxical thesis that music is a representation of that which can never be representation (and so never represented) is, as I have already said, to understand the doctrine that music is a representation of the will in a non-literal fashion. For Schopenhauer, music is not a representation of the will in the strict sense he attaches to the word 'representation' ('*Vorstellung*'): music is neither an abstract representation of the will presenting its nature by means of concepts nor a perceptual representation with a non-perceptible being-in-itself. In particular, a melody is not strictly speaking a representation of the will as it is experienced in emotion, desire and satisfaction of desire. The sense in which music is a representation of the will is that the most important elements of musical structures are close counterparts of the essential features and forms of the will as it manifests itself in time and, consequently, the experience we have in listening to music is formally analogous to the will's nature. Hence, our experience of music more closely relates us to the will than does any perceptual representation of something whose being-in-itself is the will. But when we listen to music our experience is not as closely related to the will as it is possible for it to be — in our immediate awareness of our own acts of will and pleasure and pain. Our experience of music is not literally experience of the will. Thus music mediates between the world as representation and the world as will: it enables us to experience the innermost nature of the world as it were from within — not from without, as is the case when the will is objectified in the material world and we experience it as representation — yet without our paying the normal price when the will is experienced from within, the price of suffering. We experience a psychological counterpart of the activity of the will in which the will has been rendered free from pain. We undergo an experience which is analogous to what we experience when we experience desire and satisfaction of desire, but no sacrifice is required. And it is precisely because this is the nature of musical experience that Schopenhauer thinks so highly of music as an art-form. The specific value of music is not that it provides pain-free episodes in the vale of tears Schopenhauer considers life to be. That is a value common to all aesthetic experience. The singular importance of music is that it offers the closest approximation to the experience of the will without the usual drawback. The processes which compose musical works are analogues of the temporal manifestations of the will and the experience of music resembles the experience of the will in being essentially non-representational and unconceptualised: when we listen to music our consciousness is filled with uninterpreted sounds and we can grasp the forms these sounds compose without bringing them under concepts. But musical experience is preferable to our immediate consciousness of the will since the experience of music is devoid of pain. In sum: the importance for Schopenhauer of the metaphysical significance he finds in music lies in the fact that (i) our immediate consciousness of the will in our own bodies is essentially painful, (ii) our awareness of the will in anything else is indirect, and (iii) in music we undergo an experience of which it is true both that it involves the awareness of processes that are closely analogous to the activities of the will and that it is free from pain.

This interpretation of Schopenhauer's thesis that music is a representation of that which can never be representation makes clear the meaning of his remark:

The inexpressible depth of all music, by virtue of which it floats past us as a paradise quite familiar and yet eternally remote, and is so

95

easy to understand and yet so inexplicable, is due to the fact that it reproduces all the emotions of our innermost being, but entirely without reality and remote from its pain.[16]

And Schopenhauer's claim is that the effect of music is so powerful because this fact obtains, but music's power does not depend on the listener's realisation that this is the fact of the matter. The listener can fully respond to the music without understanding the significance of that which induces his response — the significance it was Schopenhauer's mission to articulate.

11   We must now decide how much truth there is in Schopenhauer's theory of music. Unfortunately, there is very little. In the first place, his theory of music inherits many of the defects of his metaphysics. These defects, some of which are plainly visible and widely recognised, render his metaphysical conception of the nature of the world unsupportable. I shall not rehearse the arguments that tell decisively against certain of Schopenhauer's most cherished and characteristic doctrines. But it will be necessary for me to list some of the principal weaknesses in his world-view:

(i) The assumption of something — the thing-in-itself — that exists neither in space nor in time but which nevertheless 'objectifies' itself in our spatio-temporal world.

(ii) The identification of material objects, considered as spatio-temporal items, with perceptual representations in our brains.

(iii) The postulation of the will, the essence of which is striving, as the innermost nature of everything in the natural world.

(iv) The conception of the pure knowing subject, which does not lie in space or time, but which is present whole and undivided in every individual knowing subject, and in whose representation the entire spatio-temporal world has its only existence.

(v) The characterisation of the state of aesthetic contemplation as an awareness of Platonic Ideas (non-spatial, non-temporal items), and the associated idea of the pure knowing subject as the correlative of the aesthetic state.

Now if we regard these ideas as unacceptable, how much of Schopenhauer's theory of music can be salvaged? It is clear we shall have to jettison a large amount of his doctrine that music is a representation of that which can never be represented. We must reject all the parallels Schopenhauer draws between aspects of music and alleged manifestations of the will, except those which relate music to phenomena in which there is pleasure and pain, desire and genuine striving for a goal. And this means that the theory that music reveals in a peculiarly intimate way the innermost nature of the world must be replaced by the theory that music reveals in the most direct fashion what it is like to strive, desire and experience pleasure and suffering. It is for this reason I have concentrated upon Schopenhauer's treatment of the melodic aspect of music, for only melody is brought into relation with what is regarded by Schopenhauer as the foundation of every animal consciousness: the immediate awareness of a longing and of its alternate satisfaction and non-satisfaction in many different degrees.

If his conception of music is understood in this diminished form it asserts a likeness between music and conscious goal-directed activity – a likeness which has often been exploited by musical theorists in their attempts to describe basic features of music or musical experience. Now it is not easy to characterise the various elements of the experience of listening to music and it is unsurprising that recourse has often been had to terminology drawn from other areas. The capacity to undergo certain experiences does not go hand in hand with the possession of a language which has words intended to apply to these experiences specifically, and the lack of words designed to fit a particular subject matter is overcome by transferring words from other domains and using them in ways to which they are not accustomed. This procedure is open to misunderstanding, not least by those who practise it. Schopenhauer himself falls into difficulties when he tries to give an accurate description of the experience of music which at the same time conforms to his requirement that the will should not be excited in aesthetic experience. In his account of the nature of melody as a constantly renewed discord and reconciliation of its rhythmical with its harmonious element, he speaks of the various kinds of satisfaction these elements can achieve. But he also says that when the two elements of a melody are disunited we feel disquieted; the effect of a suspension is to strengthen the longing for the delayed consonance, whose appearance gives a greater satisfaction; and consonant chords are more or less quieting and satisfying, whereas dissonant chords are more or less disquieting – they excite desire – and have an almost painful effect. If these apparent references to the effects of music were intended to be understood strictly, the experience of music would not be merely an analogue of the will's activity – it would essentially involve it: if a dissonant chord arouses a desire for a further chord, when we listen to music our will is not at rest. This uncertainty in Schopenhauer's account is mirrored by the uncertainty we sometimes experience in reading musical theorists as to whether they are describing in figurative terms features we hear in music or, instead, are describing literally our responses to what we hear.

But the indication of a likeness between music and the experience of desire, effort and satisfaction would yield little by itself. For without the addition of two of Schopenhauer's most characteristic theses the diminished form of his theory would fail to explain any of the value he attached to the music. This value is of two kinds: the general value of aesthetic experience and the value specific to music as an art-form. Now the value music shares with the other arts is its capacity to provide experiences which are entirely free from the pain with which, according to Schopenhauer, most of human life is consumed. Music is an occasional consolation in the midst of the misery of life: it delivers us from life for a brief period, we no longer suffer, we experience pleasure. But we will acquiesce in Schopenhauer's assignment of a high value to this capacity only if we accept his extraordinarily pessimistic assessment of human life − taken all in all life is not worth living, since suffering greatly outweighs happiness − and, more importantly, only if we accept his doctrine of the negative nature of pleasure or happiness, which underpins his evaluation.

This doctrine maintains that only pain or desire can be felt positively and that pleasure consists in being freed from pain or desire. And it is used to support Schopenhauer's assessment of human life and the high value he assigns to aesthetic experience by means of the following chain of argument. If someone desires something he suffers from not having what he wants. If this desire is satisfied, either he desires something else or he desires nothing at all. But if he continues to desire something then he continues to suffer. If, however, there is nothing he desires there are two possible states he might be in. It might be that nothing interests him and he is bored. But in that case there is after all something he desires. For someone who is bored experiences a desire for a new desire. But if that is so he continues to suffer. The other possibility is that his consciousness is lost in the contemplation of something and he is in the painless state of aesthetic contemplation. And this last link in the chain gives Schopenhauer the conclusion he desires: aesthetic experience provides the only respite from the suffering integral to human life. But this train of thought is unconvincing, for it rests upon three unfounded suppositions. The first is that the presence of a desire in someone implies that the person is suffering. The second is that the most the satisfaction of a desire can achieve is the removal of the suffering involved in the existence of the desire. The third is that each pleasant experience or condition, except that involved in the state of aesthetic contemplation, is the satisfaction of a preceding desire. The plain fact of the matter is that the relation between pleasure and pain is not the relation between the absence of something and the presence of that thing.

But if we reject Schopenhauer's doctrine of the negative nature of pleasure we require a new explanation of why the disinterested attention to music should be experienced with pleasure. And if we have a less pessimistic view of the possibilities of human life than the view Schopenhauer advocates the supposed quiescence of the will in the aesthetic experience of music will mean correspondingly less to us. We need a more positive conception of the value of musical experience than the one provided by Schopenhauer's general theory of aesthetic experience. Now it might be thought that if we turn to the value specific to music as an art-form we will find this more positive conception. For in the case of the other arts Schopenhauer has maintained that the pleasure of aesthetic experience is sometimes dependent not so much on the state of pure will-less contemplation as on the correlate of this state – the level of that grade of the objectification of the will which one is aware of when in this state. But music goes one step beyond the presentation even of the highest grade of the objectification of the will. Hence, the value of music and the special pleasure it provides might be thought to be largely dependent on music's displaying in the most perspicuous fashion the nature of the will itself. But in the reduced form in which we are considering Schopenhauer's theory of music the significance of the function ascribed to music is greatly diminished and it is unclear what value should be attached to an art-form that embodies analogues of effort, desire and satisfaction and why we should experience its products with delight. For what it makes manifest to us does not have the scope of Schopenhauer's more ambitious conception and each of us is already familiar with much of the variety of its manifestations.

12   This conclusion is given greater force by a defect in Schopenhauer's theory I have so far concealed. Schopenhauer's claim is that music affects us exceptionally powerfully because it presents analogues of the will's activity without causing us pain. But the generality of this explanation guarantees its inadequacy. For much music has no such effect. The theory Schopenhauer puts forward is a theory of the nature of music as an art-form: the essential function of music is to mirror the nature of the will. His thesis about the melodic aspect of music is that it is a representation of conscious goal-directed activity. He asserts that in every melody there is a constant discord and reconciliation of its rhythmic and harmonious elements and that this is an analogue of the origination of new desires and of their satisfaction. But if this is true of each melody the fact that a melody is an analogue of the will's activity is not sufficient to endow it with value, for many melodies have no value. Schopenhauer's theory cannot explain how some but not all musical analogues of the experience of effort, desire and satisfaction can have value, and how some melodies can be finer or more appealing than others, for his theory locates the value of the melodic aspect of music precisely in something that all melodies have in common. In fact, Schopenhauer's account of musical value does not even allow for the possibility that there should be differences of value within the class of melodies. It is true that Schopenhauer deprecates monotonous and meaningless melodies, which are analogous to delay in the excitement of the will and so correspond to boredom. But it is unclear what reason he has for disapproving of the musical representation of boredom whilst commending the representation of the will-aspect of sadness. And although bad music is boring its content is unlikely to correspond to boredom: there are indefinitely many ways in which desire can be checked and then satisfied and which a piece of bad music can be analogous to. The fact that a melody is an analogue of some way in which the will makes itself known in our self-consciousness is insufficient to make it interesting.

13 We have already noticed an uncertainty in Schopenhauer's treatment of music: sometimes he seems to be referring to the effects of music on our feelings and not merely to the analogues of these feelings present in the music.[17] Now what this appears to be indicative of is an obscure awareness on Schopenhauer's part of an unargued transition in the development of his theory of aesthetic experience. For there are two senses in which a person's state can be said to be will-less and Schopenhauer slips from one to the other. On the one hand, a state can be said to be will-less if it is entirely taken up in the contemplation of something disconnected in thought from anything we want in life; on the other hand, a state can be said to be will-less if it is free from any experience of tension, excitement and release. Accordingly, a musical experience is will-less in the first sense if it consists in attention to the sound-patterns of a musical work in themselves and not as indicative of any other things which might be of concern to us. But a musical experience is will-less in the second sense if we are not in any way emotionally affected in undergoing it. Schopenhauer dismisses imitative music as a debasement of the art and insists that the medium of music when properly used is entirely severed from the phenomenal world: phenomena of the world of perception should not be imitated by the sounds of music and in listening to music our attention should be bound to the tones themselves without any thought about the instruments in the phenomenal world which in fact produce them. But if music is considered to be completely independent of the phenomenal world this might encourage the belief that pure music, when listened to in the appropriate manner, is unsuited to produce any disturbance in the individual knowing subject's breast. But this would be false encouragement. For the independence of music from the phenomenal world implies only that the model listener will not be agitated by or about any items other than the sound-patterns of the music. It does not imply that his state of mind will be quite calm. It is plausible to believe that Schopenhauer's desire to represent aesthetic experience as unemotional was fed in the case of music by his view that music is independent of the phenomenal world. But the lack of cogency in the transition from the assertion that aesthetic experience consists in disinterested contemplation to the assertion that aesthetic experience is free from emotion would be liable to make itself felt particularly strongly in the case of music because of the manifest emotionality of much musical experience. And this might occasion the kind of uncertainty in Schopenhauer's writing about music I have indicated.

But even if this speculation is misplaced, Schopenhauer's requirement that musical experience should be free from emotion is unjustified. Let us consider a simple case: the repetition of a musical figure at increasing pitch, volume and tempo. In accordance with Schopenhauer's theory, this can be regarded as an analogue of increasing tension as a desire presses towards fulfilment and the experience of the music can be undergone serenely. But there is another way in which the music might naturally be heard. For the music might build up tension in the listener which is released when the music reaches its climax. And there is no reason to insist that tension and release can enter an aesthetic experience of music only through the experience's containing an analogue of the experience of tension and release. The listener is not debarred from experiencing these feelings themselves; and if he does experience them he violates

Schopenhauer's requirement of aesthetic experience that the world as representation should be entirely separated from the world as will.

14 There is one final feature of Schopenhauer's attitude to music that I have not mentioned. Although he assigns a high value to music as an art-form, this value is in fact equivocal. For his account of the metaphysical significance of music construes the melodic aspect of music not only as representing the nature of the will as it is known in self-consciousness, but as always representing its complete satisfaction and contentment in the final reconciliation of the rhythmic and harmonious elements of a melody. Accordingly, music 'always holds out to us the complete satisfaction of our desires' and it 'penetrates our hearts by flattery'. Now Schopenhauer believed that the prospect of real happiness in life is a delusion: as long as we continue to have desires we will never achieve complete peace of mind. The wise man will therefore wish to free himself from life in the only way in which, according to Schopenhauer, this can truly be accomplished – through resignation in the face of the inevitable misery of life and renunciation of the will-to-live. But music flatters the will-to-live by showing us an image of an ultimate harmony and contentment which in fact cannot be realised in our desires. Hence, music is an occasional consolation in life but not a deliverance from life.

The Prelude to Wagner's *Tristan und Isolde* has rightly been said to be the perfect musical expression of Schopenhauer's philosophy of human life: as life is a process in which each desire is replaced by another as soon as it attains its object, so the Prelude expresses 'endless yearning' – a longing that renews itself without ever receiving final satisfaction. But the Prelude does not fully conform to Schopenhauer's philosophy of music. For, as we have seen, Schopenhauer thought that music always ends by representing the will as gaining complete satisfaction, whereas the continual striving of the music is never fully resolved in the Prelude. And this is not an isolated counter-example to Schopenhauer's view that music penetrates our hearts by flattery. For there are many ways in which music can present a picture of emotional progress that does not inspire us with unfounded hope in the possibility of happiness. If Tchaikovsky's *Pathetique* Symphony pierces our hearts it does not do so by holding out to us the satisfaction of all our desires.

15   Schopenhauer is the musician's philosopher. But Schopenhauer's
philosophy of music is not a fitting monument to the art.

VI
MUSIC AS
UNCONSUMMATED SYMBOL

1   The significance of music as an art-form has often been thought to derive from the fact that some or all musical works are symbols of states of mind or character, attitudes to life and other kinds of extra-musical phenomena. In particular, many pieces of music have been considered to be symbols of the emotional life and to acquire their special importance from their symbolic function. Now this thesis about the significance of music requires amplification, not acceptance or rejection. For the common idea of a symbol is not something clear and distinct: it is a vague, fluctuating, uncertain concept. If a symbol is understood as anything which stands for or represents something else, our understanding of the idea of a symbol will be only as definite as our understanding of the idea of one thing's standing for or representing another. If a symbol must stand for or represent something in some particular way, what is needed is a specification of the required mode of representation. In either case, since the expressions 'stands for' and 'represents' have many different uses, some strict and some loose, an explanation of the idea of a symbol merely in terms of one thing's standing for or representing something else fails to clarify the idea of a symbol to any significant degree. Moreover, it is clear that the class of items to which the term 'symbol' is applied — or, more accurately, the set of relations in which something that is thought of as a symbol stands to what it signifies — is heterogeneous.

Some symbols stand for what they represent in virtue of a convention. It is in this sense that a ring can be a symbol of one person's commitment to another: it is an outward and visible sign of a state of affairs that cannot be directly perceived, and its symbolic function stems from the person's conforming to a common practice. Some symbols are essentially members of a system of symbols: they possess a symbolic function only by virtue of their being members of a symbolism. Pre-eminent amongst symbols of this class is the word: a word possesses its meaning in virtue of belonging to a language; and a language is a particular kind of symbolic system in which the meaning of a compound symbol is determined by the meanings of its constituent symbols and the syntactical rules in accordance with which the constituents are combined. Some symbols stand for what they represent in virtue of their role in a work of art or some other human artefact, where this role is determined by an intention and a nonconventional relationship between the symbol and what it symbolises. In *The Divine Comedy* Dante uses the character of Virgil to symbolise human wisdom; a guttering candle has frequently been used in a film to symbolise the process of dying; Christian paintings have used the butterfly to symbolise the resurrection of Jesus: in each case the symbol fulfils its intended function only because the symbol and what it represents stand in a natural relation which allows the symbol to suggest what it represents. Some symbols stand for what they represent in virtue of there being, within a certain kind of context, a constant correlation between the symbol and what the symbol represents, the thought of what the symbol is representative of being expressed in a disguised form in the symbol. Thus a dream-symbol is an item that, when present in the manifest content of a dream, is constantly correlated with a particular element in the latent dream-thoughts expressed in the hallucinatory experience of the dream.

Now these examples show that different kinds of symbols stand for what they represent in virtue of different kinds of fact. But they also show that not everything that is thought of as a symbol stands for what it represents in the same sense. Furthermore, when an object is understood as a symbol, or when it functions as a symbol, the object may have no interest or importance in itself on that occasion but only as a symbol — so that it would be possible to replace, without significant loss, one symbol by another symbol which stands for the same thing; or those features of the symbol without which it would not symbolise what in fact it does may be interesting in their own right; or those features of the symbol which are not responsible for its semantic function may also make a significant contribution to the symbol's effectiveness as a symbol or to its overall effect. Hence, it is essential that the nature of the supposed symbolic function of music should be clarified before we can assess the thesis that it is integral to the value of some or all musical works that they are, in the intended sense, symbols. The most notable attempt to effect such a clarificä'ion is the theory of music elaborated by Susanne Langer in *Philosophy in ͵' New Key.*[1]

2   The following set of propositions encapsulates Langer's theory of music:
(i) Each significant piece of music is a symbol.
(ii) But it is not a discursive symbol.
(iii) It is a presentational symbol.
(iv) But it has a peculiarity not possessed by most presentational symbols: it is an unconsummated symbol.
(v) It symbolises the mere form of a feeling.
But the concepts of a symbol, a discursive symbol, a presentational symbol, an unconsummated symbol and the form of a feeling need to be explained, and in the next four sections I shall expound Langer's account of these notions.

3   *The concept of a symbol.* The account Langer gives of her concept of a symbol proceeds in the following way. An item is a symbol only if it is employed as a symbol: it must be a symbol to or for someone. A necessary condition for one thing to be a symbol of something else is that the two items should have a similar structure: there must be a one-to-one correspondence between the structures of the elements of the two items. Put differently: there must be a rule of 'projection' that projects the structure of the one item into the structure of the other. Or: the items must have the same 'logical form'. Now if a symbol and the object it symbolises must share a common logical form, each would be a symbol of the other if it were not that there is a feature the one possesses and the other lacks and which makes the one a symbol of the other and not vice versa. What distinguishes a symbol from its object is the state of mind of the person for whom the symbol is a symbol of that object. He finds one item — the object — more interesting than the other — the symbol — but he finds the second item easier to take in: the symbol facilitates the knowledge the person requires of the symbol's object. The symbol is the vehicle for the conception of the object: the instrument someone uses to think of the object. The essential function of a symbol is that it leads a person to conceive, to think of, what it symbolises. Therefore, an item is a symbol of something if it has a similar structure to that thing and is used by someone to conceive that thing.

Accordingly, each picture, musical score, map and proposition is a symbol. A picture is a symbol, not a duplicate, of what it represents because it leads people who perceive it to conceive the object it represents and it does so by virtue of its possessing an arrangement of elements analogous to the arrangement of salient visual elements in the object represented by it. A musical score is a symbol of a symphony because it is used to conceive the symphony and there is a rule of projection that projects the symphony into the score: in the existence of such a rule lies the internal similarity between the symphony and the score — two items which at first seem so different. A map is a map of a particular region because the structure of the relevant geographical features corresponds, via some rule of projection, with the structure of the elements of the map and this enables people to use it to conceive the region. It is therefore a symbol of the region it maps. Finally, a proposition is a symbol because it has the same structure as a state of affairs and is used to conceive that state of affairs.

4 *Discursive and presentational symbols.* According to Langer, there are two kinds of symbol: linguistic (or discursive) and non-linguistic (or presentational). A language in the strict sense is a symbolic system that functions symbolically in a particular way. It has a vocabulary and a syntax: it has elements (words) with fixed meanings, out of which can be constructed, according to syntactical rules, new units with meanings determined by the meanings of the elements and the syntactical rules. Some words of the language may be equivalent in meaning to combinations of other words in the language and different single words may have the same meaning. Hence, words can be defined and there can be translation from one language into another. A discursive symbol is a symbol that belongs to a discursive symbolism: a symbolism which is such that the symbolic function of its symbols is determined in the same way as that of language. A wordless, non-discursive, presentational symbol, on the other hand, does not belong to a symbolism and does not symbolise by means of discrete, fixed units of meaning. The elements of a presentational symbol are understood only through the meaning of the whole symbol: through their relations within the total structure of elements — as in the case of a picture. The coloured marks that compose a picture are not independent items with fixed meanings, possibly equivalent in meaning to other primitive or compound sets of marks. In order to appreciate what a picture is a picture of we do not need to remember, from previous pictures we have encountered, what certain coloured marks conventionally represent and understand what this picture represents on the basis of our memory of the fixed meanings of these elements and our understanding of the rules of syntax in accordance with which these elements are combined. We understand the coloured marks of a picture holistically: we do not credit each of them with a meaning that is independent of the marks which are adjacent to or which surround it, and through understanding one by one what each mark means understand the complete configuration: we understand a particular mark only in the context of adjacent marks, each of which in turn we understand only in its context. A picture represents what it does in a different manner from a sentence. A picture is not a discursive symbol: it is a presentational symbol.

A presentational symbol must lack elements with fixed meanings which, in accordance with rules of combination, determine the meaning of the symbol itself; but, like any symbol, a presentational symbol must consist of interrelated elements, so that it can be taken to represent some other item whose elements have the same structure: some other item for which there exists a rule of projection that projects the structure of the one item into the structure of the other. Now each kind of projection has a limited range: it ranges over some, but not all, kinds of thing. Mercator projection, for example, is applicable only to spatial objects and even then only to their spatial features. The particular form of language is discursive form: the presentation in a linear, successive order of a complex symbol consisting of discrete items with fixed meanings which determine the meaning of the symbol. If there is anything that cannot be projected into discursive form (and Langer believes there is), it is inconceivable by means of words. If it is capable of being symbolised it must be projectible into a presentational symbol. And if it is so projected it is made conceivable. Hence, if there is anything that cannot be projected into a discursive symbolism but can be projected into a presentational symbol, propositional thought is not the only way in which something can be conceived.

5 *Music as a presentational symbol.* Now what is the primary artistic function of music? Its main artistic function is not to serve as a symptom or an expression of the composer's emotions. Nor is it to evoke emotions in those who listen to it. Langer's thesis is that the principal artistic function of music is to symbolise feelings: emotions, moods, mental tensions and resolutions and other kinds of mental state. In music feelings are made conceivable: they can be envisaged and understood. It is not the composer's emotions that are expressed in music but his knowledge of emotional life; and what music provides the listener with are not feelings — his own or the composer's — but insight into feelings.

If the artistic function of music is symbolic, music must form a set either of discursive symbols or of presentational symbols. But it is clear that music cannot properly be thought of as a language in the strict sense, for it lacks a true vocabulary and syntax. A musical work is therefore a presentational symbol. But if it is a symbol it must possess a structure analogous to the structure of the phenomenon it symbolises: it must share a common logical form with its object. And the way in which a musical work can resemble some segment of emotional life is by its possessing the same temporal structure as that segment. The dynamic structure, the mode of development, of a musical work and the 'form' in which emotion is experienced can resemble each other in their 'patterns of motion and rest, of tension and release, of agreement and disagreement, preparation, fulfilment, excitation, sudden change, etc.'.[2] Music is a presentational symbol of emotional life.

6 *The forms of feeling and the unconsummated symbol.* But if we reflect upon the nature of emotions it is clear that experiences as classified by the most general emotion terms have no special 'forms'. Each instance of a certain emotion will have a particular form — a particular manner of development — but different instances of the same kind of emotion can have different forms and instances of different kinds of emotion can have the same form. Anger, for example, can take many different forms: it can suddenly flare up and be as quickly dissipated or it can be slow to grow and, perhaps, slow to disappear; and each of these forms are ways in which fear and other emotions can manifest themselves. And this conclusion holds also for emotions and feelings for which we do not have simple terms. How, then, can music be thought of as symbolising different feelings and emotions?

There are two important qualifications that Langer introduces to her thesis that musical works are symbols of feelings, and these serve to answer this question. The first qualification is that the feelings music articulates have forms which cannot be represented in language. According to Langer, language is a very poor medium for expressing how we feel. Its inadequacy is due to its discursive nature. A symbolic medium can represent anything that is congruent with it (by some rule of projection). Anything that is not of the same logical form as language is not discursively formulable. But there is a lack of fit between the nature of the felt process of life and the symbolic nature of language:

> the forms of feeling and the forms of discursive expression are logically incommensurate, so that any exact concepts of feeling and emotion cannot be projected into the logical form of literal language. Verbal statement . . . is almost useless for conveying knowledge about the precise character of the affective life. Crude designations like 'joy', 'sorrow', 'fear' tell us as little about vital experience as general words like 'thing', 'being', or 'place' tell us about the world of our perceptions. Any more precise reference to feeling is usually made by mentioning the circumstance that suggests it — 'a mood of autumn evening', 'a holiday feeling'.[3]

Since language cannot articulate the structure of our emotional life we can refer to it in language only in a highly general, vague and superficial manner. But the dynamic form of our emotional life perfectly corresponds with the nature of music and, Langer writes, 'because the forms of human feeling are much more congruent with musical forms than with the forms of language, music can *reveal* the nature of feelings with a detail and truth that language cannot approach.'[4]

The second qualification to the thesis that musical works are symbols of feelings is that it is only the 'morphology' of feeling that music can actually reflect. Now feelings of different kinds can share the same morphology: a feeling of sadness and a feeling of happiness can rise and decline and intertwine with other feelings in similar ways. Hence, music has all the features of a true symbolism except the existence of a fixed import: some musical forms can bear a sad and a happy interpretation equally well. And so music, although it is a symbolic form that represents feeling, is an 'unconsummated symbol': it symbolises not the different feelings — by means of the different forms of the different kinds of feeling — but instead the common forms that different kinds of feeling sometimes share. Music is a presentational symbol of feeling; but it represents only the morphology of feeling and not its complete nature.

With these qualifications Langer's theory of musical significance is complete.[5] And I now turn to criticism.

7   The requirement Langer imposes on a discursive symbol — that it should have a similar structure to the structure of whatever it symbolises — is taken from the theory of language put forward by Wittgenstein in the *Tractatus Logico-Philosophicus*.[6] In this work Wittgenstein thought

of a discursive symbol as a 'picture' of a fact and a fact as the existence or non-existence of a state of affairs. A state of affairs was thought of as a combination of 'objects'; the determinate way in which objects are connected in a state of affairs was the structure of the state of affairs; the form of a state of affairs was the possibility of its structure; the structure of a fact consisted in the structures of states of affairs; the determinate way in which the elements of a picture are related to one another was the structure of the picture; and the possibility of this structure was the pictorial form of the picture. And he claimed that in order for a picture to be able to depict a fact – correctly or incorrectly – it must have the same form as the fact. Now although Langer takes over Wittgenstein's terminology, she does not use his terms of art 'fact', 'state of affairs', 'object', 'structure' and 'form' in the same way. For Wittgenstein, an object is both simple (non-composite) and unalterable. But Langer uses the term 'object' in such a loose fashion that anything at all can be called an object. Hence she produces only a verbal imitation of Wittgenstein's view when she writes:

> a proposition fits a fact not only because it contains names for the things and actions involved in the fact, but also because it combines them in a pattern analogous, somehow, to the pattern in which the named objects are 'in fact' combined. *A proposition is a picture of a structure   the structure of a state of affairs.*[7]

Her notion of the pattern in which named objects are combined, or the structure of a state of affairs, appears not to have been thought through.[8] The crucial concepts of the structure of a discursive symbol and the structure of a state of affairs stand in need of explanation, and this obligation cannot be discharged by appeal to Wittgenstein's work. But Langer does not give a clear, alternative explanation of these ideas, and in consequence her requirement that a discursive symbol should have the same structure as the 'object' it symbolises cannot be assessed.

8   The requirement imposed on a discursive symbol is also imposed on a presentational symbol. And it is used to make a case for the importance of presentational symbols. Langer's claim is that there are certain phenomena that language cannot symbolise because of a disparity between the form of these phenomena and the discursive form of language. Consequently, these phenomena cannot be conceived through language. But, so the argument continues, presentational symbols have the necessary structure to symbolise – and so to yield insight into –

these phenomena. In the case of music the insight it provides – an insight that language cannot rival – is said to be the capacity to conceive the so-called forms of feeling. But in fact the claim that the dynamic structure of our feelings cannot be captured in a discursive symbolism has no foundation. It is certainly true that we often find it difficult to describe exactly how we feel. But the difficulty rarely concerns the mode of development, the 'morphology', of our feelings. And it is this that Langer denies language can represent. But there is no inherent difficulty in describing the form of our feelings (in Langer's sense). When we find it difficult to describe our feelings it is the nature or quality of our experience – rather than its temporal pattern – that eludes our attempts at articulation in language. One reason for this difficulty is that our feelings are sometimes in an inchoate state and the difficulty we experience in precisely rendering them in language is due to the fact that the feelings are themselves imprecise. In this kind of case it is only when we become conscious of the exact nature of what we feel that our feeling becomes exact. But whatever the reason for the difficulty there is no plausibility in the view that the present quality of our feelings has a structure that is incommensurable with that of any discursive symbol and that this structure can be more perfectly reflected by a presentational symbol. And although there is sometimes a difficulty in describing how we feel, the nature of our feelings is not something that in principle resists representation in language.

The view that verbal statement is almost useless for conveying knowledge about the precise character of our affective life is made plausible only by an underestimation of the resources available in language for describing how we feel. Langer is misled by the emphasis she places on generic words for emotions into thinking that language must be unspecific in its description of feelings – and this alleged inadequacy is then explained as a consequence of the discrepancy between the mode of representation of language and the structure of our emotive life. But the explanation is redundant. For it is not true that we are restricted in the characterisation of the way we feel to the common words for the various kinds of emotion, supplemented only by reference to some circumstance that suggests the feeling. Feelings of the kind Langer refers to in her discussion of the significance of music derive their articulation and complexity from the articulation and complexity of the thoughts they are founded upon. Hence, precision can be introduced to the characterisation of a feeling by the specification of the thoughts integral to it. And since there is no thought which has a content that cannot be represented in language, there is no difficulty of principle in characterising precisely the particular nature of a feeling.

9   But Langer's theory of the significance of music might still be thought to be substantially correct, despite the defects in her account of language. It is therefore necessary to examine in more detail the claims she makes about the nature and value of music. She believes that the main value of art in general, and music in particular, consists in its presenting feeling in such a manner that we can reflect on it and understand it. The aim of art is to provide insight into the essential nature of felt life. Now one way in which art can achieve this aim is by the creation of analogues of the feelings we already have. But there is another, more important way in which art can perform its function: it can make us aware of new feelings which we can incorporate into or impress on our life. The theory she puts forward maintains that discursive symbolism — language in its non-poetic use — transforms our awareness of and relation to the physical world, imposing patterns on our experience, whereby William James's 'blooming, buzzing confusion' of sense perception in its infancy is broken up into units and groups, events, things and relations, causes and effects. And what discursive symbolism achieves for our awareness of the physical world the arts achieve for our awareness of emotion and feeling: 'they give inward experiences form and thus make them conceivable . . . a musical person thinks of emotions musically'.[9] And so the arts not only give us knowledge of feelings, but form or shape our emotive experience. The arts educate feeling by developing its scope and quality. They construct forms for feeling to assume, as language provides forms for sensory experience to realise. Through art we acquire insight into feelings we already have; but we also become aware of new possibilities for our feelings to adopt.

But Langer's theory of music asserts music to be an unconsummated symbol and her idea that art educates feeling by making us aware of new, perhaps more subtle, ways for us to feel breaks down in the case of music. For all an unconsummated symbol can do to make us aware of further possibilities of feeling is to present new forms for feelings to follow: unfamiliar modes of development, change and intermingling. And this seems to have no importance. In fact, there appear to be no possibilities of this kind we are ignorant of and music could manifest to us. If we are unaware of varieties of feeling it is not the possible ways in which feelings might alter that are unfamiliar to us. (This complements the criticism of the supposed recalcitrance of feeling to discursive symbolism.)

10   The justification for Langer's emphasis on the forms of feeling is weakened by the fact that feelings have no special forms which distinguish them from many other kinds of phenomena. We have already noticed that the various emotions and feelings are not differentiated from each other by their forms: instances of the same kind of emotion or feeling can have different forms and instances of different kinds of emotion or feeling can have the same form. But neither is the class of emotions and feelings differentiated from all other classes by the kinds of forms they follow. The ways in which emotions and feelings can develop have nothing distinctive about them that is not shared with the modes of development of the rising and setting of the sun, the mounting of a storm, the explosion of a volcano and countless other natural and artificial processes.[10] Hence, even if musical works have structures congruent with the forms in which feelings can be realised these forms are not specific to feelings (and works of art). And if all that a musical work can represent is something not specific to feeling Langer's view of a musical work as a presentational symbol of a form of, specifically, feeling is unwarranted. Just as the fact that sadness and happiness can follow the same form led Langer to the view that music reflects only the morphology of feeling, the further fact that feeling has no special forms should have forced an additional retreat from the idea of music as in some sense a representational art: music reflects only the morphology of processes. If feeling is the desired object of music and music can present only its form and not its nature, the musical symbol is certainly unconsummated. But its plight is worse than Langer's theory allows. For it is twice-removed from the condition it desires: it not only lacks the ability to make the content of feelings part of itself, but the forms it can assume do not unite it more closely with the life of feeling than with the course of processes it does not care to be joined to.

In fact, Langer's derivation of the unconsummated nature of the musical symbol is imperfect. It would be an obvious mistake to conclude from the fact that some music bears equally well a sad and a happy interpretation that music can reflect only the morphology of feeling. For much music is susceptible of just one of the two interpretations. And this is not because some happy conditions possess a form not shared with any sad conditions, or vice versa, but because music is not restricted to reflecting the morphology of feeling. Now Langer does not commit the mistake mentioned above. Her conclusion that music is an unconsummated symbol is derived from the premiss that an instance of happiness and an instance of sadness can have the same morphology.

And if this premiss is to have the implication Langer requires its meaning must be that each instance of happiness can be correlated with a possible instance of sadness which has the same form, and each instance of sadness can be correlated with a possible instance of happiness which has the same form. But even if it is understood in this way it does not deliver the required conclusion that music is an unconsummated symbol without the addition of the further premiss that no part of the content of any feeling can be reflected in music. And this is neither argued for nor manifestly true. Moreover, there is at least one aspect of many feelings that music has been thought to be as well suited to present an image of as it is to reflect the forms of feeling — and that is their hedonic aspect. If happiness and sadness are understood as episodes people experience, each instance of happiness involves the experience of pleasure or contentment and each instance of sadness involves the experience of pain or discontentment. Hence, if music can represent pain and pleasure, happiness and sadness do not need to be distinguished by their forms for a musical work to be susceptible of only a happy as opposed to a sad interpretation, or vice versa. It would only be if the hedonic aspect of our emotive life were incapable of representation in music that music would be restricted to being a mirror of the morphology of feeling. Langer fails to show that the limits of music's power to represent feeling must be drawn in this fashion and Schopenhauer's more liberal view, which denies to music only the capacity to represent the thought a feeling may involve, is clearly more penetrating.

11   Langer's thesis that music is a presentational symbol of the morphology of feeling therefore does not assign to music as great a significance as she believes. And several further considerations rob her theory of music of any lingering appeal it might have.

In the first place, it follows from Langer's account of the concept of a symbol that, characteristically, we do not experience music as any kind of symbol at all. Her requirement is that one item is for a certain person a symbol of another item if, and only if, the two items have a similar structure and the person uses the first item to conceive the second item: his interest in the symbol is only instrumental — it allows him to acquire knowledge of the item it stands for, and it is this that really concerns him. Now it is true that when we use a map to find our way in a strange country, or when we listen to the sounds someone utters in order to find out what his opinion is, our interest is not in the map or the utterance *qua* physical object or event. In so far as we treat

115

the map or the utterance as a symbol we interpret its semantically significant physical features, and do not attend to the intrinsic nature of
the symbol as something interesting in its own right. But when we listen
to music we do not in general attend to it in the way we attend to
something we are using as the vehicle for the conception of something
else. The music fills our consciousness and no thought of anything else
is present to our mind. We do not conceive the form of a feeling by
listening to the music, as we do conceive a person's opinion by hearing
him speak, or as we do form a conception of our route by looking at a
map. The music is intrinsically appealing, and there is nothing we find
more interesting and are listening to the music to acquire knowledge of.
Consequently, it is not in general true for the listener that music is any
kind of symbol (in the sense given to the idea of a symbol by Langer).
Furthermore, this manner of listening to music in abstraction from the
symbolic function Langer assigns it can enable the listener to understand
the music and it can provide him with an experience he values for its
own sake. Hence, even if it is possible to listen to music as an unconsummated symbol it is not necessary to do so in order to understand it
as a work of art; and even if music has a value as the iconic representation
of the form of our inner life this is not the only value it has as a work
of art.

12   Now this leads naturally to the second consideration. For the
value Langer's theory assigns to music as an unconsummated symbol is
purely cognitive, and a purely cognitive theory of art, as has often been
argued, fails to do justice to the significance art has in our lives. If
music is an unconsummated symbol that provides us with knowledge of
the forms of feeling, there seems to be no reason why we should value
the experience of music intrinsically, rather than merely instrumentally,
and no reason why we should listen repeatedly to music we know well.
The acquisition of knowledge is not always an intrinsically rewarding
activity, and if the knowledge is retained there is no reason to repeat an
activity the sole aim of which is to acquire that knowledge. If knowledge
is extracted and retained – the extraction being rewarding or unrewarding – a return to the source of the knowledge must be motivated by
some desire other than the desire to acquire that knowledge.

To meet this objection it would be necessary to maintain, firstly,
that the kind of insight music can provide us with is something we find
rewarding to receive and, secondly, that the knowledge we acquire in
listening to music cannot be extracted and retained. Now Langer does

not appear to offer any reason why we should find it rewarding to gain knowledge of the form of a feeling through listening to a musical work which has an analogous structure to that form. But she does have available an explanation for the frequency with which we return to works we admire. For she believes that the forms of our feelings vanish from our consciousness immediately and collapse into highly condensed versions of themselves: they escape the efforts of our memory to retain them in detail.[11] These forms can be made permanent in works of art, to which we can turn in order to recover them. Now if the forms of feeling are elusive the analogous forms of musical works that symbolise them will also, it seems, be elusive. And in that case the knowledge we acquire in listening to music cannot be extracted from the music and retained in our memory. Hence, a musical work that fixes the form of a feeling is never redundant: it must be returned to whenever we want knowledge of that form (if nothing else symbolically presents the same form). But this explanation is inadequate on two counts. In the first place, it misrepresents our motivation for listening to music we are familiar with. We return again and again to the same musical work not to acquire knowledge that slips from our memory at the very moment we acquire it − which would be extremely frustrating; our reason is to undergo once more an experience we find intrinsically rewarding. Secondly, the explanation would fit only those musical works which have a structure of such complexity we can never fully remember it. But there is some music − an attractive melody, for example − whose relative simplicity allows us to remember its form perfectly; and the appeal of such music is not essentially different from that of less simple music.

13 The third consideration concerns Langer's requirement that the structure of the elements of a presentational symbol must correspond to the structure of the elements of the item it symbolises. This requirement is not so much unjustified, as unclear. For in the case of music − and we need consider no other case − the idea of the structure of a musical work is indefinite, if for no other reason than the possibility of considering musical structure in greater or less detail or with reference to a different specification of the elements of a musical work. There is no determinate context-free answer to the question, What, exactly, is the structure of Beethoven's *Diabelli* Variations? It might be suggested that each musical work can be considered at different levels of generality and, accordingly, its structure thought of in a more or less specific way. And more or less

117

specific forms of feeling will correspond to the various characterisations of the work's structure. But this would not solve the problem. For in one sense — at a high level of generality — the *Diabelli* Variations consists of a theme and thirty-three variations — and that is a form it is extremely unlikely any person's feelings will ever follow. And if the structure of the work is analysed in greater detail the probability of someone's feelings taking that form is not raised but lowered. In fact, the likelihood of feeling assuming the form of a musical work is always inversely proportional to the detail with which the structure of the work is specified: the less detailed the structure the greater the likelihood; and the highest value of this likelihood may still be extremely low — as in the case of such musical forms as theme and variations or fugue. The truth is that if the structure of a musical work can be fitted to some form feeling is likely to follow this will only be in so general a manner as to omit most of the detail that gives the music its value.

14 The final consideration that tells decisively against the view of music as an unconsummated symbol is the fact that the view does not allow for the manifest possibility that different works have different musical values. We have already indicated the latitude with which the notion of the structure of a musical work must be interpreted to make plausible the claim that it is congruent with a form of feeling. But in any case there is just as much reason to regard each undistinguished work as reflecting a possible form of feeling as to regard each significant work as doing so. However the idea of the structure of a musical work is to be understood, and whatever the level to which it is to be applied, distinguished and undistinguished works will stand in the same relation to the forms of feeling. But if it is not true that each impressive musical work, and no other musical work, is a presentational symbol of the morphology of feeling, the significance of music as an art-form cannot consist merely in music's being an unconsummated symbol. For an explanation of the significance of music is an explanation of its value as art; and just as not every discursive symbol has literary value, not every musical presentational symbol has musical value. If each musical work is an unconsummated symbol its musical value must depend upon further features of the work: the nature of the form of feeling it symbolises, the particular manner in which it represents this form, or some characteristic unrelated to its being an unconsummated symbol. But neither of the first two possibilities appears suitable to serve as a basis for the evaluation of music and acceptance of the third possibility would imply the abandonment of the theory of music as unconsummated symbol.

Now in fact Langer maintains that any work which articulates and presents feeling to our understanding is artistically good; a work of art expresses feeling well or badly and is accordingly good or bad; and bad art is corruption of feeling.[12] But in order to draw a distinction between a musical work which expresses a feeling well and one which expresses a feeling badly there must be a means of determining the structure of the feeling a work is designed to represent other than by identifying it as a form that is analogous to the structure of the work. And if corruption of feeling is understood as distortion of feeling then a bad work of music must have a different form from the feeling it distorts, and this could be shown to be so only if it is possible to establish the form of the feeling distorted other than by reading it directly off the form of the work itself. But if it is necessary to determine in a manner independent of the form of a musical work itself the form of feeling that is supposed to be the subject of the work — if it is necessary to do this in order to establish the accuracy of the work — what method is available? Although Langer believes that '"artistic truth", so called, is the truth of a symbol to the forms of feeling',[13] she fails to see the need to answer this question.

If an art-form is supposed to be able to provide us with knowledge of a certain kind then, unless reason is given to the contrary, it should equally be possible for it to misinform us. If a musical work can be true to a form of feeling, and its musical value reside in this fact, then it seems that a musical work could be false to a form of feeling, and this should be a defect in the work. For, as I have argued, there is no plausibility in the view that either a musical work possesses musical value, in which case there is a possible form of feeling it is congruent with, or it lacks value, in which case there is no form of feeling it is congruent with. But in fact we make no use of the conception of such a kind of falsity or, correlatively, such a kind of truth.[14] We have no independent means of access to the form a musical work is intended to symbolise and by reference to which we can measure the music's success or failure in embodying the form of a feeling.[15] According to Langer's theory we could not have recourse to the composer's intention, for the composer cannot specify the form in words and the only articulated symbol available to him is the work itself (unless, as is unlikely, he regards another work of art as symbolising the same form his work has attempted to capture). And if we cannot reach the intended form by way of the composer's intention, and if in the case of good and bad music alike the possibility of fitting the structure of the music to some form feeling might follow is the same, the idea that the significance of music lies in its ability to symbolise forms of feeling is quite empty.

VII
MUSIC AS THE EXPRESSION
OF EMOTION

1　The expression theory of art has assumed many forms. These changes
of appearance have been necessitated by the inadequacy of its original
leading idea. This maintains that the creator of a work of art undergoes
an experience which he wishes to transmit or communicate to others.
He wishes to communicate the experience to others in the sense that he
wishes others also to undergo the experience; and to this end he creates
or imagines an object which is or can be made perceptible – a painted
canvas, a complex of musical sounds, a structure of words – and which
is so designed as to make it possible for someone who experiences the
object in the right manner thereby to undergo the very experience the
artist intended to transmit. His experience is inside him; in order to
make it available to others he must externalise it; and by expressing it
he hopes to pass it on to others. To the extent that the artist is successful in his enterprise, and in so far as the experience he communicates is
worth experiencing, the work of art he creates is valuable.

Tolstoy put forward a theory of just this kind in *What is Art?*:

> To evoke in oneself a feeling one has once experienced and having
> evoked it in oneself then by means of movements, lines, colours,
> sounds, or forms expressed in words, so to transmit that feeling that
> others experience the same feeling – this is the activity of art.
>
> Art is a human activity consisting in this, that one man consciously
> by means of certain external signs, hands on to others feelings he has
> lived through, and that others are infected by these feelings and also
> experience them.[1]

And for Tolstoy it is the best and highest feelings that are expressed in

121

and communicated through the finest works of art: the better the feeling transmitted the better is the art that transmits it.

2   Whenever something is transmitted from A to B it must be possible to distinguish what is transmitted from its mode of transmission; if information is what is transmitted, the message is not the medium. An expression theory of art of the transmission kind is therefore committed to giving an account of what general kinds of experience are transmitted by the different art-forms and what more specific kinds are transmitted by the different works of art within these forms — an account which must fully characterise the intrinsic nature of the experience without reference to the medium or work of art by which it is transmitted.

3   It is usually held by adherents of such an expression-transmission theory that the experiences music transmits are moods, feelings and emotions. Accordingly, the composer is conceived as transforming his emotions into musical sounds which are transformed into patterns in a score which, in turn, are transformed back into musical sounds which, finally, are transformed back into emotions that the sympathetic listener experiences as he hears the music.

By far the most substantial version of the transmission form of the expression theory of music was constructed by Deryck Cooke in his *The Language of Music* — from which I have taken the preceding account of the process of musical communication.[2] Deryck Cooke's distinctive contribution to the expression theory of music was his attempt to analyse the elements of musical expression, and to establish the essentials of a musical lexicon which would specify the emotive meaning of the basic terms of musical vocabulary and by reference to which music's ability to serve as a vehicle for the communication of emotion could be vindicated. He tried to demonstrate (within Western tonal music since 1400) correlations between emotions and particular musical patterns of sound which have been used to express these emotions: the expressive meaning of such a sound pattern is constant — and the sound pattern therefore forms part of the vocabulary of music. Now the idea that music is a language of the emotions is often criticised on the ground that music lacks an essential requirement of a language: a syntax. A dictionary which defines the basic vocabulary of the supposed language of music by assigning emotions to primitive melodic phrases omits a necessary feature of a language — a feature without which the so-called 'language' can say nothing — for it provides only a vocabulary and not rules which determine the meaning of a whole in virtue of the

122

meanings of its semantic elements and their arrangement. Of course, if music is not a true language then it has no true vocabulary. And this is indeed the case; the 'meanings' of what are believed to be its basic terms do not need to be learnt in the way the meanings of the words of a language − which are conventionally determined − must be learnt; nor do they need to be remembered − as the meanings of words must be − in order to understand uses of them. Nevertheless, this criticism is misdirected if the idea of music as a language is intended only as a metaphor, the force of which is that music is a means of communication of moods, feelings and emotions.[3] But the fact that this objection is misconceived does not put the theory of which Deryck Cooke's version is the most distinguished representative in the clear. For the truth is that his version of the theory − whatever its merits and other defects − inherits the critical weakness of all forms of the theory.

4   The fundamental error of the transmission form of the expression theory of music is its separation of what gives music its value − according to the theory, the experience it transmits from composer to listener − from the music itself. It represents a musical work as being related in a certain way to an experience which can be fully characterised without reference to the nature of the work itself. It therefore regards music purely as a tool: the function of the tool is to arouse in the listener the experience the composer wishes him to feel. But the obligation to provide an independent description of the experience can never properly be discharged. For the theory misrepresents the nature of the value music has for those who appreciate it as music. It implies that there is an experience which a musical work produces in the listener but which in principle he could undergo even if he were unfamiliar with the work, just as the composer is supposed to have undergone the experience he wishes to communicate before he constructs the musical vehicle which is intended to transmit it to others; and the value of the music, if it is an effective instrument, is determined by the value of this experience. But there is no such experience.

If we suppose that there is such an experience we must, as we have seen, concede the possibility that the experience a particular work transmits − the transmission of which is its *raison d'être* − should be transmitted in some other way. But if the value of the music really were determined by the nature of this suppositious experience, we would have no special reason to listen to the music if this alternative mode of transmission were available to us. The music would be replaced by this other mode of transmission or by anything else which equally achieved the same end. But it is certain that we value music for its own sake and not merely as a means to some end that can be characterised without reference to the music. When we are eager to listen to Elgar's *Violin Concerto* our reason is not that it happens to be the sole means available for producing in us an experience which does not itself involve hearing the music: we value the experience of the music itself.

5   The separation of what gives a musical work its value from the intrinsic nature of the work – a separation that is entailed by the idea of music as merely a vehicle for the transmission from composer to listener of something other than and independent of itself – prevents expression theories of the transmission kind from doing justice to the appeal of music in general and of music which really is expressive of emotion in particular. For even in the case of music which is expressive of emotion and which is valued for its expressiveness, the reason the music is attractive to us is not because it yields an experience which in principle could be detached from the experience of the music. In fact, music can be valued as music in virtue of its expressive aspect only if the experience of music as expressive of a state of mind is not thought of as a mere combination of experiences – an experience of the music which does not relate it to the state of mind and an experience of the state of mind – each of which would be possible without the other. For if someone's experience of a piece of music is a compound of two experiences, one of which is an experience of hearing the music in which the music is not related to a certain kind of emotion, for example, the other of which is an experience of that emotion – the first experience giving rise to the second experience – then either the person's experience of the emotion has the music as its object or it does not. But, to take the first alternative, if it does have the music as its object then the person does not hear the music as being expressive of that emotion or as possessing that quality of emotion: music that bores is boring and not thereby bored or expressive of boredom; music heard with admiration is admired and not in consequence admiring or expressive of admiration; music that arouses amusement is amusing and not in virtue of that fact amused or expressive of amusement. If, on the other hand, the person's experience of the emotion does not have the music as its object then the reason he values his experience of the music – an experience compounded of two elements – will be (i) solely because he values its first element, or (ii) solely because he values its second element, or (iii) because he values each

element, or (iv) because he values neither element in itself but only the two as so combined. But if (i) gives his reason for valuing his experience, he does not value the music *as expressive of the emotion in question*. If (ii) gives his reason, he does not value the music *as music*. Now if (iii) gives his reason, he would value his experience if it contained only one or the other of the two elements. However, if to begin with it consisted of just the first element − and this is the only relevant case − then although he would then value the music as music, the addition of the second element (as an effect of the first) would not make his total experience one in which he values the music as expressive of the emotion in question. For, as we have seen, when an emotion has the music as its object the experience of the emotion as an effect of the music is insufficient for the music to be heard as expressive of that emotion. And this conclusion holds with equal force in the case of an emotion that does not have the music as its object: music that saddens is not thereby sad or expressive of sadness.[4] Finally, if (iv) gives the person's reason for valuing his experience, he would not value his experience if it contained only the first element. And it is clear that the addition of the second element to the first is insufficient to constitute an experience in which the music is valued as music, and, moreover, as being expressive of the emotion it arouses. Therefore, as I claimed, music can be valued for its expressive aspect only if the experience of music as expressive of an emotion (more generally, a state of mind) is not thought of as a mere combination of experiences of the kinds indicated.

Hence what is needed from a theory of musical expression is a less external, a more intimate, connection between the experience of what music expresses and the experience of the music itself: it is necessary in some way to fuse the experience of the mood, feeling or emotion expressed by a musical work with the experience of the music which gives it expression, or to integrate the experience of what music expresses with the experience of the music. It is necessary to avoid the heresy of the separable experience.[5]

Now my interest here is not the expression theory of music itself but, instead, a correct theory of musical expression: a theory which explains what it is for music to be expressive of emotion, what it is for music to be heard as expressive of emotion and what kinds of value can attach to musical expressiveness.[6] In what follows I explore the possibility that an accurate account of the musical expression of emotion should be based upon something which itself can be expressive of emotion: the human voice.

6 The natural model for a theory of artistic expression, if we take the term 'expression' seriously, is the expression of inner states in and by the human body: by facial expression, posture, gesture, movement, words and cries. It is in some cases easy to exploit this model by the construction of an artefact that can be imagined to stand – and which is intended to be experienced as though it stood – to an inner state in a relation similar to one or the other of the relations in which the real expression in and by the human body may stand to the state of which it is the expression.[7] There are some works of art that can properly be experienced as if they were human expression. For example, there is a form of poetry – lyric poetry (in one sense of the term) – that consists in the representation in an arrangement of words from the point of view of the first person of someone's outward verbal expression of his mental condition or of the internal counterpart of this. A lyric poem is a particular kind of verbal representation of a person expressing his thoughts and feelings in speech or a representation of his process of thought and feeling itself. A lyric poem can therefore be experienced as if it were the speech or internal voice of someone giving expression to others or to himself to some complex of thoughts, attitudes and emotions. When we experience a poem in this way we imagine someone experiencing an emotion – I shall concentrate on this element – which he expresses in the words that compose the lines of the poem. But, as R. K. Elliott has insisted,[8] when we experience a poem as if it were the human expression of emotion our imagination can proceed in one or other of two ways: we can experience the poem 'from within' or 'from without' (or we can alternate between these different imaginative modes). To experience the poem from within is to place oneself, in imagination, in the situation of the poem's 'speaker' and to experience the expression and the emotion expressed from that position. One identifies oneself imaginatively with the person whom one imagines experiencing an emotion and expressing it in the words which compose the lines of the poem. To experience the poem from without one does not place oneself, in imagination, in the situation of the poem's speaker. One imagines someone giving expression to his emotion in the poem but one does not identify with him imaginatively.

7 Let the emotional condition the poem expresses be E. Then if the poem is experienced from without it is unlikely that E will itself be experienced in the reading of the poem. If, for example, this emotion is grief then in the experience of the poem from without grief is unlikely to be experienced. If any emotion is experienced the emotion will not be grief but, perhaps, pity. If, however, the poem is experienced from within then E will be experienced. But even so, characteristically, it will not be experienced exactly as it would be if E were to be experienced outside the experience of art — just as in the experience from without pity will not be experienced as it is when it has a real object. To experience the poem from within one imagines, and so experiences in imagination, E (and the expression of E). But to experience E imaginatively or in the imagination is not the same as to experience E actually or in reality. Elliott, borrowing the terms from Edith Stein, distinguishes the experience of an emotion really from the experience of the emotion imaginatively by the use of the words 'primordial' and 'non-primordial'. To experience an emotion through an imaginative assumption of another's situation and expression — whether in a poem or in real life — is not to experience the emotion primordially; it is to experience it non-primordially. If I respond empathically to another person's grief and feel his grief within me I cannot be said, unqualifiedly, to experience grief. Likewise, if I experience grief in experiencing a lyric poem from within the grief does not qualify me in the sense in which it would if it were really my own grief. In each case I experience grief only non-primordially.

8   Elliott suggests that — in a similar fashion to the way in which a lyric poem can be experienced as if it were the human expression of emotion — music can sometimes be experienced as, or as if it were, literally the expression of emotion. Such music is susceptible of each of the two modes of experiencing expression, from within and from without. And when emotion is felt in the experience of the music it will be felt, characteristically, in the non-primordial manner.

9   Before examining the idea that some music can be heard as if it were the expression of emotion I want to consider further the matter of experiencing an emotion not really but through an imaginative assumption of the situation and expression of the lyric 'I'. For Elliott offers no explanation of the distinction between experiencing an emotion primordially and experiencing it non-primordially. He merely provides labels for these two different ways in which an emotion can be experienced. And the nature of the non-primordial experience of an emotion is left in an obscure state: if a lyric poem expresses sadness then when I experience the poem from within I am supposed actually to feel this

sadness; but at the same time it would be false to say that I am sad or even, unqualifiedly, that I feel sad. This experience can be clarified, I believe, by introducing the notion of make-believe in a manner similar to that recommended by Kendall Walton in his work on psychological attitudes ostensibly directed towards fictional things.[9] But it is, I believe, necessary to modify the account Walton presents.

10 Walton's concern is with those psychological attitudes which are such that a person cannot have an attitude of one of these kinds towards something without believing that that thing exists. In the case of these attitudes it cannot be literally true that we have an attitude directed towards an entity we know is merely fictional. It cannot be literally true that we pity Desdemona, or are horrified by Oedipus's self-blinding, or are envious of Orpheus's musical talent, or are distressed by the death of Anna Karenina – even if there should be tears in our eyes when we read the account of her suicide. For, as we know, these people never existed. But – this is Walton's thesis – it can be make-believedly true that we experience pity, horror, envy or distress at these people or the events in which they participate. For when we experience a representational work of art we can use the work of art as a prop in a game of make-believe in such a way that it can be true that, make-believedly, we experience a certain emotion, and, make-believedly, the object of this emotion is something represented in the work of art. In this game of make-believe what happens, typically, is that when we experience the work of art we imagine something's being the case and we react in a certain way to what we imagine – and it is in virtue of this reaction to what we imagine that, make-believedly, we experience a certain emotion, and, make-believedly, this emotion is directed towards a fictional entity.

What is it for someone in this sense make-believedly to experience an emotion in reaction to a work of art? Let p be what someone must believe or must have the thought of if he is to be in emotional state E. And let us give the name 'quasi-E' to the physiological/psychological state which is characteristic of someone who is in state E: the set of bodily processes and their associated feelings that someone who is in E typically undergoes. Then Walton's thesis is that for someone who experiences a work of art make-believedly to feel E he must experience quasi-E and his quasi-E must be caused by his awareness that make-believedly p. For example, a person make-believedly is afraid for himself if his quasi-fear – increased flow of adrenalin, faster pulse-rate and muscular tension (for example), and their associated feelings – is caused by his realisation that make-believedly he is or might be in danger. Make-believedly someone feels fear for himself if the awareness that make-believedly he is in danger causes him to have feelings of his heart pounding, his muscles tensing . . .[10]

Now this account of what it is to feel an emotion make-believedly in response to the content of a work of art is acceptable only if the difference between feeling emotion E really and feeling it make-believedly is that whereas in the first case quasi-E is caused by the belief or the thought that p, in the second case it is caused by the belief that make-believedly p. The rationale for Walton's account of feeling E make-believedly must be that quasi-E is all that needs to be brought about — and that it is necessary that it should be brought about — by the belief or the thought constitutive of E for it to be true that one feels E really. Therefore, if one does not need to experience quasi-E when one feels E really, or if one experiences more than quasi-E, then Walton's account of feeling E make-believedly is partly inaccurate. And in fact this is the case: an emotion is not a set of bodily feelings brought about by a belief or thought. For example, the combination of the belief that one is in danger and the experience of quasi-fear as an effect of this belief is insufficient for one to experience fear: this is consistent with one's being unafraid but, instead, pleasurably excited by the danger. The truth is that one experiences fear for oneself only if one is distressed or made uneasy by the belief or the thought that one is in danger. Hence, the account Walton presents of what feeling an emotion make-believedly consists in must be modified in the case of fear to accommodate the element of distress or unease that fear involves. Furthermore, it is in general intrinsic to the concept of a certain kind of emotion that someone experiences that emotion only if he experiences a specific form of satisfaction or dissatisfaction, pleasure or displeasure, agreeableness or disagreeableness, delight or distress.[11] Moreover, the hedonic tone of an emotion is a more important feature of the concept of the emotion than any bodily changes/feelings which might be characteristic of the emotion: many emotions lack characteristic bodily feelings, and the bodily feelings which are characteristic of a certain emotion are not — unlike the hedonic tone of the emotion — dictated by the concept of the emotion: their nature is determined by the particular constitution of the body of the kind of creature for which they are characteristic accompaniments of the emotion. Hence, the emphasis placed by Walton's account of someone's make-believedly experiencing an emotion on the person's feeling occurrences in his body is unwarranted.

A better account results if the quasi-form of an emotion is replaced by, or is redefined so as to include essentially, the hedonic tone of the emotion. Let us consider again the case of fear and let us begin with the unaided imagination of danger. Then either one can imagine being uneasy or distressed at the realisation or the thought that one is in danger or one can experience unease or distress in imagining oneself to be in danger. The first of these imaginative exercises is imagining oneself to be afraid: the emotion is imagined but not necessarily experienced. The second is experiencing fear imaginatively: the hedonic tone of the emotion is experienced when the thought-content of the emotion is imagined as being true. A similar distinction can be drawn in the more complex case in which a work of art is used as a prop in a game of make-believe. Make-believedly one is afraid if it is make-believedly true that one is uneasy or distressed at the thought that one is in danger. One experiences fear make-believedly if one experiences unease or distress as a result of the realisation that make-believedly one is in danger. The general account of what it is to experience an emotion make-believedly is this: To experience an emotion make-believedly is to experience the hedonic tone of the emotion (and perhaps its quasi-form) as a result of the realisation that make-believedly a certain state of affairs obtains, namely, whatever one would need to believe really does obtain, or whatever one would need to have the thought of, if one were to experience the emotion really. It is the notion of experiencing an emotion make-believedly − modelled upon Walton's account − that is needed to make clear the kind of non-primordial emotional response to a work of art that can be involved in experiencing a work of art as if it were the expression of emotion.

When I place myself in imagination in the position of the speaker of a lyric poem − when I experience the poem from within − I make-believe that I am in his situation. I make-believe that I am a certain person who thinks the thoughts the poem expresses and who experiences the emotion the lyric 'I' is represented as feeling towards something. I am not really in E and I do not really feel E towards this thing. But when I make-believe that I am in the place of the poem's speaker I may feel something. In particular, I may feel the hedonic tone (and the bodily symptoms) of E and what I experience will have been caused by my making-believe that I am in the speaker's place, and so by my making-believe that p, where p is what it is necessary for someone to believe or have the thought of if he is to feel E. Likewise, when I experience the poem from without I make-believe that another experiences E, and in doing this I may feel the hedonic tone of E' (and quasi-E'), where E' is a response — positive or negative — to another's E, in which case what I experience will have been caused by my making-believe that p', where p' is what it is necessary for someone to believe or have the thought of if he is to feel E'.

My suggestion, therefore, is that Elliott's talk of someone's experiencing an emotion non-primordially when he experiences a lyric poem as if it were the expression of emotion should be understood as, or replaced by, talk of someone's experiencing the emotion make-believedly, where he experiences the emotion make-believedly if his making-believe that such a state of affairs obtains as he would need really to believe obtains or to have the thought that it obtains if he were actually to feel that emotion towards something causes him to feel the hedonic tone (and a quasi-form) of that emotion. If the poem expresses E the reader who experiences the poem from within does not need to experience E really. He may experience the hedonic tone of E (and quasi-E feelings), and it will be true of what he feels that make-believedly it is a feeling of E. Although he does not actually experience E, what he actually experiences is such that make-believedly it is an experience of E: he experiences E make-believedly.

11 To experience music as if it were the expression of emotion it would be necessary to experience it as if someone were expressing his emotion in the sounds which compose the music: the music would have to be experienced as if someone's body were making the sounds of which the music is composed because the person feels an emotion, just as people do in fact make noises and in one sense thereby give expression to their emotions: it would be necessary to imagine someone giving voice to the sounds of the music and in doing so to express his emotion.

It might at first thought seem as if music could be an ideal vehicle for the artistic expression of the emotions. For music is an art of sounds and we can express our emotions in the sounds we make. It might appear, therefore, that music is peculiarly fitted to exploit the various features of the audible manifestation of emotions in the construction of works that are designed to be understood as expressions of emotions.

In fact there are two ways in which 'mere' sound is connected with emotion that music could seek to exploit. Under the stress of an emotion a human being may produce (i) a certain kind of sound, e.g. (perhaps) laughter, a shriek, a sob, or (ii) sounds in a particular manner, e.g. slowly, in a soft voice, with a characteristic inflection or pattern of intonation.[12]

Now music can in fact remind us of — it can suggest — various non-linguistic features of the vocal expression of emotion: a sudden, brief pause can put us in mind of a gasp of fear. Furthermore, music can *set out to imitate*, for example, sobs or cries of anguish, although in fact it attempts to reproduce them only in a highly stylised form: it presents only approximations and not the sounds themselves. The formalisation is necessitated by the differences between the sounds that are actually called forth by our emotions and the sounds that are used in music. And the kind and degree of formalisation of the sounds imitated in music are dictated by the particular stylistic system within which, and the instruments for which, the music is composed.

Music can, then, *sound like* the vocal expression of emotion. But even when it does it doesn't sound very much like the vocal expression of emotion. And it is clear that the difference between our reaction to such music and to the real vocal expression of emotion is partly a function of the perceived differences in the sounds.

But there is another possibility. Not only can music sound like the vocal expression of an emotion, but we can *make-believe* — and it can be intended that we should make-believe — that a piece of music M is the vocal expression of emotion E. To hear M as sounding much or quite like the vocal expression of E — even being struck by its likeness — does not imply that one makes-believe that M is the vocal expression of E. And to make-believe that M is the vocal expression of E does not imply that one thinks that M sounds much or quite like the vocal expression of E. M's sounding to X somewhat like the vocal expression of E is neither a necessary nor a sufficient condition for X to make-believe that M is the vocal expression of E, although it may make it easy for X to do so.

Now someone who wished to produce a 'work of art' that facilitated as much as possible the work's being experienced as make-believedly the vocal but non-linguistic expression of E could not do much better than to reproduce the kinds of sounds that a person characteristically makes when he experiences E and which can be said to express his E (that is, if there should be any such sounds). He would produce a work which sounded as much like the non-linguistic vocal expression of E as he could. But such a work would not be of much artistic interest. And the situation would not be materially altered if the work not only consisted of the kinds of sounds that someone characteristically makes when he experiences E but these sounds were produced in the manner in which sounds characteristically come from someone who experiences

E. Certainly, our attitude towards such a work would be very different from our attitude to the musical expression of emotion. We would probably not be eager to listen to a work of such a kind, especially if the emotion whose audible manifestations it was based upon was dispiriting or distressing. The sounds in which people express their grief, for instance, are typically not something that in themselves we would wish to listen to even if we knew that they were not in fact (then or previously) produced by a grief-stricken person. If such a work were advanced as something that is make-believedly the vocal expression of emotion there would be no question that it could be regarded in the intended light; but its artistic value would be problematic.

The mere fact that a set of sounds is for someone make-believedly the vocal expression of an emotion is therefore not sufficient to endow it with artistic value for him. If, therefore, the musical expression of emotion is ever the same phenomenon as the music's being make-believedly the vocal expression of emotion, and if the fact that a piece of music expresses an emotion can be integral to its musical value, the fact that it is *music* or music of a certain kind that is make-believedly the vocal expression of emotion must play a role in the explanation of the value of the music as art.

12 I have construed Elliott's claim that some music can be experienced as if it were the human expression of emotion as the thesis that it is possible to make-believe that the music is the human vocal expression of emotion. This thesis might appear independently plausible. For Kendall Walton is undoubtedly right that there is no literal way of paraphrasing the remark that a piece of music is anguished, say, without using or referring to some literal paraphrase of the remark taken literally; so that the remark is not a metaphor (if metaphor is understood to presuppose the possibility of such a paraphrase).[13] Hence the sentence 'The music is anguished' seems to be elliptical for 'The music expresses someone's anguish', where this sentence is to be taken not metaphorically but make-believedly. And it is natural to read this sentence which is to be taken make-believedly as: 'The music is the vocal expression of anguish.' To experience music as if it were the human expression of emotion would then be to make-believe that the music is the human vocal expression of emotion.

But it is not clear that this is how Elliott intends his theory to be understood. When we hear music as if it were expressing emotion by hearing it from without we are supposed to hear it 'as if someone were expressing his emotion in and through the sounds as a person does in and through his voice; but although we hear the sounds rather as if they were a voice, in listening to pure music we seldom if ever hear them as the ordinary human voice'. And when we hear emotionally expressive music from within – as if it were our own expression – we are supposed to experience it as if it were issuing from us as our own expression of emotion but 'not exactly as if it were our own voice but as a mode of expression *sui generis*'. These remarks appear not merely to draw attention to the fact that hearing X as if it were Y is not a matter of X's sounding just like Y (so that one might naturally take X to be Y); hence that music expressive of a certain human emotion does not sound exactly like the human voice sounds when it expresses that emotion. It is true – as I have already indicated – that one thing does not need to sound exactly or even very much like another thing in order for us in perceiving the first thing to make-believe that we are perceiving the second thing. A hobby-horse does not look much like a horse and yet a child can play a game in which he makes-believe that the hobby-horse he sees is a real horse.[14] Similarly, a piece of music may not sound much like a human voice but this is no barrier to my making-believe when I hear the music that I am hearing the human vocal expression of sadness, say. The manifest differences between the sound of the human voice and the sound of emotionally expressive music therefore do not preclude the possibility that to experience M as the human expression of E is to experience it as if it were – to make-believe that it is – some human being's vocal expression of E (i.e. it issues from his mouth). But Elliott's theory appears to be different. His reference to a *sui generis* mode of expression seems to indicate that his theory is that to experience M as the human expression of E is to experience it as if it were someone's *sui generis* expression of E. Since M consists of sounds M must be imagined to issue from a person's body in some way – if not from his mouth, by means of his voice, in some other manner of sound production. But sounds *expressive of emotion* issue from human beings only vocally. If, therefore, I am to make-believe that M is someone's *sui generis* expression of E, I must imagine human beings to have some non-vocal means of making sounds come from their bodies and in which their emotions can be expressed, and I must make-believe that M issues in this way from someone as an expression of his E.[15]

These two theories therefore enjoin upon us rather different imaginative projects if we are to hear M as the human expression of E.

13   Whichever of these theories is favoured, if a piece of music M is experienced as if it were the expression of E it can be experienced from within or from without. If I experience M from within then I make-believe that I feel E and that I am expressing my E in the sounds of M: these sounds are issuing from me as a consequence of my feeling E and they bear the imprint of E. If I experience M from without then I make-believe that someone else feels E and that his E is expressed in the sounds of M. Let us concentrate upon the experience of M from within. When I experience M from within it may be that not only do I imagine or make-believe that I feel E, but I feel E make-believedly: I experience the hedonic tone of E (and quasi-E) and what I feel is caused by my belief that make-believedly p, where p is what I must believe or have the thought of if I am to feel E – in Elliott's terminology, I feel E non-primordially. Thus, to take a particular case, when I experience M from within as the expression of sorrow I become a participant in a game of make-believe in which I am sad and my sadness is being expressed in the sounds of M, and I may feel unhappiness (and quasi-sadness) as a result of my awareness that make-believedly I have lost someone who is dear to me. What would be the significance of such an experience?

Elliott offers this account:

> An extreme experience of emotionally expressive music from within is very like a real-life experience of, say, joy, when the emotion has no definite object and when we express it by voice or gesture. . . . Once the mood or emotion is present in us the experience is usually extremely pleasing, for to the extent that emotion is not tied to any external state of affairs or dependent in any other way upon the subject's representing anything to himself by means of concepts, music is an incomparably lucid and powerful means of expression. It is as if in feeling joy or sadness we were at the same time conscious of an adequacy of expression far beyond anything we could have imagined.

He here makes two very different claims. The first likens or assimilates the non-primordial experience of emotion in the experience of emotionally expressive music from within to a particular form in which this emotion – or certain emotions – can be experienced primordially in real life. The second locates a value of the (non-primordial) experience of emotion in the experience of emotionally expressive music from within in the supposed fact that the music expresses the emotion in a specially adequate manner.

The first claim refers to the expression in real-life by voice or gesture of an emotion that on that occasion has no definite object. Now there is one way that an emotion that involves a belief or thought may on a particular occasion lack a definite object: the belief or thought may remain in an indefinite form. Thus: although when I feel fear for myself I will characteristically believe of some particular thing that it is a danger to me, on occasion I may believe that I am in danger without my belief's taking on a more determinate form. I will then be afraid without there being any definite object — real or intentional — of which I am afraid. When Elliott refers to a particular experience of joy when the joy has no definite object perhaps what he has in mind is that joy is the pleasurable emotion that is awakened by the attainment of a highly desired end and the belief that joy involves — the belief that something one highly desires has been attained — may on occasion take on no more specific form. Another possibility would be that joy is to be construed merely as a state of extremely pleasurable well-being — in which case joy does not involve a belief or thought. But whichever way we understand the idea of joy being experienced when it lacks a definite object, this first claim does not itself help us with the problem of explaining the significance of the non-primordial experience of emotion in the experience of a piece of expressive music from within — as is specially clear in the case of such an unwelcome emotion as sorrow. We therefore need to examine the second claim.

The second claim offers an explanation of why in the case of music the non-primordial experience of emotion is usually extremely pleasant — an explanation that is particularly pressing whenever the primordial experience of the emotion is not in itself pleasurable.[16] Music is claimed to be 'an incomparably lucid and powerful means of expression' for emotion which has no definite object, or which is not dependent upon the subject's representing anything to himself by means of concepts; and the musical expression of such an emotion is claimed to be more adequate than the more primitive or natural expressions of the emotion. Now any emotion that involves a belief or thought involves the subject of that emotion representing something to himself by means of concepts, even when the belief or thought remains in its least specific form. If we take what Elliott says seriously we must take what he says as not applying to any emotions that involve beliefs or thoughts: as not applying to, say, sadness and joy (unless joy is just extremely pleasurable well-being). But I think we should instead concentrate upon cases where an emotion that involves a belief or thought has no definite object. The claim would then be that for an emotion that has no definite object music is a more adequate expression than the more primitive real expression of that emotion by voice or gesture. Someone can experience joy primordially when it has no definite object and he can experience joy non-primordially when it has no definite object in the experience from within of music that expresses joy: and he feels the music to be a more adequate expression of the emotion than his voice or his gestures.[17] In what sense could this be true?

One way in which we could understand the idea of adequacy is pointed to by Elliott's remark that music can be 'an incomparably lucid . . . means of expression': an expression of E is the more adequate the more manifest it makes E. The more an expression reveals what emotion it is an expression of the more adequate it is as an expression of that emotion. But this way of understanding the idea of the adequacy of an expression of an emotion is unpromising. There are three reasons for this. In the first place, if the voice is used linguistically it can be an ideally adequate means of expression (in this sense) for any emotion. Secondly, for the only emotions for which Elliott's thesis is maintained — for emotions that lack a definite object — the non-linguistic vocal and gestural expressions of emotion can fall little short of being fully adequate. A person's non-linguistic behaviour can make it perfectly clear that he is joyful or unhappy, for example. Thirdly, even if the non-linguistic expression of an emotion experienced primordially does not fully reveal the nature of the emotion, since the emotion, as we have seen, can be fully revealed by the use of language the fact that music is a more adequate means of expression of the emotion than the non-linguistic real expression would not, if it were the case, be of any great importance.

Another way of understanding the idea of adequacy is based upon the thought that we can derive satisfaction from the ways in which emotions naturally discharge themselves in non-linguistic forms of behaviour or kinds of bodily process. A natural outlet for our grief is tears, for our anger blows, for our joy bodily movement. The stronger the emotion the more difficult it is to inhibit its natural expression in the body. And if the emotion pursues its natural course and issues in overt bodily activities which express it they can provide a satisfaction that is forgone if the emotion's natural expressions are repressed. We might, therefore, understand the idea of the adequacy of a means of expression in this way: an expression of E is the more adequate the more satisfying it is for the emotion to be released in that form. But this suggestion has little to recommend it. For the thesis we are considering is that if we experience an emotion non-primordially when it has no definite object in the experience from within of music that expresses the emotion, the music may seem to us to be a more adequate expression of the emotion than the expression of the emotion by voice or gesture in real-life. But when we experience music from within we will not begin by experiencing an emotion which we keep bottled up within us and then derive satisfaction when we no longer hold it in check but allow it to emerge in the sounds of the music which make-believedly issue from our body. And it is not in general true that the effect of empathising with music which is expressive of sadness, say, resembles the experience of having a good cry: not all expressive music wears its heart upon its sleeve.

There is a further way in which we could understand the idea of the adequacy of a means of expression of emotion. When we experience an emotion we sometimes feel an inclination to some form of behaviour that is, or seems to us would be, particularly appropriate to engage in as a result of our experiencing the emotion: in acting in that manner we feel fulfilled, or we believe we will or would feel fulfilled. At other times we may feel no such inclination or we may even be unable to conceive a form of behaviour which would be particularly appropriate to, or would do justice to, the emotion we feel. And this can make a difference to how we experience the emotion – a difference of a similar kind to that which is brought about by an obstacle to our expressing an emotion in the way we would like. We feel an emotion within us and we cannot properly externalise it: as a result we may be oppressed by the emotion. So: we may feel admiration for and tenderness towards someone who is forever lost to us, and no matter how well things turn out for us in future our life has changed in a manner that will always be a focus of regret; yet we may not feel like doing anything that would be specially appropriate to – and in this sense expressive of – our feeling, or it may even be that we feel there is nothing we are capable of doing which would be particularly expressive of our feeling. If we are oppressed because we feel an emotion but have no impulse to do something we find particularly expressive of the emotion, we may experience a need to give the emotion adequate expression. One interpretation of the thesis that music can be a more adequate expression of an emotion than the real expression of that emotion by voice or gesture would therefore be that in experiencing expressive music from within we can make-believedly express an emotion in a manner we feel does perfect justice to the emotion: it seems to us fitting that these sounds should issue from us as a result of our experiencing the emotion. And this experience would be intrinsically satisfying.

But this interpretation is no better than those already considered. For the thesis we are examining is that in the case of an emotion which does not have a definite object music can be a more adequate expression of the emotion than the real-life expression of that emotion by voice or gesture. And it is unlikely that for such an emotion the expression of the emotion by voice or gesture will be felt to be inadequate (in the sense in question): if I am oppressed by my fear of nothing in particular it will be the indefiniteness of my fear and the associated thought of its apparent unreasonableness that will weigh upon me, not my inability to do something in which I can give my feeling expression; and the burden of my unfocused sense of sadness will not be occasioned by a felt discrepancy between the behaviour I am capable of and anything which would spring from my emotion in a satisfying way − the burden will lighten if I realise that my sadness is merely the residue of a dream and it will increase if I remember the reason I do have to be unhappy. Furthermore, if we imagine the sounds that compose a piece of expressive music to issue from our bodies under the impulsion of an emotion which is present in us, and we find this behaviour more appropriate to the emotion than any behaviour that might naturally spring from the emotion in real-life, it must be possible to explain our sense of appropriateness by reference to the nature of the emotion and the character of the sounds which compose the music. But it is difficult to see what this explanation could be.

14   It would be mistaken to think that if someone hears a piece of music as if it were the expression of emotion he must find his experience of the music rewarding. If he experiences, make-believedly, the emotion the music is expressive of or an emotional response − sympathetic or antipathetic − to another's experience of that emotion, the reason he fails to find his experience of the music rewarding may be just that he does not like to experience, make-believedly, emotions of these kinds (perhaps he does not like to experience, make-believedly, emotions of any kinds). But there is at least one other possibility. For someone might be dissatisfied not so much with the emotion the music expresses (or his response to this emotion) but with the emotion's expression in the music.

One way in which this might come about is by the person hearing the music as the 'oratorical', rather than the 'poetical', expression of emotion. John Stuart Mill drew a distinction — a distinction he characterised as the distinction between eloquence and poetry — between an expression of emotion that is designed to work upon the belief, feelings or will of other people and an expression of emotion that is expressed in total unconsciousness of any listener.[18] Whereas eloquence is intended to be heard, poetry can only be overheard. When he applied this distinction to music he distinguished two styles of music expressive of emotion: the poetical and the oratorical. Expressive music in the style of poetry resembles soliloquy. Expressive music in the style of oratory resembles monologue (in one sense of the term). Poetical music is music which seems to be the expression of emotion that takes place without consciousness of an audience. Oratorical music appears to the listener to suppose an audience which is to be affected by the act of expression. If music is experienced as if it were the expression of emotion it can therefore be experienced as if it were the oratorical or the poetical expression of emotion. If someone experiences a piece of expressive music from within he may find himself imaginatively expressing an emotion poetically or, instead, oratorically; and if he experiences it from without he may regard himself as hearing the expression of an emotion intended to be heard by others or as overhearing expression which is unconscious of a listener. Now expressive music that is heard as oratorical inherits the liability to certain defects that can be present in the oratorical expression of emotion. For example, there can be a discrepancy between expression and emotion: the expression is designed to convince others of a strength or depth or purity of feeling which is unreal. If there is a sense of discrepancy between emotion and expression in someone's experience of expressive music he may feel the music to be insincere and for this reason not value it.

15 I have distinguished two ways in which music could be experienced as if it were the human expression of emotion: it could be experienced as if it were the human vocal expression of emotion or as if it were some non-vocal but audible means of expression of emotion with which human beings were endowed. If the theory of musical expression according to which expressive music is heard as if it were the human expression of emotion is understood in the first of these ways then it is based directly upon the expressive character of the human voice. But is this the most plausible of those theories of musical expression which seek to exploit the expressive character of the human voice? For a theory of musical expression can use the human voice as its model in more than one way. The theory I have considered represents the listener as experiencing sad music as if it were the sad voice of a sad person: the voice of a person whose sadness causes his voice to have a sad quality. But — as this formulation makes clear — a weaker theory is available. For whether a person's voice has a sad quality is not determined by whether he is sad: he can be sad and his voice be untinged with sadness and his voice can have a sad quality when he is not sad. Hence a theory of musical expression which uses the human voice as its model can require only that the listener hears sad music as if it were a voice with a sad quality. Both the stronger and the weaker theory require the listener to imagine that he is hearing a voice; but whilst the stronger requires the listener to imagine that he is hearing someone's sadness — his sadness as expressed in his voice — all the weaker requires is that the listener should imagine he is hearing someone's voice and this voice has a sad quality.

However, although the weaker theory is available, it appears to have no advantages over the stronger theory. And, unlike the stronger theory, it lacks an explanation of the significance of musical expression and why the listener can be moved by the expression of emotion in music. (The doctrine that we are liable to resonate in sympathy with anything we experience as having an expressive character palpably fails to provide such an explanation.)

But these are not the only ways in which a theory of musical expression can exploit the expressive character of the human voice. A theory of musical expression which is based upon the expressive character of the human voice can enjoin upon the listener an imaginative project which differs from that of each of the first two theories in that it does not involve hearing expressive music as if it were a voice. All it requires is that the listener should hear sad music as having a character of the same kind as the character of a sad voice. And to do this it is not necessary, according to the theory, to hear sad music as a voice (or as something which issues in some other way from the body). The second theory strips away one layer of the first theory, retaining the idea of a voice and its expressive character but jettisoning the idea of causation by an emotion. The third theory strips away a further layer: it retains the expressive character (of the voice) but dispenses with the idea of a voice.

The three theories therefore maintain, respectively, that to hear music as sad is to hear music:

(1) as a voice that expresses someone's sadness,

(2) as a voice with a sad quality,

(3) as something (not expressed from a person's body) that has the same character as a sad voice.

But how exactly is this third theory to be understood? Let us call that feature or set of features in virtue of which a voice is experienced as sad or happy or angry (or whatever) an expressive aspect of the voice; and let us construe the theory as maintaining that sad music is heard as having the expressive aspect of a sad voice. The question is: Does the theory intend the notion of an expressive aspect to be such that the specification of an expressive aspect involves an ineliminable reference to a certain kind of thing (the voice, for example)? If the answer to this question is Yes, the theory reduces to the second theory. If the answer is No, the theory intends the notion of the expressive aspect of a voice to be detachable from the notion of a voice in the sense that it is possible to hear the expressive aspect in something which is not experienced as a voice – just as the notion of the colour of an object is detachable from the idea of any particular kind of thing that has that colour. But is an aspect detachable in this way?

In considering this question it is helpful to consider the analogous idea of an expressive aspect of a face. Now there is a sense in which the characteristics of a face in virtue of which it is experienced as pleased, say, are not detachable from the notion of a face. For we will see a pleased expression on a face only if we see it smile. And we see a smile only if we see something as lips which smile. Hence we can see a pleased expression only if we see something which we see as, or in which we see, a face (or, at least, part of a face). To see something as having the same expressive aspect as a pleased face it is necessary to see it as a face. If we see a pleased expression we see a pleased *facial* expression. Likewise, to hear a sound as an expression of agony is to hear it as, say, a shriek. Therefore, to hear a sound as an expression of agony it must be heard as the sound of a voice. And so a face and a voice each of which is sad, say, do not have an expressive aspect in common: the one aspect is a facial expression, the other an expression of or in the voice. And to hear something as having the expressive character a sad voice has it is necessary to hear it as a sad voice. Consequently, this way of understanding the notion of an expressive aspect violates the requirement that an aspect should be specifiable independently of the notion of any particular kind of thing: the expressive aspects of a face are specifically facial expressions, and the expressive aspects of a voice are specifically vocal 'expressions'. Expressive aspects are not detachable in the required manner from the kinds of thing that can possess them. In particular, the feature of a voice in virtue of which it is heard as sad is not detachable from the notion of a voice; for it can be heard in a series of sounds only if the sounds are heard as a voice.

But there is another way in which the idea of an expressive aspect, as I have introduced it, can be understood. There are combinations of features of a voice – features of speed, strength, relative pitch-level and fluctuation in pitch – in virtue of which a voice is heard as sad and which can be specified without using the idea of a voice. And therefore something that is not heard as a voice can be heard to have such a combination of features: it can be experienced as slow, quiet, low in pitch and moving within a narrow pitch-range, say. If these are features of a sad voice in virtue of which it is heard as sad then they are detachable from the notion of a voice and can be heard in sounds that are not experienced as a voice. And if all the features of the voice that make it a sad voice are likewise detachable then sounds that are not experienced as a voice can be heard to have the very same combination of features in virtue of which the voice is heard as sad. Hence it will be possible to hear music as having the character – the expressive aspect – of a sad voice without hearing the music as a sad voice.

Now there is an ambiguity in saying that something is heard to have the same character as a sad voice. Let S be the expressive character of some sad voice. Then to hear something as having the same character as that sad voice could mean (i) to hear something as having S, or (ii) to hear something as resembling that sad voice in respect of S. It is clear that the theory according to which music is experienced as sad if it is heard as having the character of a sad voice has no plausibility unless it is understood to mean not only that the music is heard to have a certain character – which in fact some sad voice has – but the listener is struck by the likeness between this character of the music and the character of a sad voice (not, of course, some particular sad voice). For music is heard as sad only if it puts the listener in mind of sadness – just as a voice is heard as sad only if it puts the listener in mind of sadness. But even if the theory is understood to include the requirement that the listener should hear the music as resembling a sad voice in those respects which make the voice sad the theory has little attraction. Firstly, it is too strong: it is not necessary to realise which features a piece of music has in common with a sad voice if the music is to be heard as sad. Secondly, the theory appears not to be able to explain the significance of the musical expression of emotion. For why should it ever matter to us that a piece of music reminds us of a sad voice by possessing those features which make the voice sad? It might be suggested that the thought of a sad voice can be sufficient for someone who has a lively imagination and the capacity for empathy to induce the feeling of sadness.[19] But even if this should be so it fails to explain the value of the musical expression of emotion. For, in the first place, if this is offered as an account of how the fact that a piece of music is expressive of a state of mind can be a reason why it is valued *as music*, it involves the heresy of the separable experience. And so even if it is a value of a piece of music that it induces sadness by reminding the sensitive listener of a sad voice, this value is not musical value. But, furthermore, it is difficult to understand why this function of a piece of music should be thought of as a value of any kind. For we are familiar with the experience of sadness; we are fully aware of our capacity to feel sadness; we will not understand the feeling any better if it happens to arise in the experience of music that reminds us of a sad voice; and the feeling is one that in itself most of us are happy not to experience if nothing has happened to give us good reason to be sad.

This third theory is therefore no improvement on the other two theories.

16 It might be thought that a more plausible theory would result if we were to make a minor modification to the third theory. Perhaps the theory is right to assert a likeness between hearing sad music and hearing a sad voice, but it mislocates the likeness. The likeness — so this suggestion maintains — does not consist in the possession of a common character by the music and a sad voice. Rather, the experience of hearing sad music is in some important way like the experience of hearing a sad voice. This is essentially the theory put forward by Roger Scruton in his *Art and Imagination*;[20] although his account of what it is to hear sadness in music is not easy to piece together.

His initial formulation is that to experience a musical passage as sad is to respond to it in a way that is like the way in which one responds to a man when one is 'touched' by his sadness.[21] Now to be touched by another's sadness is to feel some form of positive sympathetic feeling towards him on account of his being sad: it is to be distressed by his sadness or to experience a feeling of tenderness towards him because of his sadness. This response to another's sadness involves a belief that the person is sad and a feeling of sympathy founded upon this belief.

144

Hence the thesis maintains that to experience music as sad is for one's response to the music to be similar to this compound of belief and feeling. But in what respects is the response in the aesthetic case supposed to be similar to the response to real sadness?

This question is in fact premature. For in the process of development the theory receives an important qualification. As the theory is developed the concept of perception comes to be stressed in such a manner that the model is not simply that of a person being touched by another's sadness — about which he might come to learn in a variety of ways — but that of a person being touched by another's sadness as he perceives it expressed in or by his body: by his voice, for example. The phenomenon to be accounted for is the phenomenon of hearing sadness in music and this phenomenon is an experience or a perception. It is therefore to be compared to another perception: the perception of someone's sadness. And the question as to the nature of the response in the aesthetic case is partly answered by saying that the thought that is the core of the aesthetic response can be characterised by the proposition that 'the experience of hearing the sadness in the music is in some irreducible way analogous to hearing the expression of sadness — say, in another's voice)'.[22]

The theory therefore maintains that there is an 'irreducible analogy' between the experience of hearing sadness in music and the experience of hearing sadness in a person's voice. Let us provisionally represent the theory as maintaining that to hear music as sad is to hear music in such a manner that there is an irreducible analogy between the experience of the music and the experience of hearing sadness in a person's voice.

But what is meant by there being an irreducible analogy between mental states M_1 and M_2? We are given two explanations. The first is that there is an irreducible analogy between M_1 and M_2 if someone who has the concepts of the two states and is in state M_1 will want to say that M_1 is like M_2, or will want to describe M_1 in terms that are equally applicable to M_2, but will be unable to say in what way M_1 is like M_2.[23] The second is that there is an irreducible analogy between M_1 and M_2 if it is part of the concept of M_1 that M_1 should be referred to and expressed in the language appropriate to M_2, although it is impossible to say in what way M_1 is like M_2.[24]

However, the use of this idea to explain the experience of hearing sadness in music is highly problematic. The thought that forms the core of the aesthetic response is said not to be a belief or judgment but an 'unasserted' thought: it is a thought which occurs in the mind without the mind's assent to it. And this thought that is 'embodied' in the perception of the music's sadness is to be defined by the existence of an irreducible analogy between perceiving the sadness of music and hearing the sadness in another's voice. But the sadness in another person's voice is heard (in the relevant sense) only if the listener realises that the person is sad and that his sadness is affecting his voice.[25] Now there is a thought that corresponds to this belief: the thought that the person's voice is affected by his sadness. Clearly, it is not this thought that, unasserted, forms the core of the aesthetic response. If we remove from this thought any reference to a particular person we obtain the thought that someone's voice is affected by his sadness. But this thought also cannot be the intellectual heart of the experience of hearing a musical passage as sad. For this thought – like the belief embodied in the auditory perception of another person's sadness – is directly specifiable. And in fact no thought derived from this belief can be the right candidate for the role that an unasserted thought is assigned by the theory. For it too will be directly specifiable and no recourse to an irreducible analogy between perceptual experiences will be necessary. Furthermore, if the (unasserted) thought contained in the experience of hearing the sadness in the music is to be defined by reference to an irreducible analogy which obtains between this experience and the auditory perception of another's sadness, the irreducible analogy must hold between this thought and the belief embodied in the auditory perception. For the relevant element of the auditory perception that involves a thought is the belief it embodies. But the thought this belief involves is directly specifiable and a thought (unasserted) that in any way corresponds to it must be directly specifiable. Hence an appeal to an irreducible analogy between the experience of hearing the sadness in the music and the experience of hearing the sadness in another's voice in order to define the thought that forms the core of the first experience must be ineffective.

Scruton believes that the thought-content of a perceptual experience can never be fully specified independently of the perception.[26] The only way in which the thought-content of a perception can be fully captured is by reference to the perception itself: the thought-content is the thought-content of *this* perception and there is no independent way of saying what this content is. It is for this reason that he believes recourse must be had to the idea of an irreducible analogy between experiences if the thought-content of hearing sadness in music is to be made clear. Since the thought-content cannot be distilled from the experience and specified without reference to the experience; and since it cannot be specified by saying that the experience has the same thought-content as a different kind of experience (for then there would be an independent way of saying what the thought-content is); the best that can be done is to mention another kind of experience which is such that there is an irreducible analogy between the original experience and this other experience. This move is dubious even if we accept the supposition on which it is based — that the thought-content of a perception cannot be fully specified independently of the perception. For the notion of an irreducible analogy between two phenomena precludes the possibility of indicating in what way the phenomena are alike. Hence, to postulate an irreducible analogy between the experience of hearing sadness in music and the experience of hearing sadness in someone's voice is to debar oneself from saying that the experiences are alike in thought-content. But it is unnecessary to pursue this point. For it is sufficient to point out that if a perception is characterised as perceiving or seeming to perceive that . . . (or in some manner that is reducible to this form) then of course the thought-content of the perception *as so characterised* always has an independent and fully specifiable description.

In fact, Scruton's derivation of the thesis that the thought-content of a perceptual experience cannot be fully specified independently of the perception itself is imperfect. He considers a visual experience — the experience of seeing a man — that is described in a way that at most partly characterises how the perception represents the world as being. And he then insists that the perception's full representative character cannot be captured by any description which does not mention that perception. But no reason is given for this insistence and the universal generalisation of this thesis is surely false. (Furthermore, as I have indicated, it does not imply what is required: that the thought-content of a perception as characterised in a certain manner cannot be fully specified by a description that makes no reference to the perception.)

An alternative strategy would be to abandon the thesis that the thought-content of the experience of hearing sadness in music cannot be described independently of the experience in which it is embodied, whilst retaining a comparison with the experience of hearing the sadness in a person's voice. The (unasserted) thought that provides the experience of hearing music as sad with its thought-content would be the thought of someone's sadness being expressed in his voice, and this thought would be embodied in the auditory experience in the same way that the belief, or the thought it involves, is embodied in the auditory perception of someone's sadness. Hearing sadness in music would be the unasserted auditory perception of sadness,[27] but there would be no thought involved in either experience which could not be fully specified independently of the experience in which it is realised.

But this strategy would merely return us to the thesis that to hear sadness in music is to hear music as if it were a voice which expresses someone's sadness. And the position would not be materially altered if the experience of hearing sadness in music were to be likened not to a perception – the experience of hearing sadness in another's voice – but to a feeling based on a perception (Scruton's favoured model): the experience of being touched by another's sadness as this is heard to be expressed in his voice. For if the experience of hearing sadness in music is not just an auditory perception (which has a thought-content in a sensory form) but also a feeling which corresponds in some way to a positive sympathetic emotion towards another person's sadness, this feeling will be nothing but the make-believe feeling that is liable to arise when expressive music is experienced 'from without'. And to impose on the experience of hearing sadness in music the requirement that the music should be experienced 'from without' is to restrict unjustifiably the ways in which expressive music can properly be experienced.

17   My conclusion is that no theory of musical expression which uses the human voice as its model is significantly better than the theory according to which we hear expressive music as if it were the vocal expression of emotion. But I do not believe that this theory gives an accurate account of what it is to hear music as expressive of emotion – or, at least, that it does not apply to many, if any, of the occasions when music is heard as expressive of emotion. The theory can perhaps be thought of as construing an expressive musical work as the counterpart in the auditory realm of a depiction or visual icon: an expressive musical work is an audible representation of the expression of emotion in the tone of the voice and in non-linguistic vocal sounds. And hence what is true of our experience of a visual icon will apply with the necessary modifications to our experience of a musical work which is heard as if it were the vocal expression of emotion. In particular, a musical work will be heard as the representation of the vocal expression of emotion only if the thought of a voice is present to the listener. But even if it is wrong to think of the theory in this way the conclusion still holds. For a listener hears music as if it were a voice only if the thought of a voice is present to him as he listens to the music. And yet few, if any, works which consist solely of music demand for their appreciation the thought of a voice; and in our experience of music only rarely, if at all, will the thought of a voice arise. Expressive music makes the listener aware of a state of mind; but it is not characteristic of expressive music to achieve this by representing, or intending the listener to imagine, a voice which expresses this state of mind. The awareness is not in this way indirect: it is not mediated by the thought of the expressive character of the voice. And if we now return to the rather different theory according to which when music is heard as if it were the human expression of emotion it is heard as if it were some non-vocal but audible means of expression that human beings possess, it is clear that it is open to a similar objection: when we listen to expressive music it will hardly ever be the case that we think of some imaginary way in which human beings might be capable of expressing their emotions in sounds.[28]

Elgar wrote on the score of his Violin Concerto a Spanish quotation from Lesage's *Gil Blas*:

'Aquí está encerra(da) el alma de. . . . .'
('Herein is enshrined the soul of. . . . .')[29]

The difficulty of explaining the sense in which a soul can be said to be enshrined in Elgar's music does not need to be emphasised. But two things are clear. The first is that we do not experience the music as if a person's soul were being expressed through the person's voice (or through some imaginary means of sound emission) in the sounds which compose the music or in the sounds of the solo violin alone. The second is that we do hear in the music a variety of feelings, moods, emotions and qualities of mind and character: emotional turbulence, exquisite tenderness, mounting excitement, ecstatic release, passionate regret, sincerity, wistfulness. . . . And these features of mind, character and feeling are integral to the value the music has for us: our response to the music is a function of the psychological states and processes it contains. I am not suggesting that the way we hear such an extraordinarily impassioned work as Elgar's Violin Concerto is exactly the same as that in which we hear all music expressive of emotion. But much expressive music is heard as containing states of mind that create the impression of a personality whose depth or shallowness of feeling, vitality or torpor, sincerity or insincerity, warmth or coldness attracts or repels. And the fact that our ordinary human sympathies and antipathies are engaged by expressive music is dependent not merely on our being made aware of a state of mind by the music, but on our entering imaginatively into that state of mind or on our experiencing imaginatively a sympathetic or antipathetic response to that state of mind. Hence it is indeed true that we can experience the state of mind a musical passage expresses, and this experience — as Elliott insists — can be an experience from within or from without. Nothing less than this can explain the power of expressive music to move us in the manner it sometimes achieves. What we lack is a satisfying account of how music can be a humanistic art. I have argued that a theory of musical expression based on the expressive character of the human voice (or some imaginary means of making sounds come from our bodies) does not provide such an account.

VIII
MEANING, EMOTION AND INFORMATION IN MUSIC

1   A theory of musical understanding should lie at the heart of a theory of musical value. For just as an utterance can be understood, misunderstood or listened to with incomprehension, so can a musical work. And just as the listener lacks a proper basis for certain kinds of evaluation of the utterance if he hears it but does not understand it – in particular, he is not in a position to make his own estimate of the truth-value of the utterance – so the listener lacks a proper basis for certain kinds of evaluation of the musical work if he hears it but does not understand it – in particular, he is not in a position to make his own estimate of the musical value of the work. Moreover, although the listener can find the experience of a musical work intrinsically rewarding whether or not he understands the music, it is only when he hears and understands the work that the value of the music can be realised in his experience. For the musical value of a work is a function of the experience the listener has when he understands the work he hears: the listener can be aware in his experience of the value of the music as music only if he hears the music with understanding.

Now if music is something that can be understood, it must be possible for many people to share the correct understanding of a musical work. In particular, it must be possible for this understanding to be possessed both by the composer of a musical work and by a listener. For not only can a composer listen to a work he has composed and thereby assume the rôle of the listener, but he can consider his work from the point of view of the listener in the act of composition itself – he can imagine how his work will sound and he can intend that it should be heard in a certain manner. Hence, there is the possibility of musical communication. For a composer can create something that he intends should sound a certain way and that he intends the listener to hear in a certain manner; and if he succeeds in his intention, the listener understands his work and undergoes the experience the composer intended. And if the listener undergoes the experience the composer imagined, and intended the listener to undergo, the composer has communicated that experience to the listener.

I have described this process of musical communication in such a way that it is untainted by the heresy of the separable experience – the heresy embraced by the transmission form of the expression theory of music.[1] For the experience the composer communicates to the listener is an experience that consists in hearing the composition in a certain manner. And a mode of hearing a composition is neither an accompaniment to an experience of hearing the composition nor a combination of an accompaniment and an experience of hearing the composition. Hence, if a mode of hearing a composition is valued, and the value resides specifically in hearing the composition in a certain manner, the value is not detachable from the experience of the composition. The musical value of a work can be located in an experience the composer communicates to the listener only if what is communicated is nothing other than an experience that, minimally, involves hearing the sounds that compose the music. To hear a composition with understanding is to have the experience the composer intends the listener to have; and it is this experience that can be said to be communicated from composer to listener. What is communicated is an experience constituted by the experience of hearing sounds.

But what is the nature of the experience that can be communicated from composer to listener? All that has been said so far is that the experience consists in hearing sounds in a certain manner – in that manner, whatever it is, that constitutes hearing the sounds of the composition with understanding. It is necessary to characterise in greater detail the kind or kinds of experience communicated by music not only to provide a theory of musical understanding, but to provide the foundation of a theory of musical value. For it is the intrinsic value of the experience communicated by a musical work that determines the musical value of that work from the point of view of the listener. And without a deeper understanding of the nature of musical experience, it is impossible to articulate this value. Accordingly, the answer we want to the question 'Why do we find it valuable to experience music?' is a characterisation of the nature of the experience, which enables us to understand the reason music matters to us.

It is clear that the most general characterisation of the musical experience of compositions of sounds describes it as the experience of sounds in which one or more of the elements of rhythm, melody and harmony is heard (and is intended to be heard). A more detailed characterisation will attempt to describe the experience of rhythm, melody and harmony in other terms, and so to provide an analysis of these phenomena; and it will specify the variety of forms realisable in the rhythmic, melodic and harmonic dimensions. The principal attempt to characterise the kind of experience communicated by music in such a manner that it reveals the nature of the value music has for us is Leonard B. Meyer's *Emotion and Meaning in Music.*[2] In what follows I examine the account Meyer offers of the nature of the experience communicated by music.

2   Meyer conceives the problem in the following way. Music is meaningful, and the meaning of music is something that is communicated to performers and listeners. But what exactly does music communicate; what constitutes musical meaning?

Meyer distinguishes two kinds of meaning that music can possess. Music can have an absolute meaning and it can have a referential meaning. The absolute meaning of a musical work is intramusical: it concerns solely the patterns and relationships established within the work and the intrinsic nature of the processes contained within the work. The referential meaning of a musical work consists in the relation in which the work stands to any extramusical phenomena to which it refers. Now Meyer's primary concern is with the absolute meaning of music. And he wishes to resolve the disagreement between two rival views of the absolute meaning of music and the nature and value of the experience involved in the perception and understanding of the musical relationships that constitute a musical work. These two views are Formalism and Absolute Expressionism. Formalism maintains that the intramusical meaning of music is intellectual: the musical relationships contained within a musical work are grasped intellectually and provide intellectual interest and satisfaction: music communicates a meaningful process which is appreciated by the intellect. Absolute Expressionism maintains that the intramusical meaning of music is emotional: the musical relationships established within a musical work arouse emotion in the listener who understands the style of the music: music communicates a process which is experienced with emotion and its value is dependent upon its ability to arouse emotion in the listener.

Each of these positions has suffered from an important weakness. Formalism has been unable to explain the sense in which an abstract, non-referential succession of tones can be said to have a meaning that a listener can understand and which is communicated to him if he understands the composition. Absolute Expressionism has been unable to account for the processes by which an abstract, non-referential succession of tones is experienced with emotion by the listener who understands the composition.

Meyer presents an analysis of musical meaning and experience in which both the intellectual aesthetic satisfaction of the Formalist and the emotion of the Absolute Expressionist are accounted for and the relationship between them is explained. His analysis attempts to remove the weaknesses from which Formalism and Absolute Expressionism have suffered, by giving an account of the sense in which an abstract, non-referential succession of tones may be said to have a meaning, and by giving an account of the processes by which perceived sound patterns come to be experienced with emotion. According to this analysis, there is a sense in which the rival positions of Formalism and Absolute Expressionism are not incompatible: these two positions consider the same musical processes from different points of view, and the same musical processes give rise to the two different kinds of meaning, intellectual and emotional, when considered from the different points of view. In the elaboration of his account Meyer attempts to apply some of the concepts of information theory to music in such a way as both to clarify and to support his theory of the conditions that give rise to meaning in music. He also tries to establish the dependence of the relative values of different pieces of music upon their satisfying, or the way in which they satisfy, the conditions for the creation of meaning that he has previously isolated.

3   In order to ground his account of the causal conditions of the emotional, the affective, aesthetic response to music – an account, as we have seen, not forthcoming from Absolute Expressionism – Meyer needs a general theory of the *nature* of emotion and the *conditions* that produce it. For if a value of music is to be found in the fact that music is heard with emotion, it is necessary to give an account of the nature of the emotion or emotions involved in the experience of music, and an account of how it is that music can arouse this emotion or these emotions, or the conditions under which it can do so. And it is natural to suppose that the first account can be derived from a more general account of

the conditions that are responsible for the creation of emotion. I shall consider, firstly, Meyer's theory of the conditions under which emotion comes into being, and, secondly, his theory of the nature of emotion.

4   Meyer's central thesis about the production of emotion is:

> Emotion or affect is aroused when a tendency to respond is arrested or inhibited.[3]

A tendency to respond is a tendency to think or act in some way. A tendency is arrested or inhibited if for some reason it is prevented from reaching completion. And Meyer illustrates his thesis by the example of a habitual smoker who wants a cigarette, finds he has none, and cannot obtain any, and who, in consequence, will very likely begin to respond in an emotional way by feeling restless, excited, irritated and finally angry.

Meyer appears to treat the inhibition of a tendency to respond in a particular way to a certain situation both as a necessary condition and as a sufficient condition for the arousal of emotion.[4] But it is clear that it is neither.

It is not a sufficient condition. For whether the inhibition of a tendency to think or act in some way results in emotion is dependent on the nature of the tendency and what generates it. Meyer's example of the habitual smoker is tendentious: the tendency it involves has a special status, since it is produced by a pressing desire. Now it is true that the frustration of an urgent desire will produce at least tension. And, as we shall see, it is the idea of tension that Meyer exploits in his discussion of the musical arousal of emotion. But there are many different kinds of occasion when the inhibition of a tendency to respond in some way may well not issue in emotion. If I am inclined to say something in reply to what you have just said, but you go on talking, my inclination may eventually lapse without my feeling any emotion at all.

It is not a necessary condition. For there are many emotions that do not arise as a consequence of the arrest or inhibition of a tendency to respond. Admiration, amusement, joy and pride can constitute the response to a situation, and they are not dependent upon the existence of a tendency to some other response which is prevented from reaching completion. It is clear that emotion is frequently experienced when something happens just the way one wanted it to happen, or when one is doing exactly what one wants to be doing; and in neither case is there

155

any need that the emotion should result from the arrest or inhibition of a tendency to respond.

5   Meyer's thesis about the nature of emotion is that although emotional or affective experience is differentiated, emotion or affect is in itself undifferentiated.[5] Affective experience is differentiated because it involves awareness of a stimulus situation: differences in stimulus situations differentiate affective experiences of those situations. It is the character of the awareness involved in an affective experience – the fact that it is awareness of a stimulus situation of a certain kind – it is this character and nothing else that differentiates affective experiences. The different kinds of emotion normally recognised – those for which we have names – are not distinguished from one another by what it is like to feel that emotion: the experiences of these emotions do not differ in their emotional or affective aspect. Instances of emotion are grouped into the kinds of emotion designated by our names of emotions solely in virtue of similarities between the stimulus situations that are the objects of the instances: two instances of emotion belong to the same kind if and only if they involve an awareness of the same kind of stimulus situation. There is no difference in the affect involved in the different kinds of emotion: the character of affect is always the same.

Now Meyer does not offer a positive characterisation of the nature of emotion or affect itself. But he does advance a negative claim: in itself affect is neither pleasant nor unpleasant.[6] Accordingly, it is only an emotional experience, and not emotion itself, that can be pleasant or unpleasant. And the pleasantness or unpleasantness of an emotional experience is a function of belief or lack of belief in the resolution of the inhibited tendency that generates the affective aspect of the experience. If emotion results from a tendency the inhibition of which is believed by the subject to be temporary, the inhibited tendency yields a pleasant emotional experience. If, on the other hand, the subject does not expect the inhibited tendency to be resolved, the emotion generated qualifies an unpleasant emotional experience.

But Meyer's thesis about the nature of emotion is no more acceptable than his thesis about the conditions for the production of emotion. The thesis presents an account of what it is for someone to be affected by emotion in a certain situation, and it maintains, firstly, that whenever someone experiences emotion the quality of the emotion experienced is exactly the same, and, secondly, that what distinguishes different occasions when someone is moved to emotion is the person's awareness of the situations to which he is responding. But it is absurd to claim that what someone *feels* when he feels fear at the sight of a snake and when he feels pride at his daughter's success and when he feels grief at the death of his mother and when he feels love for his baby is the same, all that differs being the person's awareness of a different object, event or state of affairs that is the cause of his feeling. The fact that a person's awareness is awareness of his daughter's success is insufficient for the emotion he feels to be pride, for this awareness might be the occasion for a different emotion, hatred or envy, for example. And in general the awareness of a particular object, event or state of affairs is consistent with different kinds of emotion being experienced. Hence, the nature of the emotion experienced on a certain occasion is not determined by the nature of the stimulus situation of which the subject is aware.

It might be suggested that a more generous understanding of the idea of a stimulus situation would enable Meyer's thesis to be preserved. If the stimulus situation were to include not only the external state of affairs of which someone is aware, but also those of his desires that concern that state of affairs and affect his response to it, the thesis would become more plausible. For someone's wanting his daughter to succeed or wanting his mother not to have died would then be part of the stimulus situation, the awareness of which distinguishes the kind of emotion involved in the emotional experience: someone experiences pride only if he is responding to a situation he welcomes and he experiences grief only if he is responding to a situation he does not welcome. But even if the thesis were interpreted in this fashion – in a fashion not in accordance with Meyer's understanding of the thesis[7] – it would still be wide of the mark. For the proud response to the welcome event is in itself different from the sorrowful response to the undesired happening. The proud response involves the experience of pleasure and the grief-stricken response involves the experience of distress; and these features are not elements of the stimulus situations, but are constituents of the emotions experienced in response to them.

It is clear that Meyer's thesis about the nature of emotion is incorrect.

6   According to Absolute Expressionism, the musical value of a musical work is a function of the music's power to generate emotion in the listener who understands the music. But the emotion with which music is experienced when it is understood is not one or more of the kinds of extra-musical emotions (anger, fear, sadness . . .), each of which requires the subject of the emotion to have an awareness or conception of some

extramusical state of affairs. Meyer hoped to explain this alleged feature of musical emotion by reference to his general theory of the nature of emotion. For if emotion *per se* is undifferentiated and an emotional experience receives its distinctive character from the nature of the stimulus situation of which the subject of the emotion is aware, the existence of affective states that involve no conception of extramusical states of affairs and that are experienced in response to music is unproblematic. The absolute meaning of music is intramusical, and, accordingly, the experience of a listener who is moved by the absolute meaning of a musical work will not include a conception of an extra-musical state of affairs, the thought of which generates the emotion the listener feels and provides the emotion with its distinctive character. When a listener responds with emotion to the absolute meaning of a musical work, the stimulus situation is the music itself; and since the absolute meaning of music is intramusical, the emotional experience of the listener is intramusical. However, the conception of musical emotion put forward by Absolute Expressionism receives no support from Meyer's account of the nature of emotion – for this account has no foundation.

7   We have seen reason to reject Meyer's thesis about the conditions for the production of emotion. Now this thesis was intended to serve as a basis for the explanation of music's capacity to arouse emotion in the listener who understands the music. It is clear that this explanation cannot be derived from the incorrect general thesis. Nevertheless, the explanation Meyer constructs of the way in which musical structure can generate emotion in an aesthetic response to music survives the removal of its basis in a general account of the production of emotion. For although Meyer's account of the specifically musical arousal of emotion makes essential use of the idea that emotion is produced by the arrest or inhibition of a tendency to respond; and although not every instance of emotion results from the checking of such a tendency; and although the checking of such a tendency is insufficient in itself for emotion to arise; it is sometimes the case that the arrest or inhibition of a tendency to respond to a situation issues in emotion. Hence, it is possible that the kinds of tendency to respond that are arrested or inhibited by music, or the specific manner in which music checks these tendencies, should be such that when these tendencies to respond to music are prevented from reaching completion emotion is created. It is therefore necessary to examine Meyer's account of the musical arousal of emotion in a listener who understands the absolute meaning of music.

8   When Meyer's thesis about the conditions for the arousal of emotion is applied to music, it undergoes a silent modification that makes it more plausible. When Meyer contrasts the affective experience of music with affective experience that is non-musical, and, more especially, non-aesthetic, the notion of tension supplants the notion of emotion: the inhibition of a tendency to respond creates tension; and it is the musical creation of tension that is contrasted with ways in which tension often arises and disappears in everyday experience. In everyday experience the factors that prevent a tendency to respond from reaching completion may be different in kind from those that give rise to the tendency; and the tension created by the inhibition of a tendency to respond is often dissipated by irrelevant occurrences, or released in activities unrelated to the inhibited tendency, so that there is no meaningful relation between the onset and the disappearance of tension. But in music tendencies to respond are activated and inhibited by the same stimulus and the tensions created by the inhibition of these tendencies are themselves resolved in a relevant and meaningful manner by this identical stimulus – the music itself.

The stress on the creation of tension becomes more prominent in Meyer's further elaboration of the concept of a tendency to respond and in his account of the way in which such a tendency can be aroused and inhibited by music. A tendency to respond is an *automatic response pattern*: it is a set of responses to a stimulus, which succeed one another in an automatic fashion unless inhibited or blocked in some way. An automatic response pattern can be natural or learned and it can be conscious or unconscious. Furthermore, a tendency to respond is, in a broad sense of the term, an *expectation*; for a tendency to respond, when not inhibited, is a kind of chain reaction in which a stimulus leads through a series of adjustments to a consequent that, accordingly, is 'implied in' the tendency when the tendency is activated. Consequently, it is clear how music can arouse tendencies to respond (automatic response patterns): for it is clear how music can arouse expectations. Expectations are continually aroused in the progress of a piece of music because, within a given style, some continuations are more probable than others, and are therefore expected by a listener who is familiar with the style. These expectations can be very specific, as when a listener expects a specific chord to complete a sequence of harmonies; or they can be more general, as when, after a melodic fragment has been repeated a number of times, a listener expects there to be a change in the music. And they can be conscious or unconscious. Moreover, each inhibition

159

of a tendency or delay in the satisfaction of an expectation creates uncertainty or suspense, and so tension, if only briefly. Hence, music is a process which creates tension in the listener who understands it and which then resolves this tension in an aesthetically significant manner. If the listener's expectation remains unconscious then the tension produced when a tendency to respond is inhibited is experienced as affect, rather than conscious expectation. And in this way we arrive at Meyer's fundamental thesis concerning the musical arousal of emotion:

Affect or emotion-felt is aroused when an unconscious expectation – a tendency to respond – activated by the musical stimulus situation, is temporarily inhibited or permanently blocked.[8]

But the demonstration of this thesis is imperfect. In fact, there are five main weaknesses in Meyer's account of the conditions under which music will be heard with emotion, in addition to those which accrue from the incorrectness of the general thesis. I shall rehearse four of these weaknesses now, but it will be more convenient to reserve the fifth for later consideration in connection with Meyer's account of rehearing music with emotion.

In the first place, the transition from the general thesis about the production of emotion to the thesis about the musical generation of emotion is effected by the dubious extension of the idea of an expectation to cover the conception of a tendency to respond as an automatic response pattern. It is clear that it is integral to music that it should create intramusical expectations in the practiced listener. But these expectations – whether conscious or unconscious – are not automatic response patterns: they do not consist in series of mental or behavioural responses that succeed one another in a determined order and at determined intervals unless checked in some way. And it is certainly untrue that the frustration of such expectations as these always results in emotion: an unexpected part of a work may well fail to move the listener.

Secondly, although it is true that delay in the satisfaction of an expectation can create uncertainty and also tension, tension is not the same as emotion, it is not included in each emotion and it does not necessarily generate emotion. Hence, the fact that the inhibition of an unconscious expectation may produce tension does not establish Meyer's account of the musical arousal of emotion.

Thirdly, Meyer maintains that the greater the accumulation of tension in the listener, the greater is the emotional release upon resolution.[9] Now it would be a misrepresentation of musical experience to construe the emotional release experienced when tension is resolved as the release from, rather than the release of, emotion: the discharge of tension is experienced with emotion. But the emotional release experienced in the resolution of tension created by music is not produced by the inhibition of a tendency or an expectation, but by its eventual satisfaction. Hence, it is not possible to identify Meyer's affect or emotion *per se* with the experience of tension. For the emotion experienced when tension is resolved does not itself consist of tension.

Finally, there is a question as to the value of the experience of affect in response to music. For affect is supposed to be neither pleasant nor unpleasant in itself. Accordingly, if music does produce undifferentiated emotion of this neutral kind in the manner suggested by Meyer, it is problematic what reason the listener has for valuing the affective response to music. Now it would be in line with Meyer's view of what determines the hedonic character of an emotional experience – that the pleasantness or unpleasantness of an emotional experience is a function of belief or lack of belief in the resolution of the inhibited tendency that generates the affective aspect of the experience – to maintain that the emotion generated by music will in general be experienced as pleasant by the listener in virtue of his belief in the resolution of the tendency the inhibition of which has resulted in emotion. But Meyer's account of the conditions that are necessary for, and that ensure, the pleasurableness of an emotional experience is inadequate. For it is not a sufficient condition for an emotional experience to be pleasurable that it should be accompanied by a belief that the tendency inhibited will be resolved: belief in resolution is compatible with the experience's being unpleasant. Meyer illustrates his view by the experience of falling through space: if this experience is not accompanied by a belief that there will be a safe outcome, the experience is likely to arouse highly unpleasant emotions; if the experience is accompanied by such a belief – as when someone experiences a parachute jump in an amusement park – it may be extremely pleasurable.[10] But there is no necessity about this: a belief that an inhibited tendency to respond will be resolved may not result in a pleasurable experience. If I am starving but I am prevented from eating food within reach, I am unlikely to enjoy the experience just because I believe that I will be free to eat the food in twelve hours' time.

9   We have now examined the outline account that Meyer offers of

the way in which an abstract, non-referential succession of tones can arouse emotion in the listener who understands the composition – an account needed by Absolute Expressionism, which construes the listener as understanding the intramusical meaning of a composition if his experience is coloured by emotion generated by the music at the right time and in the right manner. It is now necessary to examine Meyer's more general account of meaning – in particular, the intramusical meaning of musical work. It is this account that explains the sense in which an abstract, non-referential succession of tones can be said to have a meaning that a listener can understand intellectually – an explanation needed by Formalism, which construes the listener as understanding the intramusical meaning of a composition if his experience is informed with an intellectual awareness of the significance of the various episodes of the music as it unfolds.

The notion of meaning that provides the foundation for Meyer's account – something is meaningful if, and only if, it points to, indicates or implies something beyond itself[11] – is too thin and loose to bear much weight. But by making use of it a distinction can be drawn between two kinds of meaning; and the kind of meaning with which Formalism and Absolute Expressionism are concerned can be further delineated.

For a stimulus to have designative meaning it must imply, indicate or point to an event different in kind from itself – as when a word designates something that is not itself a word. For a stimulus to have embodied meaning it must imply, indicate or point to an event of the same kind as itself – as when one natural phenomenon (the rumble of distant thunder and the piling up of storm clouds) announces another (the coming of a storm). Formalism and Absolute Expressionism are concerned with embodied, not designative, meaning.

From the point of view of embodied meaning, a musical stimulus implies, indicates or points to musical events that may be forthcoming: one musical event – a tone, chord, phrase, section – implies, and makes the listener expect, another musical event. Embodied musical meaning is a product of expectation: a present musical stimulus has meaning for a listener if, and only if, it leads him to expect a more or less definite subsequent musical event. Hence, music in a style with which the listener is totally unfamiliar is experienced as meaningless. For expectation is largely a result of stylistic experience, and music in an unfamiliar style will arouse in the listener no expectations as to how the music will progress. In fact, a style is basically a complex system of probability relationships: probabilities as to the occurrence of a sound or group of sounds and probabilities as to one sound or group of sounds being followed by another sound or group of sounds.[12] When these probabilities are internalised as learned habits of expectation, the listener is able to experience a work in the style as a complex of felt probabilities: he entertains expectations with varying degrees of certainty, in accordance with what he feels the probabilities of subsequent musical events to be.

In order to accommodate the fact that the expectations of the listener change and are confirmed or disconfirmed as a musical work progresses, Meyer distinguishes three forms of embodied meaning: hypothetical meaning, evident meaning and determinate meaning.[13] But it is unnecessary for us to consider determinate meaning.

Hypothetical meaning is the meaning attributed to a musical event in virtue of the fact that when the listener who is at home in the style of the composition hears that event he expects (consciously or unconsciously) a certain musical event to follow: the sounds he expects constitute the hypothetical meaning of the sounds he hears. In fact, it will rarely be the case that the listener's expectation is single and fully definite. Within a given style, there will in general be many different ways in which a musical work might continue, and the state of mind of the practised listener will be complex: he is unlikely to form just a single expectation as to the continuation of the music; his expectations will be more or less specific; and the certainty of the expectations he forms will be directly proportional to the likelihood that the music will continue in the fashion expected. Accordingly, in most cases a musical event will not have a single hypothetical meaning, but many hypothetical meanings.

Evident meaning is the meaning attributed to a musical event in retrospect, when the listener hears what in fact the event leads to and understands the relationship between the antecedent and the consequent. Evident meaning can result in a revaluation of the hypothetical meaning of the initial event and, consequently, of the completed progression within a wider context; and if such revaluation takes place it then becomes the basis for future expectations. An instructive example of a sound term that has an evident meaning very different from its hypothetical meaning is the illustration Meyer takes from the C-minor fugue from Book I of the *Well-Tempered Clavier*. A sequence is begun that is followed by a motive that is at first understood as part of the sequence and, in consequence, leads the listener to form a certain expectation. But it quickly becomes apparent that the hypothetical meaning attributed to this motive is misleading, and that the motive is not really part of the sequence, but the beginning of the fugue theme. Consequently, the evident meaning of the motive is quite different from its hypothetical meaning. But it is also clear that Bach intended the listener to be misled in this way, and, accordingly, the listener's understanding of the significance of the whole passage includes this musical 'pun' as one of its meanings.[14]

Now the embodied meaning of a musical work can be understood in one or the other of two different ways. It can be realised in the listener's experience either emotionally or intellectually. When it is realised emotionally the listener has a meaningful experience but not, thereby, an experience the meaning of which he articulates. When it is realised intellectually the listener is conscious of the meaning: the thought of the meaning is present to his mind: the meaning is the object of the listener's consideration: the meaning has been objectified by the listener. This conscious objectification takes place only in the case of a certain kind of listener, and usually only under certain conditions. The listener must possess a mastery of musical theory and be disposed to reflect on the nature of his experience in order that he should understand it; and he will be inclined to realise the embodied meaning of a musical work intellectually when a normal, automatic response pattern is disturbed in some way – when a tendency to respond is inhibited or blocked. And so we reach the conclusion – a conclusion that effects a reconciliation between Formalism and Absolute Expressionism – that the same processes or the same stimulus conditions that give rise to affect also give rise to the objectification of embodied meaning – the aesthetic intellectual response to music. Musical meaning, whether affective or intellectual, arises when a tendency to respond is inhibited:

> the inhibition of a tendency to respond or, on the conscious level, the frustration of expectation, is the basis of the affective and the intellectual aesthetic response to music.[15] While the trained musician consciously waits for the expected resolution of a dominant seventh chord the untrained, but practiced, listener feels the delay as affect.[16]

10   This reconciliation is undoubtedly neat. But Meyer's thesis about the objectification of embodied meaning and the conditions that create intellectual aesthetic meaning cannot be taken seriously. For it is easy for the listener to adopt the self-conscious approach to musical meaning and objectify this meaning at moments other than those when a tendency to respond is blocked. Consequently, Meyer cannot maintain in the case of the intellectual aesthetic response to music the counterpart of the thesis he advances in the case of the affective response to music. Whereas it is plausible to assert that the inhibition of a tendency to respond is a necessary condition for the listener to respond to music with affect, it is not plausible to assert that the inhibition of a tendency to respond is a necessary condition for the listener to respond to music by objectifying its meaning. And in more guarded moments Meyer does not maintain this.[17] In fact, the strange nature of Meyer's thesis about the objectification of embodied meaning and, especially, the conditions that create intellectual aesthetic meaning is explained by the fact that Meyer oscillates between a wider and a narrower conception of the intellectual meaning of music. The wider conception is in accordance with Meyer's guiding idea that a sequence of tones has a meaning if it implies, indicates or points to other tones: if, for example, it gives rise to a conscious expectation. The narrower conception credits music with intellectual meaning only where the music is interesting, or where the nature of the music excites the trained musician to reflect on what is happening in the music. It is this more restrictive conception of meaning that is operative in Meyer's account of the conditions that give rise to musical meaning.

Meyer's position can be reconstructed in the following manner. There are two ways in which music can be experienced as meaningful: the music can arouse emotion in the listener or the music can arouse the listener's intellect. In the first case, the music is experienced affectively; in the second case, it is experienced with conscious conceptual awareness of the music's intramusical significance. When music is experienced affectively the meaning of the music is affective; when it is experienced with conscious conceptual awareness of its intramusical significance the meaning of the music is intellectual. The musical listener will be affected by a musical work or he will become interested in the nature of the music's intramusical significance when his expectation as to how the music will develop is not confirmed by the music. Hence, musical meaning, whether affective or intellectual, arises when a tendency to respond is blocked, or, more perspicuously, when an expectation is frustrated.

Thus Meyer's theory of the conditions for musical meaning is a theory of the conditions under which music is found interesting or moving, rather than trite or unaffecting. Music that is neither interesting nor affective is not meaningful — as when music progresses in just the way it has led the listener to expect. Music becomes meaningful when the expectation it has engendered in the listener who has internalised the style of the music is temporarily frustrated by an unexpected novelty of development. And the meaning of the music for the listener is affective or intellectual according as the music generates emotion in him or stimulates him to conceptualise the music's progress. Hence, the wider conception of meaning, which attributes meaning to the most banal musical progression, is replaced by the narrower conception in Meyer's theory of the conditions for musical meaning.

Now although it is true that a trained musician may consciously wait for the expected resolution of a dominant seventh chord, whilst an untrained listener will experience the delay only as affect, Meyer's account, which opposes the two responses, is mistaken. For the fact that the trained musician's expectation is a conscious conceptual awareness of the significance of the dominant seventh chord does not imply that he will not experience affect as its resolution is delayed. The conceptualisation of an expectation does not preclude the experience of affect. And this underscores a weakness in Meyer's thesis about the producion of emotion.[18] His thesis is that emotion is created when a tendency to respond is inhibited, unless the mental tension is rationalised as conscious conceptual awareness of the implication of the stimulus to which the subject is responding.[19] But such a process of rationalisation does not prevent an experience from being qualified by affect.

I have previously made the point that emotion can be produced not by the frustration of an expectation, but by its eventual satisfaction.[20] A similar point applies to Meyer's thesis about the Formalist's intellectual response to music. His thesis is that a trained musician is inclined to rationalise his experience of music through conscious conceptual awareness of the nature of the music he is listening to: he responds on the aesthetic intellectual level and experiences aesthetic satisfaction rather than affect. But the intellectual satisfaction of the Formalist must be a product not of the formation of a conscious expectation at a moment when his unconscious expectation is upset, but of the eventual satisfaction of this conscious expectation at a later stage of the music.

11   We are now in a position to consider Meyer's application of information theory to music. The essential features of information theory that Meyer attempts to exploit concern a 'message' sent from a transmitter to a receiver. A message is a finite, structured set of elements taken from a repertoire. Information theory provides a measure of the amount of 'information' transmitted by a message. The concept of information that information theory operates with is a technical concept:

it is the concept of a certain measurable quantity. The measure of this quantity depends upon the probability of the occurrence of the constituents of the message. The basic principle of the theory is that information is the reciprocal of probability: information and probability are inversely correspondent. The occurrence of the most probable element generates the least information; the occurrence of the least probable element generates the most information. The greater the probability of an element in a message, the less information it transmits; the smaller the probability of the element, the more information it transmits. The degree of redundancy of an element in a message is directly proportional to its probability: the more probable it is that a certain position in a message will be occupied by a particular element, the less necessary it is to transmit that element and the easier it is to reconstruct that part of the message if the element is omitted. Unwanted additions or alterations to a message that occur in transmission and that make it more difficult for the receiver to understand what the message is are called 'noise'. Hence, redundancy counteracts noise: the chance of reconstructing a message through a gap or distortion caused by noise is directly dependent on the probability that the element of the message occupies that position in the message. And redundancy reduces information: the greater the degree of redundancy, the less information is generated – for degree of redundancy is directly proportional to probability and probability and information are inversely correspondent.

Now we have seen that Meyer's thesis about musical meaning is that musical meaning, whether affective or intellectual, arises when a tendency to respond is blocked – when an expectation is frustrated. And this implies that musical meaning arises when the listener is confronted by an uncertain situation: his latent expectations as to the progress of the music are upset and his expectations become active either as affective experience or as conscious conceptual awareness.[21] Accordingly, Meyer's thesis about musical meaning can be reformulated as the thesis that musical meaning arises when the music makes the listener uncertain about its immediate development and the listener is forced to estimate, consciously or unconsciously, the probabilities of the possible ways in which the music will continue.[22] The listener experiences music as meaningful when, and only when, something less probable than expected happens. Hence, Meyer concludes, the conditions that give rise to musical meaning are the same as those that communicate information: the less meaningful the music, the less information it carries; the more meaningful the music, the more information it carries. For music is meaningful to the degree that the way it develops, although possible within the style of the work, is less probable than other possible continuations. And this is to say that music is as meaningful as it is informative.

Meyer develops the relation between musical meaning and information in a number of ways. In the first place, a musical work is not only a stochastic process — a system that produces a sequence of elements according to certain probabilities — it is a Markoff process — a stochastic process in which the probabilities depend upon the previous elements. Accordingly, a musical work is a message of just the kind to which the principles of information theory apply. Secondly, music contains considerable redundancy, and tones can be omitted from a musical passage without affecting the listener's ability to understand its meaning, if what has been omitted is probable with respect to the style of the work. Moreover, redundancy in music counteracts not only noise in the literal, technical sense of the word, but also 'cultural noise': disparities between the tendencies to respond required by a musical style and those possessed by a particular listener. (Meyer suggests that some of the difficulties that listeners experience with modern music result from the fact that the redundancy rate of the music is too low to counteract the inevitable cultural noise.) Finally, there is a positive correlation between information and musical value: what creates or increases the information transmitted by a piece of music increases its value as music.[23]

It is clear that Meyer's application of information theory to music stands or falls with its capacity to provide a satisfactory account of musical value — a topic I have just broached, but not yet explored. It is therefore necessary to examine the account that Meyer offers of the features that determine the value of a musical work.

12   Meyer's theory of musical value is a simple development of his theory of musical meaning. For he considers musical value to be a straightforward function of musical meaning. A musical work possesses embodied musical meaning when and only when it creates an expectation in the practised listener as to how it will continue and which it then frustrates: when and only when the practised listener feels that it is probable that the music will have a certain continuation which, in fact, it does not. Accordingly, a work that creates no expectations lacks embodied meaning; one in which the most probable goal is reached in the most direct way consistent with the style of the work possesses little or no meaning; and one in which the goal is never reached or is reached only after over-elaborate or irrelevant diversions loses the meaning it promised to sustain. Now Meyer maintains that musical value is directly proportional to musical meaning and, consequently, to musical information. In accordance with this view, a work that creates no expectations as to how it will continue lacks musical value; and one in which the most probable goal is never reached or is reached in the most direct manner consistent with the work's style or is reached only after superfluous diversions has little value.[24] In short, musical value is a product of the temporary inhibition of goal-oriented musical processes. And the correlative in the listener of the temporary inhibition of a musical process is the temporary inhibition of his tendency to respond − the temporary frustration of his expectation.

This account of musical value enables Meyer to explain the essential difference in musical value between sophisticated and primitive music. A primitive, immature person cannot tolerate frustration and uncertainty and seeks immediate gratification for his inclinations and desires. A sophisticated, mature person is willing to forgo immediate gratification in order to obtain a future gratification that he values more highly and he is capable of withstanding the frustration and uncertainty that this involves. Corresponding to this, primitive music provides almost immediate gratification and minimises uncertainty by limiting its tonal repertory, limiting departures from the tonic note, or frequent use of hackneyed musical devices: the listener is not required to experience lengthy delays in gratification of the kind integral to the appreciation of sophisticated music. Hence, the essential difference in musical value between sophisticated and primitive music is speed of tendency gratification.[25]

Now this account of musical value is entirely syntactical: it is based solely upon the embodied meaning of music and ignores both designative meaning and the sensuous appeal of music. Meyer defends his exclusive concentration upon syntactical considerations by arguing, firstly, that a response to the syntactical relationships of a musical work is more valuable than a response to the sensuous aspect of the music or a response to its designative meaning (its associative aspect), and, secondly, that sensuous-associative considerations are of minor importance in connection with musical value − music must be evaluated syntactically. The syntactical response is more valuable than either of the other responses because, unlike those other responses, it enables the listener to achieve self-realisation. The syntactical response involves the evaluation of various probabilities and the retrospective understanding of the relationships among musical events, and, consequently, it leads the listener to self-awareness and a sense of his individuality — the more so the more that immediate gratification is withheld by the music. In contrast with the syntactical response, each of the other responses involves the dissolution of the listener's self, which loses its identity either in voluptuous sensation or in day-dreaming. And syntactical considerations are of supreme importance in connection with musical value for a threefold reason: firstly, it is a completely subjective matter which of two works has the greater sensuous or associative appeal; secondly, syntactical relationships play an important role in all except the most primitive musical works, even in those works that strongly emphasise the sensuous; thirdly, it is the superior syntactical organisation, not the superior sensuousness, of a work that emphasises the sensuous that makes it superior to another work that also emphasises the sensuous.[26]

But Meyer's justification of the view that the syntactical response to music is more valuable than the sensuous or the associative response is inadequate. For there is no reason to believe that the syntactical response to music leads the listener to self-awareness and individualisation. If the syntactical response is affective, rather than intellectual, then the evaluation of alternative probabilities of musical development occurs unconsciously and, consequently, appears not to be significantly related to increased self-awareness. And whether the syntactical response is affective or intellectual, it cannot have the status that Meyer wishes to credit it with. For the ability to make complex assessments of occurrences within a particular domain is compatible with a crude and unreflective attitude towards the nature and lives of human beings; in particular, it is easy for it to co-exist with a radical ignorance or misapprehension of one's own self. And this is especially true when the events that are being assessed are being considered in abstraction from any reference they might make to, or any relevance they might have for, human life — as is the case with the syntactical response to music. The truth is that the kind of ability Meyer regards as being exercised in the syntactical response to music is only a necessary condition of the capacity for self-awareness, and the form this ability assumes in the syntactical response is not specially suited either to the more general development of this ability or to the development of the form in which it is realised in self-awareness.

Now it follows from Meyer's theory of musical value that a syntactically simple musical work — one that involves few intricate or subtle interconnections between musical events — must be of little musical value. But there seem to be syntactically simple musical works that induce extremely moving syntactical responses. Furthermore, a musical work that is syntactically simpler than another work can have a much greater musical value than that other, more complex, work. Meyer meets the first of these two points with a speculation: when a syntactically simple musical work induces an extremely moving musical response, the response is associative, not syntactical, and the response indicates an appeal to childhood, remembered as untroubled and secure.[27] But the truth of this speculation would not provide a defence of the supremacy of syntactical considerations over associative considerations. And if the speculation is false, there can be musical works whose syntactical musical value is not dependent upon the particular syntactical feature that Meyer indentifies as the vehicle of that value – the creation and inhibition of tendencies to respond. Meyer meets the second of the two points with a refinement or clarification: syntactical musical value varies in direct proportion not to amount of information, but to the ratio of amount of information to the means used to generate the information.[28] Accordingly, two works that yield the same amount of information will have different syntactical musical values if one uses less means than the other to generate that information.

At this point Meyer's theory of musical value takes an unexpected turn. For he maintains that a purely syntactical theory, whilst appropriate to musical value *per se*, is inadequate as an account of musical greatness. It must be replaced by a theory that assigns a high value to the 'content' of musical experience. Musical experience acquires a content through the interaction between the syntactical relationships and the associative aspect of the music. And Meyer specifies the content of the experience of a great work as an awareness of a number of fundamental features of human life:

> man's sense of the inadequacy of reason in a capricious and
> inscrutable universe; his feeling of terrible isolation in a callous and
> indifferent, if not hostile, nature; and his awareness of his own
> insignificance and impotence in the face of the magnitude and power
> of creation.[29]

Meyer's theory of greatness in music allows that a work that has a syntactical musical value no more, perhaps less, than the syntactical musical value of a second work might, nevertheless, be the greater work; and it maintains that the greatest works are those that combine the highest order of syntactical musical value with the most profound content. And the importance of the content of the experience of great music lies in the fact that the suffering involved in the acknowledgement of the fundamental features of human life leads the listener to self-realisation: self-awareness, individualisation and purification of the will. Just as Meyer maintains the superiority of the syntactical response to the associative and the sensuous responses on the ground that, unlike those responses, it is conducive to self-realisation, so he maintains the supremacy of the experience of great music on the ground of its special suitability to induce self-realisation. The ultimate value of music is the same as the ultimate value of all art: its ability to individualise the self.[30]

But Meyer's theory of musical greatness is infected with a vagueness that minimises its attractiveness. Musical experience is said to acquire its content through interaction between the syntactical relationships embodied in a musical work and the associative aspect of the music. But the process of interaction is not characterised in such a manner that it is understandable that musical experience can have the kind of content that Meyer attributes to the experience of great music.[31] And it is unclear how the listener's appreciation of the purely musical syntactical features of a work is informed with the consciousness of extramusical facts that Meyer considers to be integral to the experience of great music. Furthermore, the basis of the association between the syntactical character of a musical work and the facts of human existence that Meyer highlights is not specified, and, in consequence, it is impossible to determine whether the association is well-founded and relevant to the music's value. Moreover, Meyer has argued that the syntactical response to music is superior to the associative response in that, whereas the syntactical response encourages self-realisation, the associative response involves the dissolution of the self in the reverie of day-dreams. Hence, an explanation is needed of how the associative aspect of music can assume the importance Meyer credits it with in his theory of musical greatness. Finally, Meyer's reason for assigning such importance to the alleged content of the experience of great music is inadequate. For the experience of a listener will have this content only if he is already aware of the features of human life that define this content. And the listener is unlikely to realise this awareness in his experience of great music more forcibly than in his experience of much else — when the immensity of the universe is visibly present to him as he contemplates the stars on an unclouded night, for instance. If the experience of great music is specially conducive to self-realisation, it possesses this character in virtue of a nature different from that assigned to it by Meyer's theory.

13 I have reserved till last a consideration of what might seem to be an insuperable difficulty for Meyer's theory of emotion and meaning in music. It appears to be a consequence of his theory that the significance and emotional impact of a musical work will inevitably decline the more the listener becomes familiar with the music. For his theory is based on the idea that music is meaningful only when, and to the extent that, it creates expectations in the listener that are held temporarily in suspense as the music progresses in a manner somewhat different from what was expected. But with repeated hearings the expectations formerly created in the listener and which the music did not satisfy immediately or even at all will be replaced by more accurate expectations, the unexpected will become the expected and uncertainty will give way to certainty. If musical significance is inversely proportional to the degree of probability that a musical event is felt to have, it seems that musical significance must decrease as a listener becomes increasingly familiar with a particular work; and if music is heard with emotion only when uncertainty about the nature of the course of the music arises, it seems as if the listener's experience of music with which he is well acquainted must be emotionally neutral. And yet it seems undeniable that music with which a listener is thoroughly familiar can retain its power to move him.

Meyer attempts to meet this apparent difficulty for his theory by advancing four main considerations. In the first place, the listener tends to forget the less well-structured parts of a work and to regularise in memory the irregular parts. Consequently, various features, including those responsible for affect or interest, are likely to remain unexpected through a number of hearings. Secondly, a listener's expectations are dependent upon his past musical experience: each musical experience affects the expectations aroused in later acts of listening to music. Accordingly, the expectations that a particular work will generate in a listener are being continually modified, if only slightly, by whatever musical experiences he has. Thirdly, different performances of the same musical work involve differences in the manner and timing of the sounds required by the score. Hence, a listener's expectations will not be satisfied exactly by an unfamiliar performance or they will be sufficiently indefinite for each new performance to yield new information. Finally, the listener can hold his knowledge of a musical work in suspension and abandon himself anew to the surprises and delays the work contains. And if he does so, the expectations he experiences will be satisfied by the work as imperfectly as they were satisfied when he was less familiar with the work.[32]

Now it is certainly true that where these considerations are applicable, and in proportion to the force with which they can be applied, the listener will be able to rehear music with emotion and interest in the manner prescribed by Meyer's theory. But a question remains. For suppose that these considerations do not apply to a listener or apply with minimal force: the listener remembers each part of a work in great detail; his 'internalised probability system' − his set of tendencies to respond to musical stimuli − is minimally affected by additional musical experiences; he has repeatedly listened to a certain recorded performance that he can recall perfectly; and his experience is now informed with his knowledge of how the music (as performed) will develop. Must his experience of the performance now be unrewarding: must it be devoid of interest and emotion? Meyer's theory of emotion and meaning in music stands or falls according as this question should be answered affirmatively or negatively.[33] But it is not easy to determine the correct answer to the question. Meyer draws attention to a number of facts: composers develop and transform the stylistic traditions they inherit; performers tend to vary their performances of familiar works; and the more complex of two works of equal excellence can be reheard with enjoyment more often than the simpler work.[34] But it is unclear that these facts dictate the correct answer to the question. Each is an indication of the need for novelty that is integral to human life: we tend to lose interest in undergoing exactly the same experience we have had many times before. But there are some experiences, especially those that spring from biological needs, for which this is not so. Hence, the facts Meyer cites do not preclude the possibility that the listener we are considering should be able to derive emotional satisfaction from his familiar experience. In so far as I have been able to assume the position of the imagined listener myself − and it is relatively easy to do this for short works or for parts of works − I have found it possible to derive the same satisfaction from familiar works. Of course, if I were to listen to the same performance time and time again without break, my interest would eventually flag and I would find myself unable to respond emotionally to the music. But that is not what is at issue: it expresses only the need for novelty in the particular form of satiation. The point in question is whether the syntactical feature that Meyer's theory identifies as the source of musical emotion is the sole syntactical cause of emotion. If any weight should be attached to my own experience of rehearing music with emotion, Meyer's theory is an inadequate explanation of the emotional appeal of music.

SUMMARY CONCLUSION

I have argued that there is a requirement that must be observed by any acceptable theory of musical value: the theory must respect the autonomy of music. From the point of view of the listener, the value of music is intrinsic, not merely instrumental: the listener values the experience of a musical work in itself; the experience he values can be specified only by reference to the music that is experienced in undergoing the experience; the experience is not replaceable by a different experience that offers the listener exactly what he values in the original experience − for it is the experience itself, not some separable component or effect of the experience, that is valued. It is the failure of the transmission form of the expression theory of music to meet this requirement that disqualifies the theory.

I have also claimed that it is mistaken to think of each valuable piece of music as owing its value as music to the fact that the music is expressive of emotion: this is sometimes, but not always, so. Accordingly, a viable theory of musical value must not only respect the autonomy of music, but must allow music to possess different kinds of value: in some cases, but not all, music is valuable partly because it stands in a certain relation to an emotion − the music is an expression of the emotion. I have argued that the nature of this relation cannot be clarified by basing the explanation on the model of the expression of emotion in the human voice.

If the nature of this relation cannot be elucidated by a comparison with the expression of emotion in the human voice, one reason that might be suggested as an explanation of this fact is that music can penetrate beneath the surface of emotion to its innermost core: music is not restricted to the outer world of the expression of emotion but reaches as far as the inner world of emotion itself. I believe that this is so; but I have argued that Schopenhauer's theory of music, which construes music as a certain kind of representation of the essence of emotion, has too many defects, even when it is stripped of its metaphysical extravagances, to serve as a foundation for a theory of musical value.

A different approach, that continues to regard music as being essentially related to emotion as it exists outside the experience of music, proposes that music should be thought of as some kind of symbol of the emotional life. Now there are many senses of the word 'symbol', and in some of these senses it is undoubtedly true that at least some musical works are symbols of states or aspects of the mind. But I have argued that it is mistaken to suppose that the value of music is to be located in music's capacity to symbolise the morphology of feeling — something that supposedly eludes the non-poetic use of langauge — by music's exemplification of forms possessed by life as life is felt to unfold in time.

An alternative solution to the problem music presents maintains that the basis of music's value and the secret of its emotional appeal is not to be found in some relation in which music can stand to an extramusical emotion, but in the fact that music, when it is valued, is experienced with an emotion specific to it: the value of a musical work is dependent upon the music's power to generate a certain intramusical emotion in a listener who understands the absolute meaning of the music. This theory appears in two forms. The first asserts that the emotion specific to music is a quality of emotion that nothing other than the experience of music can be clothed in. The second claims that the intramusical emotion is emotion that is differentiated from other emotion only by the fact that it involves the awareness of music as its stimulus. But I have tried to show that these emotions are myths. And I have also argued that the musical generation of emotion is not illuminated if it is viewed in the light of the principles of information theory.

If my arguments are correct, a new theory of music is needed; and if this theory is to be revealing it will, I believe, have to be less monolithic than the theories I have rejected.

NOTES

I   THE EMOTIONS

1 See Aristotle's definition of the class of emotions and also his definitions of the individual emotions anger, fear, shame, pity, indignation, envy and emulation in his *Rhetoric*, 1378a19–22, 1378a30–2, 1382a21–2, 1382b14–6, 1385b13–6, 1386b11, 1387a9, 1386b17–20, 1387b20–2, 1388a30–4. His (rough) definition of the class of emotions involves a reference to pleasure and pain, and each of his definitions of the individual emotions involves a reference to a thought experienced with pleasure or pain.
2 Sigmund Freud, *Three Essays on the Theory of Sexuality*, trans. James Strachey (London, 1962), pp. 71–2.
3 For the distinction between immediate and long-term wants see Anthony Kenny, *Action, Emotion and Will* (London, 1963), p. 124.
4 Compare R. G. Collingwood's view that emotion can be a charge either on a sensum or on a mode of consciousness. See *The Principles of Art* (Oxford, 1960), p. 162, pp. 231–2.
5 See C. D. Broad's definition of the concept of extensive magnitude in his *Kant, An Introduction* (Cambridge, 1978), p. 149.

II   THE REPUDIATION OF EMOTION

1 Eduard Hanslick, *The Beautiful in Music*, trans. Gustav Cohen (London and New York, 1891).
2 The thesis that the beauty of music is specifically musical does not follow solely from the thesis that musical value is unrelated to the emotions. For musical value might be related to some other extra-musical phenomenon. But Hanslick believes that the most significant opposition to the view that the beauty of music is specifically musical stems from the idea that the musical value of a work is in some way a function of the emotions.

177

3 *The Beautiful in Music*, pp. 11, 18, 32f.
4 *The Beautiful in Music*, pp. 33–5.
5 *The Beautiful in Music*, p. 34.
6 *The Beautiful in Music*, p. 19.
7 *The Beautiful in Music*, p. 37.
8 See, for instance, *The Beautiful in Music*, pp. 37–8. This is also what Hanslick is concerned with in his discussion of music's ability to depict other kinds of natural phenomena.
9 I am here concerned only with the matter of copying features of the emotions themselves and I am ignoring the possibility of copying features of phenomena other than the emotions but which are intimately linked to the emotions. For an excellent discussion of the possibility of copying features of the natural expressions of the emotions in bodily movement and the human voice, see Edmund Gurney, *The Power of Sound* (London, 1880), Chapters XIV, XXI.
10 See *The Beautiful in Music*, Chapter VII. In one place Hanslick asserts that the 'aesthetic inquirer', confining himself to what the music itself contains, 'will . . . detect in Beethoven's Symphonies impetuousness and struggling, an unsatisfied longing and a defiance, supported by a consciousness of strength' (pp. 87–8). But he fails to integrate this thought into his theory that the beauty of music is specifically musical, and that the most that music can do is to reflect the dynamic properties of feelings.
11 See Chapter V.
12 *The Beautiful in Music*, pp. 56f.
13 *The Beautiful in Music*, pp. 18–27, 107f., Chapter V.
14 See, for example, Ludwig Wittgenstein, *The Blue and Brown Books* (Oxford, 1960), p. 178.
15 Compare the argument developed in the fourth and fifth sections of Chapter VII.
16 I return to the issue of the musical arousal of definite extramusical emotions in Chapters IV and VII.
17 Edmund Gurney, *The Power of Sound*.
18 Leonard B. Meyer, *Emotion and Meaning in Music* (Chicago, 1956).
19 See Chapters IV and VIII.
20 The ascription to music of emotional qualities is an instance of a more general phenomenon: the ascription to music of essentially human or animal characteristics. To establish that the beauty of music is specifically musical it would be necessary to extend the account Hanslick advances of the ascription of emotional qualities to music to the ascription of any features that might be thought integral to the value of music and which apparently involve a reference to what are essentially human characteristics. It is clear that Hanslick insists on such an extension.
21 *The Beautiful in Music*, pp. 74–5.
22 But see the fourth section of Chapter III.
23 This is only one possibility. For others, see Ludwig Wittgenstein, *The Blue and Brown Books*, pp. 129–41.

24 I. A. Richards, *Practical Criticism* (London, 1964), pp. 221-2.
25 See J. O. Urmson, 'Representation in Music' in *Philosophy and the Arts, Royal Institute of Philosophy Lectures* 1971-2 (London, 1973). The only difference between this thesis and Hanslick's position is that whereas the thesis is unspecific as to the kind of purely audible feature that emotion terms are used to attribute to music, Hanslick's position maintains that they attribute dynamic features.
26 This claim is also a presupposition of Nelson Goodman's theory of expression as applied to music. See 'Some Notes on *Languages of Art*' in his *Problems and Projects* (Indianapolis and New York, 1972). In my view there is no reason to believe the presupposition of the purely sensible description thesis that there must be some description in purely audible terms that is satisfied by each sad melody and by no non-sad melody.
27 See O. K. Bouwsma, 'The Expression Theory of Art' in *Philosophical Analysis*, edited by Max Black (Ithaca, 1950).
28 The denial of this possibility seems sometimes to arise from a conflation of the grounds of justification for the transferred use of the word with what is to be understood by the application of the word in the new context.

III   MOTION AND EMOTION IN MUSIC

1 Carroll C. Pratt, *The Meaning of Music* (New York, 1931), pp. 157f.
2 John Ruskin, *Modern Painters*, Volume III (London, 1856), Chapter XII.
3 *The Meaning of Music*, p. 184.
4 Even if movement need not be continuous – so that an object could change its position without tracing a continuous path between its different positions – an object moves from A to B only if *it* is first at A and then at B.
5 '. . . in addition to the purely qualitative pitch-character by which tones are readily placed with respect to each other along a scale there may be discovered an intrinsic spatial character in tones . . .'. *The Meaning of Music*, p. 54.
6 Edmund Gurney, *The Power of Sound* (London, 1880), p. 139.
7 *The Power of Sound*, pp. 139-40.
8 Differently coloured patches of paint on a canvas can be seen as at different distances from the plane of the canvas. But this does not imply that the experience of seeing colours does provide a proper parallel to the experience of pitch. For (i) the sense in which one colour can be seen as behind another colour is not the same as that in which one note can be heard as higher or lower than another, and (ii) difference in pitch *is* difference in distance and direction: difference in colour is difference in kind which may *in addition* involve perceived differences in distance.

9   There are many respects in which the analogy fails to hold. For example: more than one sound (with the same timbre) can have the same pitch at the same time but not more than one chair can occupy the same spot at the same time; two sounds of different pitch cannot change their distance apart unless one of them changes intrinsically (namely, with respect to pitch), whereas two chairs can change their distance apart without either of them changing intrinsically.

10 It will be clear from what I have said that the words 'up' and 'down', and their relatives 'high' and 'low' and the comparative forms of these words, are not needed in the description of the material of music. When the predicate 'is higher than' is used to describe pitch relations it does not stand for the same relation as it does when it is used to describe spatial relations, and the relation it stands for can be fully characterised without using the predicate or any predicate synonymous with it. Its use in the domain of pitch no more co-incides with its use in the domain of space than it does with its use in the domain of numbers. Furthermore, it is in general unnecessary to bring the concepts high and low to the appreciation of music. Only if music has a certain kind of representational intent will it be necessary to hear sounds as specifically high or low. And the prime manifestation of the experience of hearing a note as high will be the inclination to apply the word 'high' (or a synonym) to the note.

11 For the purpose of the following argument it is not in fact necessary to accept this thesis. There would be little loss of plausibility if it were replaced by the account I have offered of the experience of pitch.

12 A similar misrepresentation is found in the works of Susanne K. Langer. See her *Feeling and Form* (London, 1973), pp. 107–8.

13 We talk of perceiving movement in cases where continuity of change of position is manifestly lacking. But it is clear that in such cases we do not literally see an object moving from one position to another. Rather, we draw this conclusion from what we do see.

14 *The Meaning of Music*, p. 198.

15 *The Meaning of Music*, p. 189.

16 *The Meaning of Music*, pp. 197–8.

17 *The Meaning of Music*, p. 203. See also 'Structural vs Expressive Form in Music', *The Journal of Psychology*, 1938.

18 Carroll C. Pratt, 'Objectivity of Aesthetic Value', *Journal of Philosophy* Vol. XXXI (1934).

19 Pratt believed that music is intrinsically an autonomous art. But it can be given an extraneous meaning by listeners and treated as a heteronomous art which is representative of phenomena external to itself. And there is one kind of meaning that music is often given which is only a short step away from the intrinsic nature of music's formal structure and that is closely related to the fact that music and bodily movements that are involved in moods and emotions can have common characteristics: the kind of significance that is

accorded to music by Schopenhauer's theory of music demystified. And this kind of meaning can have a special importance. See *The Meaning of Music*, Part III. I consider Schopenhauer's theory of music in Chapter V.

20 *The Meaning of Music*, p. 204.

IV   SEXUAL EMOTION IN IDEAL MOTION

1 Edmund Gurney, *The Power of Sound* (London, 1880).
2 *The Power of Sound*, p. 317.
3 *The Power of Sound*, p. 120.
4 *The Power of Sound*, pp. 116–24, 315–17.
5 Charles Darwin, *The Descent of Man* (London, 1874), Chapter XIX.
6 See also Charles Darwin, *The Expression of the Emotions in Man and Animals* (Chicago, 1965), pp. 87, 217. Darwin's explanation is based not on principles of natural selection, but on the Lamarckian principle that associations can be inherited.
7 *The Power of Sound*, p. 533.
8 *The Power of Sound*, p. 316.
9 *The Power of Sound*, p. 123, and especially 'The Psychology of Music' in Edmund Gurney, *Tertium Quid* (London, 1887) Volume II, pp. 297–8, where Gurney confesses that this difficulty seems to him 'scarcely less than that of leaving Darwin's suggestion on one side'.
10 *The Power of Sound*, p. 369. The description is unsurprisingly reminiscent of sexual pleasure.
11 *The Power of Sound*, p. 530. Compare Gurney's remarks on the use of the term 'vulgar' to describe music at *The Power of Sound*, p. 378, where he maintains that our condemnation of a tune as vulgar must rest on its vulgarising musical taste – and so tending to decrease the capacity for and the chance of greater pleasure – and not on its vulgarising moral character. A taste for tunes that yield only a trivial and fleeting pleasure is no more incompatible with a high moral character than a taste for bad puns or garlic. Ethics and aesthetics are here two, not one.
12 It is entirely consonant with this stance that Gurney should declare that it would be nothing but a gain if he could now enjoy a melody that he once found impressive but no longer does. *The Power of Sound*, p. 233 fn. 1.
13 The idea quickly loses its appeal if we consider some reaction to music other than delight. I may be bored by the music to which I am listening but I am not thereby acquainted with a kind of boredom that can be found only in the experience of music. In any case, it could not be a matter of necessity that the sublimated quintessence of sexual emotion that Gurney finds in the experience of music should be aroused only by music. In principle, it could be experienced in response to many kinds of thing.

14   *The Power of Sound*, pp. 312–13.

15   *The Power of Sound*, p. 313 n.

16   *The Power of Sound*, p. 352.

17   *The Power of Sound*, p. 131 n.

18   This applies equally to a theory that identifies emotional expression with the suggestion, and not the arousal, of emotion. In fact, there is a further defect in Gurney's account of musical expression. If M arouses F, what is it that determines whether M expresses F or M expresses Q, where F ≠ Q but F is the feeling with which Q is contemplated? Does awe-inspiring music express awe or, instead, the quality of greatness to which awe is directed?

19   Gurney discusses this phenomenon at *The Power of Sound*, pp. 207f.

20   The term 'synaesthesia' can be used less strictly than this, so as to cover the mere association of a phenomenon experienced in the exercise of one sense-modality with a phenomenon experienced in the exercise of a different sense-modality, or to cover any 'felt resemblance' between phenomena specific to different senses, or so as to include every metaphorical use of a word.

21   *The Power of Sound*, p. 375.

22   In his consideration of the means whereby music can express emotions Gurney examines the possible contribution of four features: timbre, certain harmonic features, the major and minor modes, and the dynamic characteristics, speed and rhythm. He finds the expressive capabilities of the first three features to be slight.

23   *The Power of Sound*, p. 341.

24   *The Power of Sound*, pp. 337–8. Gurney's uncertainty about the musical expression of emotion is here manifest. For he appears to allow that music can arouse the feeling of triumph (for example) and yet not express triumph. Perhaps he wished to maintain that M expresses E if and only if M both suggests and arouses E, and that music might not express the emotion it arouses because it suggests a different emotion.

25   Deryck Cooke, *The Language of Music* (London, 1960).

26   *The Power of Sound*, pp. 339–40.

27   But Gurney's arguments can sometimes be given a wider reference by not restricting the musical expression of emotion to the musical arousal of the emotion expressed.

28   *The Power of Sound*, p. 495.

29   *The Power of Sound*, p. 512.

30   *The Power of Sound*, p. 314. Compare: 'what is lugubrious or violent has of course an exceptionally good chance of being "expressed" by what is ugly, shiftless, or abrupt as music.' *The Power of Sound*, p. 517. The distinction between melancholy and lugubriousness is perhaps the distinction between, on the one hand, pensive sadness and, on the other hand, misery, gloom, dreariness or cheerlessness.

31   See the tenth section of this chapter.

32   *The Power of Sound*, p. 338.

33 *The Power of Sound*, p. 342 n.
34 Ludwig Wittgenstein, *The Blue and Brown Books* (Oxford, 1960), pp. 158 f.
35 Although Gurney would reject this position, he occasionally approaches it when explaining the expressive character of some music by reference to the nature of the process by which the listener realises it: as when he explains the contrasting characters of the major and minor modes and the yearning character of the opening of Schumann's *Des Abends*. *The Power of Sound*, pp. 272 f, 330 f.
36 *The Power of Sound*, p. 341.
37 *The Power of Sound*, p. 342.

V   THE WORLD AS EMBODIED MUSIC

1 Arthur Schopenhauer, *The World as Will and Representation*, trans. E. F. J. Payne (New York, 1969).
2 Thomas Mann, 'Schopenhauer' in his *Essays of Three Decades*, trans. H. T. Lowe-Porter (London, 1947).
3 *The World as Will and Representation*, Volume II, p. 195.
4 *The World as Will and Representation*, Volume II, p. 318.
5 Schopenhauer does little to make clear the concept of an Idea. But in one place he illustrates his conception: 'When clouds move, the figures they form are not essential, but indifferent to them. But that as elastic vapour they are pressed together, driven off, spread out, and torn apart by the force of the wind, this is their nature, this is the essence of the forces that are objectified in them, this is the Idea. . . To the brook which rolls downwards over the stones, the eddies, waves and foam-forms exhibited by it are indifferent and inessential; but that it follows gravity, and behaves as an inelastic, perfectly mobile, formless, and transparent fluid, this, *if known through perception*, is the Idea'. *The World as Will and Representation*, Volume I, p. 182.
6 *The World as Will and Representation*, Volume I, pp. 178–9.
7 *The World as Will and Representation*, Volume I, p. 196.
8 *The World as Will and Representation*, Volume I, p. 257.
9 *The World as Will and Representation*, Volume I, pp. 260–1.
10 *The World as Will and Representation*, Volume II, p. 202.
11 *The World as Will and Representation*, Volume I, p. 261.
12 *The World as Will and Representation*, Volume I, pp. 164, 250, 260. Also: '*joy and sorrow* are not representations or mental pictures but affections of the will'. *Parerga and Paralipomena*, trans. E. F. J. Payne (Oxford, 1974), Volume II, p. 606.
13 *The World as Will and Representation*, Volume II, pp. 593, 275.
14 *The World as Will and Representation*, Volume II, p. 451.
15 *The World as Will and Representation*, Volume II, p. 451.
16 *The World as Will and Representation*, Volume I, p. 264.
17 Another example: 'Because music does not, like all the other arts,

exhibit the *Ideas* or grades of the will's objectification, but directly the *will itself*, we can also explain that it acts directly on the will, i.e., the feelings, passions, and emotions of the hearer, so that it quickly raises these or even alters them'. *The World as Will and Representation*, Volume II, p. 448.

VI MUSIC AS UNCONSUMMATED SYMBOL

1 Susanne K. Langer, *Philosophy in a New Key* (New York, 1951).
2 *Philosophy in a New Key*, p. 193.
3 Susanne K. Langer, *Problems of Art* (London, 1957), p. 91.
4 *Philosophy in a New Key*, p. 199.
5 In her later (1951) preface to *Philosophy in a New Key* Langer refers to 'the unsatisfactory notion of music as an essentially ambiguous symbol' and to a possible replacement. But a study of her later writings reveals that all she feels is an uneasiness about the term 'unconsummated symbol'. Accordingly, she no longer characterises music as an unconsummated symbol but, instead, as a significant form, the significance of which is its 'vital import', i.e., the pattern of felt life it presents. But the theory itself is unchanged.

    It is not quite true that the text presents a complete account of Langer's theory of musical significance. *Feeling and Form* (London, 1953) contains a curious, and badly motivated, addition to her theory of music as an unconsummated symbol. The essence of music is here located in Hanslick's 'tönend bewegte Formen', 'sounding forms in motion', a motion of forms that can only be heard because the forms only seemingly exist and are elements in a 'purely auditory illusion'. But it is clear that Langer has been misled by the fact that music is described in terms of words drawn from the language of motion, and there is no need for the theory of pure duration she is led to advance. For she concludes from the fact that music does not literally possess the features metaphorically attributed to it that it must therefore present an illusion or apparition of these features. And this is a *non sequitur*.
6 Ludwig Wittgenstein, *Tractatus Logico-Philosophicus*, trans. D. F. Pears and B. F. McGuinness (London, 1961).
7 *Philosophy in a New Key*, p. 67.
8 Her position may well be vulnerable – as Wittgenstein's would not – to the objection brought against it by Ernest Nagel in his review of *Philosophy in a New Key* in *Journal of Philosophy*, Vol. XL (1943).
9 *Problems of Art*, p. 71.
10 Compare the point made in the last paragraph of the sixth section of Chapter II.
11 See, for example, *Mind: An Essay on Human Feeling* (Baltimore and London, 1975). Volume I, p. 67.
12 *Problems of Art*, pp. 25, 126, 74.

13 *Philosophy in a New Key*, pp. 221-2.
14 We may sometimes fault a work on the ground that it violates 'the logic of emotion': the emotions it expresses follow one another in an unnatural manner. But this criticism concerns not the form of an emotion, but the nature of different emotions.
15 Compare and contrast the case of a map. For each map there is a possible world that the map accurately represents (in accordance with some given system of projection). Nevertheless, a map can be inaccurate.

VII   MUSIC AS THE EXPRESSION OF EMOTION

1 Leo Tolstoy, *What is Art?*, trans. Aylmer Maude (London, 1959), p. 123.
2 Deryck Cooke, *The Language of Music* (London, 1959), pp. 200-1.
3 For an explicit statement of this point, see Deryck Cooke, 'Wagner's Musical Language' in *The Wagner Companion*, ed. Peter Burbidge and Richard Sutton (London, 1979), p. 241. This was clearly Cooke's point of view in *The Language of Music*.
4 If the emotion aroused by the music not only does not have the music as its object, but has a different object, it is especially clear that the music is not valued for being expressive of that kind of emotion. In fact, a theory that locates music's capacity to express an emotion in its ability to arouse in the listener an instance of that emotion is likely to hold that the emotion it arouses in the listener − like the emotion it expresses − lacks a definite object: the emotion it arouses is directed neither towards the music nor towards any other particular thing. But even in this case, so I have argued, the music is not valued for being expressive of that kind of emotion.
5 Compare A. C. Bradley's 'heresy of the separable substance' in his 'Poetry for Poetry's Sake' in *Oxford Lectures on Poetry* (London, 1909).
6 A theory of musical expression in this sense should be distinguished from a theory of musical expression that is concerned (i) to specify the principal means by which music expresses emotion, or (ii) to provide a psychological explanation of why we are inclined to characterise musical passages with words drawn from the language of the emotions.
7 Perhaps the most important way in which bodily expressions can be differently related to the states that are expressed in them is that whereas some bodily expressions are voluntary acts, others are not. Compare Collingwood's distinction between psychical expression and imaginative expression: the distinction between those bodily occurrences that issue from a mental state as automatic, uncontrolled, involuntary (even unconscious) changes, and those that are controlled, performed 'on purpose'. See R. G. Collingwood, *The Principles of Art* (Oxford, 1960), pp. 228-41.

8 R. K. Elliott, 'Aesthetic Theory and the Experience of Art', *Proceedings of the Aristotelian Society*, Vol. LXVII (1966–7), reprinted in *Aesthetics*, ed. Harold Osborne (Oxford, 1972).

9 Kendall Walton, 'Fearing Fictions', *Journal of Philosophy*, LXXV, No. 1 (January 1978). Walton has developed the idea of make-believe truths more fully in his 'Pictures and Make-Believe', *Philosophical Review*, Vol. LXXXII, 3 (July 1973).

10 I am here following the letter of Walton's account. A simpler formulation that captures much of the account would be: Someone make-believedly feels fear for himself if his making-believe he is in danger causes him to feel quasi-fear.

11 See the discussion in Chapter I.

12 In fact, few emotions are expressed in characteristic kinds of sound (and few, if any, emotions have sounds specific to them).

13 Kendall Walton, 'Pictures and Make-Believe', *Philosophical Review*, Vol. LXXXII No. 3 (July 1973).

14 Compare E. H. Gombrich, 'Meditations on a Hobby Horse or the Roots of Artistic Form' in his *Meditations on a Hobby Horse and other Essays on the Theory of Art* (London, 1963).

15 Another possibility would be that M could be heard as the non-human expression of E. Rather than making-believe that M is the human vocal expression of E, or that it is the human non-vocal expression of E, I could make-believe that it is the non-human vocal (or perhaps non-vocal) expression of E. If I were to experience the music from within this would involve my making-believe that I am not a human being but a person or creature of another kind.

16 Our conception of what exactly needs to be explained will depend on our view of what is involved in the primordial and the non-primordial experiences of emotion. If we agree with Kendall Walton's view, we will require an explanation most urgently whenever the experience of the quasi-form of the emotion is not in itself a pleasurable experience. Now this will nearly always, perhaps always, be so. The bodily sensations we experience in feeling an emotion are characteristically neither pleasant nor unpleasant, even when the emotion is joy or sorrow. The problem will therefore not be that of explaining how sensations that are normally distressing or unpleasant can be experienced as pleasant, but rather how sensations that are neither pleasant nor unpleasant can be an integral part of an extremely pleasant experience when they are aroused in the course of experiencing a piece of expressive music from within. If, on the other hand, the hedonic tone of an emotion is thought to be what we experience essentially when we experience the emotion, then the explanation will be required whenever this hedonic tone is not a form of pleasure. For if we experience, make-believedly, an emotion that has a negative hedonic tone, we experience, really, an unpleasant affect.

17 If the music is valued as the most adequate expression of the emotion, to value it for its expressiveness is not to embrace the heresy of the separable experience.

18 J. S. Mill, 'Thoughts on Poetry and its Varieties' in *Autobiography and Literary Essays*, ed. John M. Robson and Jack Stillinger (Toronto, 1980).
19 Compare Friedrich Nietzsche, *Daybreak*, trans. R. J. Hollingdale (Cambridge, 1982), section 142.
20 Roger Scruton, *Art and Imagination* (London, 1974), Chapters 6-9.
21 Ibid., p. 72.
22 Ibid., p. 127.
23 Ibid., p. 104. I have improved the formulation slightly.
24 Ibid., p. 110. Hence, 'being irreducibly analogous to' does not signify a symmetrical relation.
25 To talk of hearing the sadness in another's voice is to speak ambiguously. The model of being touched by another's sadness invites us to construe this as I have done in the text. On the other hand, the idea might be that the sadness that is heard in a person's voice need not be the person's sadness. But with the necessary alterations the argument in the text will apply with equal force to this suggestion.
26 Roger Scruton, *Art and Imagination*, p. 119.
27 Ibid., p. 127.
28 R. K. Elliott does not claim that this theory provides a general solution to the problem of the musical expression of emotion, but only that it gives a correct account of how we hear some music. The claim that we hear expressive music as if it were the vocal expression of emotion forms the core of Peter Kivy's theory of musical expression in *The Corded Shell* (Princeton, 1980).
29 See W. H. Reed, *Elgar* (London, 1946), p. 103. The score has 'encerra', not 'encerrada'. It seems probable that the soul Elgar had in mind was Alice Stuart-Wortley's. See Michael Kennedy, *Elgar Orchestral Music* (London, 1970), pp. 43-4.

VIII MEANING, EMOTION AND INFORMATION IN MUSIC

1 See the first five sections of Chapter VII.
2 Leonard B. Meyer, *Emotion and Meaning in Music* (Chicago, 1956).
3 *Emotion and Meaning in Music*, p. 14.
4 The condition is supposed to be sufficient if the mental tensions that result when a tendency to respond is inhibited are allowed to remain unconscious and are not rationalised as conscious intellectual awareness of the nature of the stimulus.
5 *Emotion and Meaning in Music*, pp. 18-9.
6 *Emotion and Meaning in Music*, p. 19.
7 *Emotion and Meaning in Music*, pp. 8, 20.
8 *Emotion and Meaning in Music*, p. 31.
9 *Emotion and Meaning in Music*, p. 28.
10 *Emotion and Meaning in Music*, p. 20.
11 *Emotion and Meaning in Music*, p. 34.
12 *Emotion and Meaning in Music*, p. 54. See also Leonard B. Meyer, *Music, The Arts, And Ideas* (Chicago, 1969), p. 116.

13 *Emotion and Meaning in Music*, pp. 36-8.
14 *Emotion and Meaning in Music*, pp. 48-9.
15 *Emotion and Meaning in Music*, p. 43.
16 *Emotion and Meaning in Music*, p. 40.
17 See, for example, *Emotion and Meaning in Music*, p. 39.
18 See the fourth section of the present Chapter.
19 *Emotion and Meaning in Music*, p. 31.
20 See the eighth section of the present Chapter.
21 *Music, The Arts, And Ideas*, p. 9.
22 *Music, The Arts, And Ideas*, pp. 10-11.
23 *Music, The Arts, And Ideas*, pp. 14-28.
24 *Music, The Arts, And Ideas*, p. 26.
25 *Music, The Arts, And Ideas*, pp. 32-3.
26 *Music, The Arts, And Ideas*, pp. 34-6.
27 *Music, The Arts, And Ideas*, p. 37.
28 *Music, The Arts, And Ideas*, p. 37. I am not sure that I have represented Meyer's refinement accurately. His view may perhaps be that syntactical musical value does not vary in direct proportion to amount of information, or in direct proportion to the ratio of amount of information to the means used to generate the information, but in some more complex (unspecified) manner.
29 *Music, The Arts, And Ideas*, p. 38.
30 *Music, The Arts, And Ideas*, pp. 37-40.
31 In a number of places Meyer draws attention to the fact that there is interaction between the syntactical relationships and the associative aspect of a musical work. See *Music, The Arts, And Ideas*, pp. 7, 34, 44. But it remains obscure how a musical work can acquire the kind of content that Meyer believes is integral to musical greatness.
32 See *Emotion and Meaning in Music*, pp. 58, 74, 90 and *Music, The Arts, And Ideas*, pp. 46-8.
33 It is assumed that the listener's response to the music is purely syntactical, not sensuous, associative or that combination of syntactical and associative that Meyer regards as being characteristic of greatness in music. Of course, if an affirmative answer to the question should be given, Meyer's theory is not thereby *established*.
34 *Music, The Arts, And Ideas*, pp. 49-52.

INDEX

Aristotle, 4, 90, 177

Bach, J.S., 163-4
Beethoven, L., 18, 92, 117, 178
Bouwsma, O.K., 179
Bradley, A.C., 185
Broad, C.D., 177

Collingwood, R.G., 177, 185
composer, 16-19, 151-2
Cooke, D., 66, 122-3, 185

Darwin, C., 56-9, 61, 181

Elgar, E., 18, 124, 149, 187
Elliott, R.K., 126-7, 131, 133-9, 150, 187
emotion: and bodily feelings, 9-10, 128-9; and bodily movement, 39, 46-50; and desire, 7-9, 22; experienced make-believedly, 128-31; expression of, 62ff, 135-40; musical arousal of, 28-31, 53, 56-74, 122-5, 135-9, 154-6, 158-66, 173-4; and pleasure and pain, 4-15, 22, 25-6, 129-30, 156, 161; sexual, 56-9; specifically musical, 56ff, 176; and thought, 4-15, 21-5, 128-31

Freud, S., 6, 177

Gombrich, E.H., 186
Goodman, N., 179

Gurney, E., 31, 41-3, 53ff, 178

Hanslick, E., 20ff

information theory, 154, 166ff, 176

James, W., 113

Kant, I., 79
Kenny, A., 177

Langer, S., 106ff, 180
lyric poetry, 126-7

Mann, T., 76
melody, 53-6, 58-9, 71, 87-92
Mendelssohn, F., 18
Mill, J.S., 140
Mozart, W., 18, 36
music: and communication, 121-5, 151-3; emotive description of, 31-51; expression theory of, 121-5, 152, 175; as expressive of emotion, 124-5, 127, 131-50; as a language of the emotions, 89, 122-3; listener, point of view of, 16-17, 19-20, 51, 151-2, 175; and meaning of, 153ff, 158, 162-74; and movement, 39, 43-50; as representation of definite emotions, 21-7; as representation of the will, 86ff; and space, 39-43; as symbol, 104ff; value as music, 99-100, 151-3, 168-72, 175-6

189